'This book has eloquently captured a contempora:
rightly so, places children as paramount and central
"must read" for seasoned practitioners and school le
early career teachers, researchers and policy makers in ... ... .. ......

**David J. Malachi**, Deputy Headteacher (Transforming the
Curriculum), London Enterprise Academy, UK

'This book is a game-changer in terms of modern-day educational approaches.
I cannot remember a time recently where I have read something so honest yet
straightforward. Whilst it is open and clear about the restraints of the National
Curriculum, it makes many references to its purpose and fundamental positives.

As a teacher and school leader the ideas described are exactly what we, as
educators, have been wanting for 10+ years. A curriculum that is not "one-size
fits all". So many educators across the country feel let down by the current
regime and genuinely break their hearts when they see ex-pupils fail to fulfil
their potential. I can only imagine if some of my ex-pupils were able to have
access to a personalised secondary curriculum. It would most definitely have
positively impacted their lives.

Pupil-Progress Reviews and the link to CPD is excellent. There is so much
confusion surrounding this idea that the clarity and importance the book gives
to this, is enlightening. I can imagine many young teachers reading this book in a
few years time, wishing they had these ideas when they were NQTs.

As someone who has trialled the idea of Pupil Progress Reviews across two
continents, I can say that they work magnificently in bringing the community
of staff, pupils and parents together. They provide clarity where it is lacking
and support pupils in seeing their potential, should they choose to use it. I'm
delighted that these ideas have been highlighted in the book.

So well written, clear, with an easy approach, this book will help teachers and
leaders transform their schools.'

**Jennifer McGuigan**, School Improvement Partner,
United Arab Emirates

'This unique book is a must read for those that want to realign the curriculum to
their vision and values. It captures a range of case studies and examples that are
relevant and thought provoking, designed to support leaders at all levels. Above
all else, this is a reflective guide to help us to improve the educational outcomes
of all.'

**Wasim Butt**, Principal TBAP, UK

'*Secondary Curriculum Transformed* is one of those rare books, that clearly unpicks
why the importance of curriculum is now, more than ever, so integral to the
success of schooling in the UK. Throughout the text, we are guided through the
ever changing landscape of education, and through the use of clear case studies
and underpinned with the best of research, a compelling argument for why it is
important to equip our students with both the knowledge and the skills to be
successful in an ever changing world. The case is made articulately for a curriculum which balances traditional academia with the need for creative thinking and

critical literacy. Importantly, this book also begins to unravel the need for schools to balance the academic curriculum with the wider cultural capital which is so important in building successful learners and allowing social mobility. This is an absolute must read for any school leader rethinking the purpose and intent of schooling in the UK and for anyone committed to reviewing what is taught and more importantly how it is taught in our schools.'

**Elroy Cahill**, Headteacher, Kingsley Academy, UK

# Secondary Curriculum Transformed

More than ever, secondary curriculum requires greater flexibility and adaptability so young people learn the relevant knowledge and key skills they need for the evolving world of training and employment. This practical guide, both radical and progressive, makes a compelling argument for a secondary curriculum that addresses the needs and aspirations of all students. A balanced approach will help reform students' attitudes and behaviours and re-ignite their curiosity and motivation for learning.

*Secondary Curriculum Transformed* proposes an ambitious GCSE five-year journey inclusive of academic, creative and technical subjects, including T-Levels and mandatory key skills. To equip young people with this critical knowledge and key skills, the book:

- transforms the 11–19 curriculum so it does not disadvantage, marginalise or exclude young people;
- showcases excellent practice case studies from British and international contexts;
- provides curriculum models which schools can adapt to their own context;
- signposts educational research and listens to the 'student voice'; transforming them into leaders of their learning.

Offering a comprehensive model for leaders and teachers to put the evidence into practice, this is essential reading for all education professionals.

There are also additional templates, PowerPoints, useful links and other resources which can be downloaded from www.routledge.com/9780367900878. Offering a comprehensive model for leaders and teachers to put the evidence into practice, this is essential reading for all education professionals.

**Meena Kumari Wood** has worked across the British and International Education sectors. She is an Educational Consultant. She was a former HMI (OFSTED), DfE Adviser and Principal in secondary schools and of an Adult College. Her insights into education are shaped by placing learners' aspirations at the heart of curriculum.

**Nick Haddon** is Vice Principal of 11–19 Academy. His impactful QCDA research on deprivation and attainment inform his commitment to whole school curriculum and behaviour reform.

# Secondary Curriculum Transformed

## Enabling All to Achieve

Meena Kumari Wood and Nick Haddon

Routledge
Taylor & Francis Group

LONDON AND NEW YORK

First published 2021
by Routledge
2 Park Square, Milton Park, Abingdon, Oxon OX14 4RN

and by Routledge
52 Vanderbilt Avenue, New York, NY 10017

*Routledge is an imprint of the Taylor & Francis Group, an informa business*

*British Library Cataloguing-in-Publication Data*
A catalogue record for this book is available from the British Library

*Library of Congress Cataloging-in-Publication Data*
Names: Wood, Meena Kumari, author. | Haddon, Nick, author.
Title: Secondary curriculum transformed : enabling all to achieve /
Meena Kumari Wood & Nick Haddon.
Description: Abingdon, Oxon ; New York, NY : Routledge, 2021. |
Includes bibliographical references and index. |
Identifiers: LCCN 2020038747 | ISBN 9780367900861 (hardback) |
ISBN 9780367900878 (paperback) | ISBN 9781003022534 (ebook)
Subjects: LCSH: High schools–Curricula–United States. |
Curriculum change–United States.
Classification: LCC LB1628 .W66 2021 | DDC 373.19–dc23
LC record available at https://lccn.loc.gov/2020038747

ISBN: 978-0-367-90086-1 (hbk)
ISBN: 978-0-367-90087-8 (pbk)
ISBN: 978-1-003-02253-4 (ebk)

Typeset in Bembo
by Newgen Publishing UK

Access the Support Material: www.routledge.com/9780367900878

For all young people in these challenging times, who deserve a secondary education that prepares them for an uncertain future, and to the education professionals who enable them to achieve this.

# Contents

# Preface

'There should not be two routes but a multiplicity of interrelated pathways, all of which can lead to higher education and/or a good job, but which recognise that different people want and need different things as they develop' (Sir Christopher Ball, 'Papering Over the Cracks', *Guardian*, 28 May 1991).[1] This citation concluded my previous book, written 25 years ago on a pathways curriculum for Further Education that recognised the starting points of learners. The debates on the existence of, or lack of, relevant employability skills possessed by young and mature employees have been raging for decades, firmly linked to education.

It seems like we have come full circle at this time. 2020 is a historic watershed as the UK and the world have been shaken by some seismic events that will change the course of society, education, and employment forever.

During the writing of the book, we have lived through a unique time of uncertainty, characterised by Brexit, catastrophic environmental natural disasters, and an acceleration in the Fourth Industrial Revolution, with a heavier reliance on digital technologies permeating every aspect of our life. The latter, especially key during the global pandemic of COVID-19 'lockdowns'. This has clearly influenced our writing as we are acutely aware that the model of education from 2020, owing to social distancing, examinations and other factors, will never be the same again.

The original inspiration for this book came from a passion to see the secondary school curriculum transformed so that it meets *all* young people's needs, inclusive of their aptitude, aspiration, skills and knowledge. As a former HMI, I was deeply influenced by seeing students 'off task' in lessons, where they either did not understand, could not retain information, or had no interest in the subject. As a Principal, I observed a number of excluded 'repeat offenders' appearing daily in a 'remove room', facing the wall and being 'contained' for the duration of a lesson for a day or more. These students rapidly became what I call 'square pegs in the round hole of education' as they tragically lost out on learning. Witnessing my daughter's education and employment history, on the other hand, was an eye opener! A high performing student in Science and Arts at GCSE and A-levels, she aspired towards a career in medicine. However, surprisingly, from conducting cancer research during her Masters, she then carved out a successful career as a digital entrepreneur and founded a healthcare tech-enabled start-up. None of the Careers Education, guidance, or importantly, the knowledge-based teaching that she had in either school or university would have prepared her for this! Her example is not atypical of young people's destinations today as they exit from education.

Now, more than ever, our education system should instil the skills and competencies that young people need for their future life and work through recognising the zigzag pattern of employment paths they may take. Education professionals, leaders and teaching staff do their very best to develop these skills in young people at schools and colleges. Yet what is most striking to us is that they are doing this *in spite* of a narrowing of the curriculum that seeks to design out exactly the skills and behaviours young people need.

Much is written about curriculum, learning and assessment models that focus on looking at schools through an introverted lens. We wanted this book to think outside the box, to imagine the 'what if' scenarios and for education to look outwards. We want to pose the prickly question of how well we prepare our young people for the next stages of their lives at 16 onwards; for the brave new world of post-COVID-19, post-Brexit, and living in a digital society.

This book is thought provoking and possibly controversial at times, particularly in the solutions proposed to the challenges we face. We do not aim to provide all the answers but would like to commence an educational and societal debate that revisits the curriculum from the students' perspective – not as individual tabula rasa, but with a recognition that students, as leaders of their learning, should influence the shape and direction of their education. Above all we would like to see the curriculum transformed so that it reignites the 'curiosity for learning', thereby fulfilling every young person's aspirations.

## Note

1     M. Wood (1995) *Assessment of Prior Learning: APL and Bilingual Learners.* London: Routledge.

# Acknowledgements

The authors would like to thank the staff, students and schools of the following schools for providing brief case studies from their websites:

Westminster Academy, Chelsea Academy, Cabot Federation, Schools21.

Our sincere appreciation of the following education professionals for their valued contributions and comments:

Elroy Cahill, Headteacher, Kingsley Academy; Colette Doran Hannon, Executive Principal, St Thomas More Catholic Primary School; Andrew O Neill, Headteacher, Rob Mahon and Sarah Marshall, Assistant Headteachers, All Saints Catholic College; Dr Trevor Papworth, Headteacher, Roberto Giovanelli, Head of English, St Thomas More Academy; Wasim Butt, Principal, Michelle Burgess-Allen, Deputy Headteacher, Beachcroft Alternative Provision –TBAP; Carolyn Roberts, Headteacher, Thomas Tallis School; Sam Gorse, Headteacher, Turton School; Mark Anstiss, Headteacher, Felpham Community College; Dave J. Malachi, Deputy Headteacher, London Enterprise Academy; Jennifer McGuigan, School Improvement Partner, United Arab Emirates; Ty Goddard, Education Foundation; Elizabeth Tweedale, Founder of EdTech start-up Cypher; Devika Wood, Founder of the tech-enabled care start-up Vida; and School-Home Support (SHS).

Our special thanks to Jamie Hanson (Director of Coda Studios) and Catalina Ionita (Architect at Coda Studios) for the designs of the Octoweb Graphic Organiser and the Iceberg Learning Model.

Cover design courtesy of Catalina Ionita (Architect at Coda Studios).

# Abbreviations

| | |
|---|---|
| A8 | Attainment 8 |
| ADHD | Attention Deficit Hyperactivity Disorder |
| AI | Artificial Intelligence |
| AP | Alternative Provision |
| AR | Accelerated Reader |
| ASC | Autistic Spectrum Disorder |
| ASCL | Association of School and College Leaders |
| ASDAN | Award Scheme Development and Accreditation Network |
| BREXIT | British Exit |
| CBI | Confederation of British Industry |
| CEIAG | Careers Education, Information, Advice and Guidance |
| COVID-19 | Coronavirus |
| DARTs | Directed Activities Related to Texts |
| DEAR | Drop Everything and Read |
| DfE | Department of Education |
| EAU | Engage and Achieve Unit |
| EBacc | English Baccalaureate |
| EF | Executive Function |
| EHC | Education Health and Care |
| EIF | Education Inspection Framework |
| EPRA | Engaging Parents in Raising Achievement Programme |
| ESB | The English Speaking Board |
| ESFA | Education and Skills Funding Agency |
| FE | Further Education |
| FTE | Fixed-Term Excluded |
| GL Assessment | Granada Learning |
| IB | International Baccalaureate |
| LSA | Learning Support Assistant |
| NASA | The National Aeronautics and Space Administration |
| NEET | Not in Education, Employment or Training |
| NSR | Non-Secondary Ready |

| OECD | Organisation for Economic Cooperation and Development |
| OFSTED | Office for Standards in Education |
| P8 | Progress 8 |
| PASS | Pupil Attitudes to Self and School |
| PISA | The Programme for International Student Assessment |
| PPR | Pupil Progress Review |
| PRU | Pupil Referral Unit |
| RAP | Raising Achievement Plan |
| RSA | Royal Society of Arts |
| RTA | Recall, Transfer, Apply |
| RONI | Risk of NEET Indicator Tool |
| SEND | Special Education Needs and Disabilities |
| SHS | School Home Support |
| STEAM | Science, Technology, Engineering, Arts and Maths |
| STEM | Science, Technology, Engineering and Maths |
| TA | Teaching Assistant |
| TIOBE | The Importance of Being Ernest |
| T-Levels | Technical Levels |
| UCAS | University and Colleges Admissions Service |
| UTC | University Technical College |
| WEF | World Economic Forum |

# Introduction

## Secondary curriculum transformed so every student achieves

Britain's role as a political and economic world leader is pivotal. From 2020 onwards, we are at a crossroads facing new opportunities and challenges. Key amongst these are advancing technologies in the face of the Fourth Industrial Revolution, climate change, a worldwide COVID-19 pandemic, a national skills shortage and a transformed future relationship with our European neighbours and the rest of the world. The COVID-19[1] pandemic in itself is one of the biggest influencers on transforming the intent and implementation of curriculum. A spotlight has emerged on online learning; the need for a model of teaching/learning that would accommodate 'catching up' on academic knowledge for thousands of students upon return to school, as well as the disbanding of GCSE/A-level examinations in 2020.

To maintain Britain's position as a global influencer, investment in education is necessary. This is the engine room of new thinking and for tomorrow's emerging young work force. If we want to be at the forefront of future industries, we must equip our young people with the knowledge and skills they require for our evolving economy and the transforming world of employment. Is our secondary curriculum flexible and adaptable enough to meet these demands?

Before we begin to review the secondary curriculum's potential in addressing these seismic change levers, we must look at the curriculum's current intent and actual impact on young people.

Our contention is that there is a disconnect between the aspirational intent of the National Curriculum and students' actual outcomes. The impact measures demonstrate that across the country, a sizeable proportion of young people are not attaining the GCSE EBacc in line with government targets. Over half of 16 year olds in 2019 left school without a 'good' standard in English and Maths GCSE.[2] Huge gaps exist by region and between students with different characteristics, in particular, ethnicity and special educational needs. Most worryingly, are the significantly rising proportions of students marginalised from mainstream education. Forty students, many vulnerable, are excluded every day across all of the schools in the UK.[3] This is potentially about the lost life chances of these young people.

How 'broad and balanced' is the National 11–19 curriculum and does it provide a genuinely accessible, inclusive and equitable education for all our students? Students' educational experiences will depend heavily upon where their schools are located within our fragmented educational landscape. Regional variations and local inter-pretations of the curriculum all play a significant part in shaping outcomes. Most importantly, do school leaders, in designing the curriculum intent and implemen-tation accommodate the complex interplay of their students' aspirations, capabilities and socio-economic backgrounds?

In response, this book aims to empower educationalists and school leaders in recon-ciling the constraints and the scope offered by the National Curriculum. We explore the intent, implementation and impact of what constitutes a 'broad and balanced' curriculum. In doing so, our starting point is modelling a knowledge and skills-based curriculum that we believe lies in the best interests of all students, especially those currently demotivated by aspects of their education. This means moving away from funding-led curriculum to a context that is genuinely funding the *knowledge and skills* of students through academic, technical and vocational pathways.

For ease of reference, the book is divided into seven parts; the first of which, explores the levers for change. This includes the blend of face-to-face teaching and online learning, necessary for flexible curriculum implementation. The other sections focus on key aspects of the curriculum, including an Extended Learning Community and the points of transition at 11 and 16. Good practice in preparing students for their curriculum choices and destinations in KS3/4 is profiled, including post-16, technical and vocational sector-based pathways with the onset of T-levels. Careers Education, Information, Advice and Guidance (CEIAG), benchmarked through the internationally informed Gatsby Measures, must not uniquely focus on an outdated and static idea of a jobs market, but should keep pace with the changing national and global employment trends that young people face.

In line with this continuing trajectory, in the age of AI and technologies, the 'human skills' that comprise creativity, critical and conceptual thinking, originality, persuasion, problem solving and negotiation are much in demand by further/higher education and employers. A knowledge-based curriculum, by definition, does not structure opportunities for all young people to develop these necessary skills. The key skills underpinning Citizenship – critical literacy, digital competence, oracy and financial literacy – are neither mandatory nor accredited within the KS4 National Curriculum. Unless a school believes in the value of placing these as an entitlement for all of its students, it is left to each school to include, or not, within its curric-ulum intent.

Only when we actively focus on these skills and the metacognition 'learning to learn skills'(as these are integral within the assessment/feedback processes), do our students become more motivated, skilled and knowledgeable.

As our students lie at the heart of the curriculum, we reflect their educational experiences through their 'voice'. In particular, we focus on students, who may not have a 'voice', such as the disadvantaged, those with special educational needs and disabilities, and those who are excluded from lessons, or school. We consider practical strategies for 'hard to reach' students, through partnerships with their parents/carers, the Third Sector, local businesses and national agencies, and make a strong case for re-defining 'human, social and cultural capital'. Throughout, we signpost educational research and excellent practice case studies from English schools and international contexts.

We transform OFSTED's methodology of evaluating curriculum 'intent, implementation and impact', into a whole school quality assurance process. We refer to this as class-based Pupil Progress Reviews (PPRs). PPRs are a powerful tool that result in professional staff development, whilst systematically addressing barriers for students who are failing to reach their potential. Schools gain valuable insights into the way students respond to teaching and assessment. Meanwhile, leaders gather a wealth of information, which feeds into their self-evaluation and curriculum design.

We contend that OFSTED's preoccupation with a retracted KS3 and the 'narrowing of choice' should not be the key line of enquiry pursued on inspection. Curriculum intent is less about whether the GCSE subject choices are made at the end of Year 8 or Year 9. It is about a five-year journey that prepares our students towards their destinations and employment routes through widening the EBacc. The EBacc should be inclusive of creative, technical and vocational subjects, along with a mandatory entitlement to the key skills. In this way, we transform our curriculum towards one that is accessible, inclusive and equitable.

## Notes

1    Coronavirus disease in 2020 led to lockdown over an extensive period and school closure.
2    The Department for Education (2019) GCSE results ('Attainment 8'). Available at: www.ethnicity-facts-figures.service.gov.uk/education-skills-and-training/11-to-16-years-old/gcse-results-attainment-8-for-children-aged-14-to-16-key-stage-4/latest    (Accessed:    25 November 2019).
3    E. Timpson et al. (2018) *The Timpson Review of School Exclusion*. London: Department for Education, Crown Copyright 2019 [Online]. Available at: https://assets.publishing.service.gov.uk/government/uploads/system/uploads/attachment_data/file/807862/Timpson_review.pdf (Accessed: 1 December 2019).

PART

I

# Change levers: Transforming curriculum

# 1

# Transformational levers for change

## Introduction

The word 'curriculum' derives from a Latin word meaning a race or the course of a race. Interestingly, the verb 'currere' means to 'run' or to 'proceed'. The curriculum takes our students on a learning journey and requires them to proceed, as with all journeys, towards their destination. The National Curriculum, originally developed in 1988 and modified thereafter, was envisaged for a radically different UK society with different destinations in mind. The context was within a world economy, with very little resemblance to today's national and global stage. Why do we need to transform our curriculum? Very simply put; our curriculum no longer meets the needs of a significant number of our young people. Its relevance with regard to students' outcomes and future destinations is debatable. We contend that during their five years of secondary schooling, not all students have the educational opportunities that help fulfil their potential. Many do not achieve successful qualification outcomes at their destination points at 16 and then again at 19. We explore the reasons why.

## Disconnect between curriculum and young peoples' destinations

Today's work destination for our young people will be radically different from those of their parents or even their older siblings. By the time Year 7 students join secondary school in 2020 and arrive in Year 11 in 2025, they will be looking at a significantly different market place to their predecessors. In 2018, the World Economic Forum stated that '65% of children entering primary school today will ultimately end up working in completely new job types that don't yet exist'.[1] The potential of automation is defined in a McKinsey report as the requirement of people and technology to work in synergy. Whilst it is widely acknowledged that robots and computers perform a range of routine physical work activities better and more cheaply than humans, it is increasingly evident that AI is capable of accomplishing activities that include cognitive capabilities, such as making tacit judgments and sensing emotion.[2]

Arguably, we live in an age where digital technologies are increasingly doing for our brainpower what the steam engine and related technologies did for our muscle power during the nineteenth-century Industrial Revolution.

All school leaders, teachers, students and their families should have greater awareness of the sea changes in our national and global employment patterns. The statutory prominence of CEIAG (Careers Education, Information, Advice and Guidance) features 'school-employer links' as one of the key eight Gatsby Benchmarks measures. Surely employment trends should now influence curriculum design? This school case study illustrates the adverse impact of curriculum design: Two high-achieving Year 9 students were unable to choose the subjects they required for their future careers.

## CASE STUDY: 11–19 ACADEMY

In speaking with the Careers Adviser, the students had expressed their aspirations, influenced by their families. One wished to pursue Robotic Processing Automation (RPA) and the other, Robotic Engineering. Their curriculum options, however, were premised on an EBacc trajectory. Both wished to study Technology and Computer Science, but could only opt for one of these two subjects. For the student who wished to train in RPA, business studies would have been helpful, for design of robotic software is typically used for automating business processes. Both students then faced a Hobson's choice, but one with serious consequences for their future destinations.

## Employability skills

A wealth of opinion across the employment and education sector identifies a clear disconnect between employers' needs, in relation to current and future job trends, and the National Educational Curriculum. A recent survey amongst teachers highlighted concerns that the narrower curriculum increased content and exam focus within GCSEs and A-levels which were creating barriers for young people. They were risking leaving school without the necessary employability skills.[3]

The ACSL 2018 conference concluded that the school curriculum must reflect the breadth of knowledge and skills needed by people in their lives and at work,[4] and that schools should not have to choose between knowledge and skills in their curriculum planning. These sentiments are further reinforced by the OCED Head of Education. He reiterates the importance of digitalisation on future employment prospects, emphasising inter-disciplinary learning and a range of competencies, such as dealing with novelty and reflective practice.[5]

Similarly, the Institute of Director's 2016 Learning for Life report stated that education policy is turning 'schools into exam factories, squeezing out creativity and the joy of learning at a time when these very attributes are becoming increasingly important'.[6]

## The economy of the UK outside the European Union

A key factor for reviewing our curriculum is the economy of a post-Brexit United Kingdom. In view of migration patterns, skills shortages will occur in certain sectors such as hospitality, plumbing, building, agriculture, social care and healthcare,[7] as the government's immigration policy may limit entry of low-skilled/non-skilled migrants. To fill the gaps, future generations predictably require skills for a markedly different national economy. The RSA's recently published report proposed 'the emergence of two types of jobs: "hi-tech" ones; creating, maintaining and interpreting machines; and "hi-touch" ones; entirely resistant to automation, such as social care workers and hospitality staff'.[8] Apprenticeships are one way forward, designed to meet the future workforce's needs and are crucial in addressing the challenge. One such example is the Lloyds Banking Group offering 25 apprenticeship programmes ranging from Entry Level (equivalent to Level 2) to Level 7 (equivalent to a Master's Degree).

Living in a radically changing global economy, we are subject to a complex web of digital technologies within our labour market. This has given rise to the 'GIG' economy, the world of entrepreneurships and 'start-up' companies; fundamental contributors to our national and international economies. The young generation of today are entering a world of work where they have opportunities to create jobs rather than apply for them. This requires constant adaptation in learning knowledge and skills. The curriculum needs to shift from qualifications-based certification to knowledge and skills-based certification. This means moving from a one-size curriculum for all to highlighting what individuals can do.

Linguistic skills are going to take on greater prominence post-Brexit. The APPG[9] for Modern Languages urges 'a national plan to ensure the UK produces linguists … to become a world leader in global free trade and on the international stage'. They noted that the UK loses 3.5 per cent of GDP in lost business opportunities due to poor language skills and that SMEs who deploy languages report 43 per cent higher export/turnover ratios. Only one-third of Britons can read and write in more than one language, whereas the EU average is 80 per cent. Through studying a language, employers recognise the intrinsic value of linguistic skills-sets in furthering cultural awareness and building positive relationships. The reality today is, despite the inclusion of a language in the EBacc subjects, only half of pupils in England, Wales and Northern Ireland take a foreign language GCSE, whereas in 2002, it was three in four.

Language accreditation into apprenticeships, plus a series of different routes to gaining language qualifications in schools, would be highly beneficial for the UK. Work readiness today requires students to understand the dynamics of globalisation and to be open to people from different cultures.

## Environmentally-led learning

Green industries are rapidly evolving as employers of tomorrow. Our young people need to learn about environmental sustainability. Biology, Chemistry and Geography directly address climate and environmental issues. Through accurate guidance (CEIAG), students need to see the direct relevance of this curriculum to future green career paths. For example, taking advantage of opportunities for working with energy companies in key areas, such as renewables, smart metering and low carbon solutions as well as on-site construction. This requires flexibility for students in choosing subjects that include STEM (Science, Technology, Engineering and Mathematics) and also importantly, Design and Technology (D&T) and Computing Science. These are not part of the EBacc suite and so GCSE entries in these subjects have noticeably decreased over the last two years. Not including these as part of the EBacc suite is counter-intuitive if the sustainability agenda is to be achieved.

## Narrowing of the curriculum

Inflexibility in choice can inhibit students in making informed decisions about the range of potential training and employment pathways that may be suitable for them. We risk shoehorning our students into a curriculum that is appropriate for many, but may not be appropriate for others. Schools are under pressure to drop creative subjects such as Art and Design, and Music, usually in favour of the higher loaded academic qualifications. This has included a reduction of course hours; significant increases in class numbers (combining study); or in extreme cases, even being completely dropped from the curriculum offer. Far from broadening the curriculum, this move towards an academic knowledge-based curriculum potentially sacrifices the breadth and relevance of study.

Schools might argue that the extended or extra-curricular activities they can provide compensate for the lack of accredited opportunities in the creative subjects. In order to futureproof our students' life chances, we should not rely on this roulette of optional activities to broaden a curriculum that all our students deserve and need.

## An inclusive and equitable curriculum intent

Using the OECD's definition, equity has two aspects: (1) inclusion, meaning that all individuals reach at least a basic minimum level of skills, and (2) fairness, meaning that personal or social circumstances such as gender, ethnic origin or family background, are not obstacles to achieving educational potential.[10]

As educationalists how do we reconcile the fundamental question of curriculum intent with inclusivity and equity? Our aim must be to enable all our students to access and participate equally within an appropriate knowledge and skills-based curriculum. At present, if we apply the Henry Ford theory of 'choice' in car design to curriculum design, we must ask ourselves, how well served are *all* our students by their educational experiences in school? He famously said in his promotional branding, 'You can have any car, in any colour, as long as it's black!'(1909).[11] This mantra was successful because with the growing market in cars, what was required was a universal product that was produced rapidly, to suit *all* pockets and that sold quickly.

## Impact of the curriculum on young people

The stark reality of a potential 'one-size fits all' curriculum is that it takes little account of individual student's preferences. This can have a negative impact on those who do not fit the mould. Instead, we need to listen to the students themselves. Harriet Sweatman, a 16 year-old winner of the Scottish Schools Young Writer of the Year, asserts that schools are 'a place where you are … manufactured. You move along the conveyor belt of exam seasons, hoping for the grades you need, so you can be packaged up with a pretty label saying you got straight As and shipped off somewhere else. Capitalism tells us that if we are not fit to work, then we are worthless. There is no love in learning anymore.'[12]

If our curriculum is about a journey to a destination, surely the destination has to be *relevant* to the lives of our young people? En-route, our students must experience the curiosity for learning that inspires them, not simply as an 'awe and wonder' factor – but more critically, as relevant to their lives and ambitions. Within a context of rising school exclusions and 'off rolling' of students, there is an 'invisible', but highly significant, minority of young people who are being failed by the school system. With the increase in knife crime, gang violence and 'county lines', it is a sad indictment of our society how many of these young people who are excluded, or at risk of exclusion, become vulnerable and succumb to living on the margins of society. Whilst not ignoring external pressures such as family and personal circumstances, we strongly contend that the impact of the school curriculum is a factor in not engaging a number of students in the learning process.

All of us as educationalists have been in lessons in the role of observers or teachers, where students are disenchanted with the subject. They may not be able to access the learning because of dyslexia or ADHD. Or, they may arrive in the lesson preoccupied with worries that spill over from their everyday lives. Their behaviours and attitudes to learning may be the start of a vicious spiral of internal or fixed term exclusions. These will ensure periods of interrupted study for those students across all their subjects; even in those where they enjoy learning and can achieve. It will take a student with the greatest staying power, resilience and motivation to ensure they can keep on track and turn away from the destination towards which they are heading, marked 'exit school'.

## Not failure, but low aim is crime[13]

It is incumbent on us to explore how we can transform our secondary curriculum, so that all our young people achieve positive outcomes and aspirational targets. Meeting these challenges head on, we must ensure that our range of students are well prepared for acquiring the new knowledge and skills that they need to enter the brave new world market place.

Clearly, the imperative for us is to ensure that our curriculum does not fail any student nor must we aim low. We can justifiably argue that the current EBacc-based curriculum is about 'high aim' for all of our students, and that we must have high aspirations for our students. However, the reality is that it may not necessarily be the *correct* aim, or indeed, *an accessible and relevant aim* for some of our young people, inevitably ending in failure for too many of them. Our secondary curriculum must be an equitable curriculum that actively shapes opportunities for all our students, whatever their background, ability and capability for each to successfully fulfil his/her potential.

## Summary

We have outlined key change levers for transforming the curriculum. Of these, the most compelling reason is for the sake of our students so that all experience a relevant, broad and rich curriculum, in line with their future aspirations, interests and abilities. The key word is *relevance*; a curriculum that creates a genuine curiosity for learning for each student, leading to successful outcomes and does not marginalise any student. As we continue to lose potential future talent and skills that are sitting in our classrooms, we face challenges like other global societies. A simple focus on a knowledge-based curriculum does not give equal parity to the academic, technical and creative aspects. We ignore, at our peril, the employment trends and opportunities resulting from the Fourth Industrial Revolution, including for instance, entrepreneurship and regional production hubs linked by global chains of information and goods.

Our future generations of school children must be given the opportunities to be skilled and knowledgeable. They must be able to respond intelligently to the threats and opportunities posed by a host of complex interrelated factors. These include the challenges of climate change, worldwide pandemics, urbanisation, the radical evolution in bio-technology and artificial intelligence, globalised financial markets, 'fake news', rising societal inequalities and migration patterns.

As each school's population is unique, decisions on curriculum design should be flexibly steered by the needs of the national economy, together with the local context of students' needs and aspirations. Autonomy in decision-making at local level should in turn be balanced by what further/higher education and training, as well as what employers identify as requisite. Ideological dogma that dictates what is in the best interests for students to study, does not help *all* young people to succeed in their chosen pathways.

## Notes

1    K. Schwab et al. (2018) *The Future of Jobs Report.* London: Centre for the New Economy and Society.

2    McKinsey & Company (2017) *A Future That Works: Automation, Employment, and Productivity.* London: McKinsey (MGI).

3    E. Kashefpakdel et al. (2018) Joint dialogue: How are schools developing real employability skills? Available at: www.educationandemployers.org/research/joint-dialogue/ (Accessed: 14 October 2019).

4    Careers & Enterprise Company (2018) ASCL Conference makes strong connections between schools and business. Available at: www.careersandenterprise.co.uk/ascl-conference-strong-connections-schools-business (Accessed: 11 November 2019).

5    J. Dunford (2019) At long last, the narrow knowledge-based curriculum is being rejected across the education sector. Available at: www.tes.com/news/long-last-narrow-knowledge-based-curriculum-being-rejected-across-education-sector (Accessed: 14 November 2019).

6    International Youth Foundation (2016) *IVF Annual Report.* Baltimore: IYF.

7    L. O'Carroll et al. (2020) UK to close door to non-English speakers and unskilled workers. Available at: www.msn.com/en-gb/news/uknews/uk-to-close-door-to-non-english-speakers-and-unskilled-workers/ar-BB108gP3 (Accessed: 19 January 2020).

8    The RSA (2018) Work in an age of radical technologies. Available at: www.thersa.org/discover/publications-and-articles/reports/work-in-an-age-of-radical-technologies (Accessed: 29 November 2019).

9    Association for Language Learning (2019) APPG on Modern Languages launches Brexit & Languages: A checklist for Government negotiators and officials. Available at: www.all-languages.org.uk/news/appg-on-modern-languages-launches-brexit-languages-a-checklist-for-government-negotiators-and-officials/ (Accessed: 3 March 2020).

10    OECD (2012) *Equity and Quality in Education: Supporting Disadvantaged Students and Schools.* Paris: OECD Publishing. http://dx.doi.org/10.1787/9789264130852-en

11    H. Ford and S. Crowther (1922) *My Life and Work.* New York: Doubleday, Page & Co.

12    H. Sweatman (2019) Children must be freed from the curriculum's chokehold. www.tes.com/news/children-must-be-freed-curriculums-chokehold (Accessed: 15 November 2019).

13    J. R. Lowell (2019) James Russell Lowell quotes. Available at: www.brainyquote.com/quotes/james_russell_lowell_132684 (Accessed: 19 January 2020).

## 2

# The impact of technologies and employment trends

## Introduction

Here we examine in greater detail the impact of technologies on the changing landscape of society and employment. External and global key factors have had an impact on translating science fiction to science fact to business fact. The changing nature of work due to automation and artificial intelligence (AI) is explored in a recent report which identifies a greater focus on the 'innovative applications of technology and its resultant value'.[1] This underscores the importance of education in preparing students with academic knowledge, technical and creative skills. The internet society we live in means workers are no longer rewarded primarily for what they know, but for what they can do with that knowledge.

The fitness for purpose of the secondary curriculum for the Fourth Industrial Revolution is measured through how effectively young people are prepared for their future destinations through the relevant choice of qualifications, knowledge and skills, for further training and future employment. Schools recognising the importance of adapting to the Fourth Industrial Revolution are blending the latest technologies with teaching through their curriculum implementation.

## A key global influencer

The worldwide COVID-19 pandemic (2020) has thrown into sharp relief the vulnerability of education delivered through the traditional classroom. The continued necessity for learning during the 'lockdown' has accelerated some innovative online learning for students. This emphasises the importance of government and schools investing in a new curriculum model. A blend of technologies with teaching results in a continuity in learning that happens anyhow, anytime, anywhere!

In addition, the critical need for PPE[2] equipment for use in the health and social care sectors gave rise to countless schools across the UK helping out in 2020. This case study demonstrates the timely importance of placing the STEM subjects and creative thinking skills firmly within the school curriculum. Before the pandemic, these technical skills may not have been fully appreciated.

**CASE STUDY OF THE HIGH PROFILE OF TECHNOLOGY DURING THE PEAK OF COVID-19 CRISIS**

TURTON SCHOOL BOLTON[3]

**Sam Gorse – Headteacher**

Led by our heads of technology, a productive and skilled group of teachers have worked hard to keep up with the local demand for PPE. Producing visors, cloth masks, kit bags and headwear, staff worked from 7am to 6pm to keep up with demand.

When we started production, our aim was to produce 500 visors for local use; however, we more than tripled our production, as demand increased. As soon as word got out, the requests for PPE made us realise that we must keep producing in order to support our local community of key workers.

One week's production reached 508 visors, 140 masks, 23 scrub hats and 43 scrub bags in a day.

The PPE was distributed to a wide range of people, including doctors' surgeries, hospitals, hospices, care homes, care workers and special schools. People who were in desperate need of protection in order to fulfil their roles, but who were not on the government's priority lists.

I am so proud of our staff, who, as well as showing integrity and determination in setting daily work for our students, gave up their time, using their talents to help our community and frontline workers.

## Current and projected roles and skills in the Fourth Industrial Revolution

Transforming our curriculum cannot happen without envisaging our world economy and employment trends. The World Economic Forum's analysis of skills shortages, in the period up to 2022, include data analysts, scientists, software and applications developers, e-commerce and social media specialists. In addition, roles enhanced by technology include AI and machine learning specialists, process automation experts, information security analysts, human–machine interaction designers and robotics engineers.[4]

Surprisingly, the following disparate roles are seen as increasingly redundant over the short term. These include many routine-based, middle-skilled white-collar roles; telemarketers, electronics and telecommunications installers, bank tellers, van/motor-cycle drivers, high-street vendors, finance/insurance clerks and lawyers.

Jobs such as cyber catastrophe forecaster, algorithm bias auditor and VR arcade manager are forecast as emerging over the next ten years, presenting new options to students considering how to best prepare for their future.[5] One such job envisaged is an E-sports arena builder requiring a master's degree in architecture, construction management or a related field. The skills include 'gaining contracts for innovative "smart" foundations … erecting immersive cage gaming structures … designing biometric AR/VR displays; and massive state-of-the-art high-definition screens … that expand or contract depending on crowd size'. This is not too far-fetched a reality, as the technologies currently exist. But is our curriculum capable of training our young people with the necessary skills and knowledge?

## What of the 'human skills' in this new Fourth Industrial Revolution?

These new projected roles, critically, sit alongside an increased demand for roles that require distinctively 'human' skills; to accelerate innovation, experimentation and creative collaboration. Despite the emphasis on the STEAM disciplines of Science, Technology, Engineering, Arts and Mathematics, students also, importantly, should access the wider business and creative skills and be given opportunities to develop the key attributes of human and emotional empathy. It is ultimately how we work with and manage others that sets us apart from machines. Essentially these are the skills required for successful working in jobs such as customer service workers, marketing professionals, training and development roles, as well as transformational leaders/managers.

Sydenham High School's[6] media advert drew attention to its sixth form curriculum 'Futureproofing students in a changing landscape'.[7] The school profiled McKinsey Global Institute's 2030 prediction on 'artificial intelligence displacing one fifth of the global work force'. Future career preparation is at the heart of this school's curriculum development post-16. This is with the growing realisation that students need henceforth a generic set of skills within any workplace, rather than necessarily for one specific role. A-level students undertake the Extended Project qualification and an 'Active Citizen Programme' so that they gain creative and critical thinking skills, problem-solving and social development. Year 12 students gain corporate communication skills and a bespoke mentor who prepares them for the world of work, while working on a self-directed project.

We contend that introducing these skills from Year 7 will shape students' thinking from an early age. Training students in these skills can take place through extra-curricular activities, SMSC themed work, or by mapping subject-based knowledge and skills into a project-based approach. For instance, ensuring that every subject, and not just the humanities and English, include an assessment of a self-directed project or a collaborative peer-based project, debate or presentation.

There is a reskilling imperative as skills continue to grow in prominence, including analytical thinking and innovation. Becoming proficient in new technologies means that the soft core skills are increasingly vital. Both Figure 2.1 and Figure 2.2 evidence the synergy between the skills and competencies required in employment. Prime amongst these are communication, creativity, digital skills that are not explicitly structured into the National Curriculum.

The 'human' skills of creativity, originality and initiative, critical thinking, persuasion and negotiation are set to retain or increase their value, as will attention to detail, resilience, flexibility and complex problem-solving. Emotional intelligence, leadership and social influence are key attributes in demand. These, of course, are currently dependent on a school's individual curriculum intent and not a curriculum entitlement for all students.

As we see in Figure 2.2, the basic human skills and competencies are combined within a work context. Most importantly, knowing how to apply these in new situations becomes key through the metacognition strategies. In Table 2.1, employability skills and competencies gathered from employer led research  illustrate how these translate into actual examples in the workplace. This grid can usefully guide curriculum design through mapping these skills across  subjects and identifying teaching opportunities. In this way, students' thinking is influenced and they become more knowledgeable about the importance of the skills, competencies and strategies they require in a work context. This is clearly illustrated in Figure 2.3.

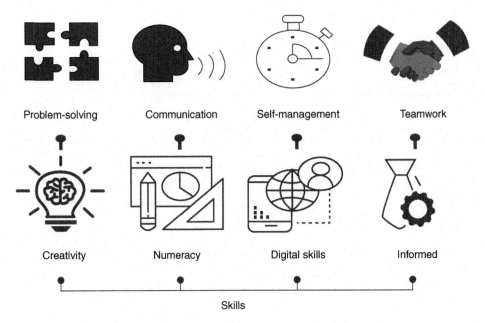

**FIGURE 2.1**  Skills required in employment
Courtesy of Joint Dialogue: How Are Schools Developing Real Employability Skills?

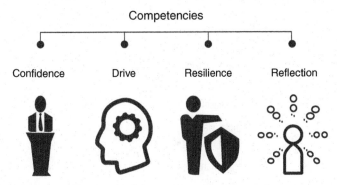

**FIGURE 2.2**  Competencies required in employment
Courtesy of Joint Dialogue: How are Schools Developing Real Employability Skills?

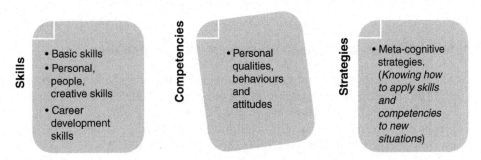

**FIGURE 2.3**  Combined  skills, competencies and strategies required within a work context

**Table 2.1** Employment 'skills grid'

| Wider skills | Examples |
| --- | --- |
| Problem-solving | Preparation for solving a problem |
| Communication | Day-to-day communication (social skills for work) Writing skills Presentation skills |
| Self-management | Organisation Dress and behaviour |
| Teamwork | Involvement Support Collaboration |
| Creativity | Original thoughts and ideas |
| Numeracy | Estimation Deduction |
| Digital skills | Confident use of digital devices Digital responsibility |
| Informed (about the world of work) | Preparation for interviews Interview skills Understanding of job market Service orientation |
| Confidence | Leading teams and groups Decision making |
| Drive | Flexibility Enthusiasm |
| Resilience | Handle criticism Dealing with workloads |
| Reflection | People management Adaptability |

Source: Fettes et al. (2018). *Putting Skills to Work: It's Not So Much the WHAT or Even the WHY, but HOW …* London: Commercial Education Trust.
Courtesy of Joint Dialogue: How Are Schools Developing Real Employability Skills?

## Potential disconnect between curriculum and job market

The educational curriculum has to be in synergy with this changing work skills profile. The growing skills instability in the workplace is affected by the wave of new technologies and trends 'disrupting' traditional business models. A whole new entrepreneurial industry with the gig economy and disrupters co-exist, across all sectors, including retail, health care, education and environmental science.

In any city or town centre, work-hub spaces, such as the London-based Media Works are occupied by 'start-ups' – establishing innovative companies using digital platforms and related technologies. A comprehensive Virgin report, 'The Start-up Low Down' identifies that start-ups contribute £196 billion to the UK economy every year and AI start-ups attracted over 12 per cent of all worldwide private equity investments in the first half of 2018.[8]

All the signs indicate that the knowledge and skills required to perform a number of roles are shifting significantly. The implications for our students is that potentially the career destinations for a number of them sitting in our lessons now could be as CEO or CTO[9] of a start-up company, or working within the disrupter industry. It is doubtful whether a solely academic knowledge-based curriculum will give them the necessary skills set they require to be successful. The start-up era is a brave new world that comes with its very own culture and language. Below is the case study of the creators of UnbOx – a start-up that came about through a desire to help those who were unsure of their next steps following school.

## CASE STUDY OF NIKITA KHANDWALA AND SOFIA VERKHOTUROVA

Our degrees taught us knowledge and theoretical skills and rarely gave us the chance to collaborate with other people. We founded UnbOx to help students align their passion to their profession. Our aim is to help undergraduates around the world make an impact, while learning employability and other transferable skills. We match self-starting students, based on their skills set, to fast-growing start-ups and real-world opportunities in the booming start-up ecosystem. So far, we have attracted 50+ students through our tailored talent matching process. There are many different paths to fulfilment in life and we want to ensure that every student is a bit closer to it by the time they graduate.

As this trend is pervasive across all sectors of society, a good starting point is all subject teachers familiarising themselves with the terminology of *start-up incubators, accelerators, business angels, venture capital* and the *eco-system*.[10] An equally important consideration is whether during curriculum planning, these 'careers' are signposted by CEIAG advisers in schools as a destination for young people and whether they are given practical advice or guidance on how they can follow this route. The DfE's statutory *Careers Guidance and Inspiration* highlights that schools must ensure all students have the 'enterprise and employability skills, experience and qualifications that employers want ... to gain the practical know-how and attributes, relevant for employment'.[11]

## Speed of evolutionary change in the workplace

The prescient Czech writer Karel Čapekand and his brother Josef coined the word 'robot' a century ago, in a play about factory androids where each did the work of two-and-a-half humans at a fraction of the cost. Science fiction has since become business fact.[12] Robots are commonplace in manufacturing, and algorithms play significant roles in companies from UPS to Amazon. The McKinsey report, cites many examples from cooking hamburgers to dispensing drugs in hospital pharmacies.[13] Artificial intelligence computers can read lips with 95 per cent accuracy, outperforming professional lip readers, who tested at 52 per cent accuracy.[14] Further examples from the RSA report, include DeepMind's software that can diagnose 50 types of eye disease with 94 per cent accuracy. The Press Association deploys algorithms to generate 30,000 monthly local news stories and a Shanghai 'fulfilment centre' can process 200,000 orders per day with just four employees.[15]

We recognise that automation is changing the daily work activities and lives of everyone, from miners and landscapers to commercial bankers, fashion designers, welders and CEOs. But how quickly will these automation technologies become a reality in the workplace? It is estimated that by 2030 the vast majority of roles will contain elements of automation and/or AI.[16]

The following evolutionary stages from the mid-nineteenth century onwards, since the last Industrial Revolution are a lesson for us. Productivity growth from the steam engine over 60 years (1850–1910) is calculated at 0.3 per cent. This is contrasted with a similar period of time (2015–2065), where productivity owing to robotics, AI and machine learning is projected to become much greater, at 0.8–1.4 per cent.

These rapid changes in obsolete technology are illustrated by this example: Japanese pagers in the 1960s, known as *pokeberu*, or 'pocket bells' were used by sales people and hospital staff. Pagers, clipped to city workers belts, demonstrated cultural status and industriousness.[17] By the 1980s, 60 million page users existed worldwide; by the 1990s, pagers' popularity was rapidly overtaken by the mobile phone and the rest is history! A YouGov survey in the UK demonstrated the swift rate of changes over a relatively short period.[18] Despite all the devices being an intrinsic part of our history and culture, the vast majority of the children were unable to identify them (Figure 2.4). Interestingly, one child, unable to identify a typewriter, described it creatively as 'a thing that you write movies on!'

The trajectory of change both nationally and internationally, as technology continues to advance, will have an impact on how we, as educationalists should prepare students for a vastly different world. This begs the question of the selection of knowledge presented to students. Students know, for instance, of the devastating impact of two world wars on our history and yet do not learn of the evolutionary changes to, and dramatic impact of technologies on, their lives and their futures.

## The role of technology in the curriculum

In an educational context, we can broadly define technology as the use of knowledge skills and values through creative practical solutions to problems, taking societal and environmental factors into consideration. If taught well, it teaches how to take risks, so that students become more resourceful, innovative, enterprising and capable. If we refer to technology within a school curriculum KS4 setting, this mostly equates to the suite of GCSE Design and Technology (D&T) qualifications (Resistant Materials, Electronic, Graphic and Food Technology), and may include Engineering and Construction. Unless a school is committed within its curriculum intent, to a STEM focus, the emphasis on technological skills development can be comparatively

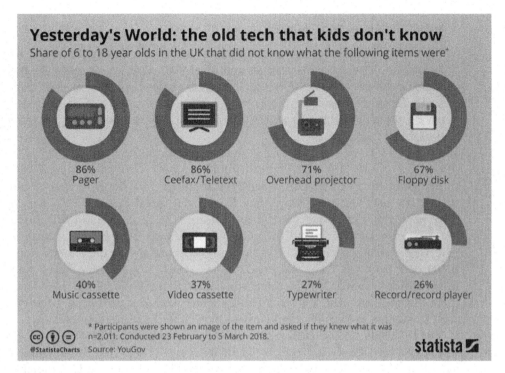

**FIGURE 2.4** What proportion of 6 to 18 year-olds are unable to recognise an image of old technology? Courtesy of 'Statista' 2018 under the Creative Commons License CC BY-ND 3.0

minimised. Despite STEM subjects being interdependent, Maths, Design and Technology and Computing are taught largely separately. Good practice in the mapping of skills and knowledge across these subjects would greatly benefit students' understanding.

The DfE EdTech strategy (2019) reiterates that 'Technology is an enabler and an enhancer.'[19] DfE funding for schools is intended for technology 'to reduce teacher workload … create efficiencies, improve accessibility and inclusion'. *Blended and interactive learning* using technologies has huge benefits. Some innovative and impactful teaching and learning are profiled in 'Edutech schools', as these pioneer the way forward. Case studies from the STEAM Edutech schools 2019 illustrate imaginative practice across the country.[20]

Transforming the curriculum means harnessing the spirit of problem solving and innovation embodied in the STEAM subjects.[21] The cross-curricular skills of observation, logical thinking, creativity and application of Maths, along with technologies, address real world issues. Schools at the forefront recognise this as part of their curriculum intent as in the examples below.[22]

For Wimbledon High Girls School, the STEAM philosophy is embedded in cross-curriculum thinking and experimentation, and explained by the school as 'at the heart of what we do. The STEAM room, it's like a sauna, but for tech'.

### WIMBLEDON HIGH GIRLS SCHOOL

This is a Microsoft Showcase School and the use of Teams and OneNote is the cornerstone of its approach.[23,24] All subject departments work with STEAM, aided by Scientists in Residence located in the school's new STEAM Lab. This enabling space can help break down barriers between subjects, ensuring pupils are confident, critical thinkers with a creative approach to problem-solving. Students are equipped to navigate a fully digital world; adding real value to transforming teaching.

According to a recent poll, teaching technology in schools is seen to outrank even Maths and Sciences. 'More than Code'[25] identified that three-quarters of the employers would encourage candidates to learn tech specialisms so that they could 'futureproof their careers and the company they work for'. A tech specialism was perceived as an 'important factor' in training others, and giving the business leaders an opportunity to learn. Technology was cited as a 'great way to enter dream industries from movies to sports, music to environmentalism'. Interestingly, the imperative is so great that the vast majority of employers would consider partnering their business with a school or college in an initiative to help close the technology skills gap.

The UTC illustrates collaboration with employers towards the next generation of 'confident, work-ready individuals'. The curriculum is delivered through employer-led AI and Mixed Reality projects making learning relevant and memorable and boosting students' academic achievement.

### LONDON DESIGN & ENGINEERING UNIVERSITY TECHNICAL COLLEGE (UTC) (14–19)

Year 13 Digital Media students gained 'Double Distinction', demonstrating real-world projects such as published apps and VR animations with organisations such as Augmentifyit, Fujitsu and Water Aid. Working with real employer briefs, the focus is on 3D printing, robotics, VR, AR and LEGO® technologies and Digital Media assignment work. The programming robots project consists of a collaborative task to get a Nao robot to ski plus a trip to the Italian Alps and 3D printing. Qualifications such as Microsoft Office Specialist and Technical Associate formally recognise the students' digital literacy. The school's pragmatic mantra is: 'try it, measure the impact, evaluate it, adopt or drop!'[26,27]

Friars Academy in partnership with local business Cummins UK, prepares students for the changing world away from life in formal education. Innovative use of technology creates another channel for sharing and receiving information.

### FRIARS ACADEMY, WELLINGBOROUGH, NORTHAMPTONSHIRE

Microsoft 365 brings different perspectives on knowledge. A junior tech team delivers an in-house mobile radio station. A vertical English intervention group uses Sway to share a student newsletter with students, parents and carers, projected in the school's reception.[28,29]

In this 'An Apple Distinguished School', tradition blended with technology across the school promotes students' digital and longer-term business skills, critical thinking, entrepreneurship and self-awareness.

## CATERHAM INDEPENDENT SCHOOL, SURREY

Technology ranges from video reflections on work, through to recording biological reactions down a microscope. An online Digital Inquiry course addresses real life problems, requiring students to apply a digital skill to developing a product. The Innovation Centre's different clubs develops pupils' technology skills outside of the curriculum: cyber security challenges, app-design competitions, LEGO® robotics, VEX robotics, a girls-only coding club.[30,31]

The DfE's EdTech strategy is largely built on 'partnerships'; within the context of the education community working with the EdTech industry. One of the ten challenges addressed is opening up communication and creating independence in learning. The use of technologies is envisaged as transformational for making learning accessible for students with special education needs, such as dyslexia or autistic spectrum disorders. This case study exemplifies how well students learn to use the technology independently.

## CITY OF LONDON ACADEMY (SOUTHWARK)

Students with dyslexia/specific learning difficulties use computers in writing; overcoming difficulties with handwriting, reading and spelling through spell checking errors and reading text out loud. Text-to-speech enables students to listen to assessment questions/instructions and proofread their answers.[32]

'By using the technology, pupils can show people what they can do. If someone has illegible handwriting or undecodeable spelling errors etc., all you're going to see are the errors and not the good work that's behind them. Using the technology means that you get a truer sense of their underlying ability.' Candida Dearing, (SENCO)

This special school is a teaching school and views education through the lens of inclusivity. Its achievements are widely disseminated through events like 'What's Special about Special,' providing insightful case studies into SEND education technology.

## SWISS COTTAGE SCHOOL RESEARCH & DEVELOPMENT CENTRE

Appropriate communication devices and specific apps – like Snap, Core and Clicker – are allocated according to students' needs. The impact of technology across the school, and for wider stakeholders, is channelled via the centre's online learning journal. This allows information on pupil progress to be tracked and records formative and summative assessment measures.[33,34]

It is intended that governmental level partnerships with the UK's innovation foundation Nesta, will lead to technological solutions on essay marking, formative assessment, parental engagement and timetabling technology – four of the ten EdTech challenges set out in the plan. In Denbigh High School, teaching through PowerPoint slides is replaced by Green Screen that creates immediacy in learning.

### DENBIGH HIGH SCHOOL, LUTON, BEDFORDSHIRE

The versatile 'Green Screen' (that combines layering of images from different sources into a single image) is used in teaching about World War I to instant video playback in PE lessons, to the development of apps by students. This includes an online safety mechanism for pupils, parents and teachers and has been selected by UNESCO as the UK case study for 'Using mobile technology to support learners from disadvantaged backgrounds'.[35,36]

In West Grantham Academy, students are trained to become leaders of their own learning and 'Sharing Good Practice Sessions' to assist staff in becoming 'Apple' teachers.

### THE WEST GRANTHAM ACADEMY

The school's use of iPads in the classroom and at home deepens the learning experience allowing independent study – via weekly e-statements, Showbie, Seesaw, Tassomai, Complete Maths and other options. Modelling through dual coding and collaborative writing focuses on extended writing skills.[37,38]

## Moving ahead – transforming curriculum potential

AI can be used to individualise learning from Maths to Languages. Feedback is tailored to match ability and tasks selected by AI that extends learning and consolidates concepts. Voice active and physical interactions potentially exist for students to try out their practical skills in PE, DT, construction and so on, or to simulate a real in-work scenario. For instance, in A-level Science, those wishing to pursue a career in medicine can experience an A&E Triage through virtual reality. These are all possible and as always complemented by teacher guidance and feedback. Google Classroom and Microsoft Teams have taken learning to be however, wherever and whenever, with teachers and students accessing class assignments, course materials and feedback. The potential is limitless.

The Google Reference School (below) wants its students to feel at ease in 'this rapidly changing climate'; Google for Education and Chromebooks help students to become well-informed, responsible digital citizens. Developing memorable learning through virtual learning and addressing subject misconceptions are key features.

**WITTON PARK ACADEMY**

Staff use of apps guide students in their learning with real time advice; individually and discretely. Cloud storage allows students to work at school, at home, between the two, nurturing them into independent and curious learners. They are empowered to virtually travel to parts of the world to experience the scenes and sites that they learn about in History and Geography. From the teachers' perspective, positive impacts are cited from the use of G Suite, including time, cost and paper savings.[39,40]

## Summary

A 2016 analysis by McKinsey & Company reported that teaching is one of the least likely professions to be automated.[41] However during the Pandemic 2020, the proliferation of Zoom, Microsoft Teams, social media and apps radically paved the way for a different learning model. An evaluation of its success or shortcomings could very usefully inform a future curriculum model with a blend of teaching and online learning at its heart. The growing number of resources devoted to tech educational tools raises the important question as to whether, in themselves, these constitute the golden panacea in the curriculum. A 2017 review conducted by Escueta et al. finds that simply providing students with access to hardware has a limited impact on learning outcomes.[42] As we saw in the case studies, the effectiveness of AI related technologies is optimised through interactive and blended learning opportunities between students, and their teachers, rather than solo working in lessons. We need to exercise a degree of caution on replacing human interaction by technology, especially, for students with special educational needs. In the impact analysis conducted by EEF of what works and what is value for money in students' learning, digital technologies were judged to be moderate impact with moderate cost based on extensive evidence. Conversely, feedback from teachers was considered as very high impact with low costs based on extensive evidence.[43] A combination of both is desirable.

Looking to other countries; Estonia[44] for instance, as a high achieving country, is transforming its education system through the use of AI with learning environments that combine academic, vocational and cultural strands. This includes boosting their start-up culture.

Deploying technologies, including learning assistive technologies, is certainly welcomed. However, ditching other teaching methodologies in favour of the new age of technological advances will not produce successful outcomes for all our students. Given the importance of 'human skills' in further training and employment, we propose a future that pairs artificial intelligence with valuing the cognitive, social and emotional skills of people.

> EdTech is not a silver bullet … (It is) an inseparable thread woven throughout the processes of teaching and learning … What we should concentrate on is when and in which ways it is best deployed to support these processes.
>
> (Dominic Norrish Group Director, United learning Trust)[45]

By investing exclusively in technology to deliver our curriculum, do we risk reverting once more to the Henry Ford model of '*have any car, in any colour, as long as its black!*' - one-size-fits-all? A more graduated approach, taking account of student cohorts and local contexts, is arguably more beneficial.

## Notes

1   B. Pring et al. (2019) Cognizant's centre for the future of work. Available at: www.cognizant.com/future-of-work (Accessed: 8 November 2019).
2   PPE – Personal Protective Equipment.
3   www.turton.uk.com
4   O. Newton et al. (2019) Skills shortages in the UK economy. Available at: www.edge.co.uk/sites/default/files/documents/skills_shortage_bulletin_4_web-1.pdf (Accessed: 7 November 2019).
5   B. Pring et al. (2019) Cognizant's Centre for the Future of Work. Available at: www.cognizant.com/future-of-work (Accessed: 8 November 2019).
6   Sydenham High School (2020) Sydenham High School. Available at: www.gdst.net/school/sydenham-high-school/?gclid=EAIaIQobChMIl4iC4p2c6AIVCbLtCh1p1AY4EAAYASAAEgI2wvD_BwE (Accessed: 19 January 2020).
7   *Guardian*: 21 September 2019.
8   Centre for Economic and Business Research (2019) The start-up low down: How start-ups are transforming Britain. www.virginstartup.org/news/start-low-down-how-start-ups-are-transforming-britain.
9   CEO – Chief Executive Officer; CTO – Chief Technical Officer.
10  https://abdoriani.com/91-startup-terms-every-entrepreneur-should-know/
11  Department for Education (2017) *Careers Guidance and Inspiration in Schools*. London: Department for Education.
12  K. Čapek (1920) *R.U.R. (Rossum's Universal Robots)* . Gutenberg [Online]. Available at: www.gutenberg.org/ebooks/59112 (Accessed: 3 December 2019).
13  M. Chui (2016) Where machines could replace humans and where they can't (yet), www.mckinsey.com/business-functions/mckinsey-digital/our-insights/where-machines-could-replace-humans-and-where-they-cant-yet.
14  H. Hodson (2016) Google's Deepmind AI can lip-read TV shows better than a pro. Available at: www.newscientist.com/article/2113299-googles-deepmind-ai-can-lip-read-tv-shows-better-than-a-pro/ (Accessed: 8 November 2019).
15  The RSA (2018) Work in an age of radical technologies. Available at: www.thersa.org/discover/publications-and-articles/reports/work-in-an-age-of-radical-technologies (Accessed: 29 November 2019).
16  K. Rooney (2019) These revolutionary technologies are now unused and forgotten. Available at: www.weforum.org/agenda/2019/10/obsolete-technology-pager-japan-walkman-floppy-disk-vcr/ (Accessed: 8 November 2019).
17  Ibid.
18  M. Smith (2018) These revolutionary technologies are now unused and forgotten. Available at: https://yougov.co.uk/topics/technology/articles-reports/2018/04/26/two-thirds-children-dont-know-what-floppy-disk (Accessed: 11 November 2019).
19  D. Hinds et al. (2019) Realising the potential of technology in education. https://assets.publishing.service.gov.uk/government/uploads/system/uploads/attachment_data/file/791931/DfE-Education_Technology_Strategy.pdf. London: Department for Education (DfE).

20    T. Goddard et al. (2019) The Ed Tech 50 Schools, www.ednfoundation.org/wp-content/uploads/EDTECH-50-SCHOOLS-2019.pdf. London: The Education Foundation.

21    STEAM Science, Technology, Engineering, Arts, Maths.

22    Visits can be arranged to the schools through the Education Foundation. The excellent sample case studies below are from the STEAM 50 Edutech schools 2019. These represent a celebration of the innovative and forward-thinking work in place in schools across the United Kingdom and Northern Ireland.

23    Wimbledon High School website (2019) Available at: www.wimbledonhigh.gdst.net/ (Accessed: 15 November 2019).

24    T. Goddard et al. (2019) The Ed Tech 50 Schools. www.ednfoundation.org/wp-content/uploads/EDTECH-50-SCHOOLS-2019.pdf. London: The Education Foundation.

25    #More Than Code (2020) More Than Code. Available at: https://morethancode.cc/ (Accessed: 19 January 2020).

26    London Design & Engineering University Technical College website (2019). Available at: www.ldeutc.co.uk/ (Accessed: 14 November 2019).

27    T. Goddard et al. (2019) The Ed Tech 50 Schools. www.ednfoundation.org/wp-content/uploads/EDTECH-50-SCHOOLS-2019.pdf. London: The Education Foundation.

28    Friars Academy website (2019) Available at: www.friarsacademy.org/ (Accessed: 14 November 2019).

29    T. Goddard et al. (2019) The Ed Tech 50 Schools. www.ednfoundation.org/wp-content/uploads/EDTECH-50-SCHOOLS-2019.pdf. London: The Education Foundation.

30    www.caterhamschool.co.uk/

31    T. Goddard et al. (2019) The Ed Tech 50 Schools. www.ednfoundation.org/wp-content/uploads/EDTECH-50-SCHOOLS-2019.pdf. London: The Education Foundation.

32    D. Hinds et al. (2019) Realising the potential of technology in education. https://assets.publishing.service.gov.uk/government/uploads/system/uploads/attachment_data/file/791931/DfE-Education_Technology_Strategy.pdf. London: Department for Education (DfE).

33    Swiss Cottage School Research & Development Centre website (2019) Available at: http://swisscottage.camden.sch.uk/ (Accessed: 15 November 2019).

34    T. Goddard et al. (2019) The Ed Tech 50 Schools. www.ednfoundation.org/wp-content/uploads/EDTECH-50-SCHOOLS-2019.pdf. London: The Education Foundation.

35    Denbigh High Luton website (2019) Available at: www.denbighhigh.luton.sch.uk/ (Accessed: 14 November 2019).

36    T. Goddard et al. (2019) The Ed Tech 50 Schools. www.ednfoundation.org/wp-content/uploads/EDTECH-50-SCHOOLS-2019.pdf. London: The Education Foundation.

37    The West Grantham Academy St Hugh's website (2019) Available at: www.wgacademiestrust.org.uk/ (Accessed: 15 November 2019).

38    T. Goddard et al. (2019) The Ed Tech 50 Schools. www.ednfoundation.org/wp-content/uploads/EDTECH-50-SCHOOLS-2019.pdf. London: The Education Foundation.

39    Witton Park Academy website (2019) Available at: https://witton.atctrust.org.uk/ (Accessed: 15 November 2019).

40    T. Goddard et al. (2019) The Ed Tech 50 Schools. www.ednfoundation.org/wp-content/uploads/EDTECH-50-SCHOOLS-2019.pdf. London: The Education Foundation.

41    M. Chui (2016) Where machines could replace humans– and where they can't (yet), www.mckinsey.com/business-functions/mckinsey-digital/our-insights/where-machines-could-replace-humans-and-where-they-cant-yet: McKinsey Digital.

42    M. Escueta et al. (2017) Education technology: An evidence-based review. www.povertyactionlab.org/sites/default/files/publications/NBER-23744-EdTech-Review.pdf: National Bureau of Economic Research.

43   Education Endowment Foundation (2019) Teaching and Learning Toolkit. Available at: https://educationendowmentfoundation.org.uk/evidence-summaries/teaching-learning-toolkit (Accessed: 11 November 2019).

44   OECD (2019) PISA 2018 Results. Available at: www.oecd.org/pisa/publications/pisa-2018-results.htm (Accessed: 19 February 2020).

45   D. Hinds et al. (2019) Realising the potential of technology in education. https://assets.publishing.service.gov.uk/government/uploads/system/uploads/attachment_data/file/791931/DfE-Education_Technology_Strategy.pdf. London: Department for Education (DfE).

# 3

# Students at the heart of curriculum

## Introduction

Both as influencer and a challenge is the 2019 OFSTED inspection framework. The principles are welcomed with the spotlight on the *single conversation at the heart of inspection* and the interconnectedness of curriculum through its intent, implementation and impact. Whilst we applaud an inspection framework that aims to get under the skin of the education received by each student, the reality is more complex.

In practice, how fit is the intent, implementation and impact of the EBacc knowledge-based curriculum for all students as measured through each student's educational experience? These are key impact measures:

- the inclusive and equitable nature of the curriculum intent;
- success through outcomes by student group and the 'disadvantage factor';
- curriculum relevance to students' future destinations, further training and employment.

## The OFSTED 2019/2020 framework: A signposted road map leads to each student's destination

It remains to be seen how accurately the inspection process evaluates the impact on the educational outcomes of different pupil groups; in particular, those with a range of special educational needs and those termed 'disadvantaged' or 'vulnerable'. However, the risk is that whilst trying to implement a curriculum that has a positive impact on all students' achievement, schools are still shackled to the National Curriculum and need to prove an academic EBacc curriculum which is deemed 'broad and balanced'. This means that they are unable to take the curriculum's relevance into account, in relation to the students' profile and local context.

Implicit in every OFSTED framework[1] has been the duty of OFSTED HMI and inspectors to inspect without '*fear or favour*' and to evaluate the quality of education through the evidence they gather based on students' experiences, progress and outcomes. The 2019 framework methodology is explicit, stating, 'Inspectors must use all their evidence to evaluate what *it is like to attend the school.*'

The translation of this intent into reality in the classroom – the implementation and its impact for each young person – will of course be markedly different.

Impact will be successfully demonstrated through how well the senior – and especially middle – leaders dovetail the curriculum's intent and implementation in line with the needs of each student. OFSTED inspectors test out whether 'curriculum *is rooted in the solid consensus of the school's leaders about the knowledge and skills* that pupils need to take advantage of opportunities, responsibilities and experiences of later life'.

Is the curriculum's intent designed to broadly serve students who are on a trajectory to successfully gain the EBacc suite of subjects-levels 4–9? If this is the case, is the curriculum sufficiently acknowledging the abilities and needs of those students with special educational needs and disabilities, others for whom the curriculum is difficult to access (owing to literacy, language and numeracy barriers), vulnerable students, as well as those from specific socio-economic backgrounds, gender and ethnicity? Amongst these might reside the sporadic attenders and/or persistent absentees and those students who are internally or fixed term excluded. Then the curriculum needs to focus on the higher ability students and those who are on a trajectory not to achieve their full potential – some of whom might well fall into the vulnerable category, or be on the spectrum of autism.

This is a complex melee of students. Even if we were to construct a Venn diagram of placing our students into the different categories, so that we start to recognise their differences and similarities, this would still not capture the full diversity sitting in our classrooms.

'Powerfully addressing social disadvantage' argues for a clear route map for all students that might, paradoxically, suggest bespoke pathways for some. Most importantly, the focus by inspectors is on 'what pupils need to know and be able to do to reach those end points'. A typical school plans and sequences so that new knowledge and skills build on what has been taught before and towards its clearly defined end points. Connections are made in learning within a subject and cross-curriculum. Therefore, it follows logically what happens in the classroom, or out of the classroom, and must reflect the school's local context by 'addressing typical gaps in pupils' knowledge and skills.

The curriculum leadership must structure opportunities for this to happen. Gaps do matter. They disrupt the sequence of knowledge and skills, and provide a true predictor of the student's P8/A8 outcomes trajectory. Over time, the gaps will, in inverse proportions, have a negative impact on the acquisition of knowledge and skills development. The result is students acquiring fragmented and superficial knowledge, and disengaging from learning, and at best, requiring rote learning intervention prior to GCSE examinations.

We all know this, but it is arguable whether all schools today can truthfully say that *consistently* addressing gaps in students' knowledge and skills across all subjects, is a *leadership priority* within the curriculum intent and implementation. The implication is that schools must ensure that those students with sporadic attendance and/or those subject to exclusions, for whichever reason, will require some form of meaningful 'catch up' learning opportunities or provision. Many schools ensure that students' behaviours are addressed, but fail to systematically address the learning that they miss. In addition, this needs careful monitoring to ensure they do not fall behind, within each year group.

The OFSTED framework promises a far greater focus on the quality of curriculum for all students' learning. The implications for schools are that the previous unique focus on examination outcomes has shifted to schools doing what they should always do – ensuring that all students experience a broad and balanced curriculum, so that each and every student's learning opportunities is optimised.

## Is the EBacc curriculum intent matching impact?

The EBacc curriculum of today is hallmarked and branded to provide world-class educational standards. It is predicated on an entitlement towards benchmarked standards in at least five academic subjects. These are judged as the bedrock of a good education and the stepping stone for each student's future destinations. Driving the successful attainment of the 'academic' GCSEs, is the government's aspirational target; three-quarters of Year 10 pupils studying EBacc subjects by 2022, rising to 90 per cent by 2025.

Yet, in 2019, under two-fifths of students were entered nationally for the EBacc suite of subjects, resulting in 14–22 per cent of these students attaining 'good' level 5 GCSEs, with stark regional variations within this. Of those students who had been excluded from schools in 2018, the harsh reality is only 2 per cent achieved a GCSE in English and Maths. One in two of excluded students do not even access education, employment or training from 16 (NEET)[2].

A further challenge to schools is the fitness for purpose of a GCSE EBacc curriculum by gender and ethnicity. 2019 outcomes indicate boys are not as successful as girls in GCSEs.[3] Interesting patterns emerge: in every ethnic group girls had a higher average Attainment 8 score than boys; White British and Black Caribbean scored below the average, whilst the highest scoring pupil groups were Chinese, Indian, Bangladeshi, Black African, Irish and White Other.

In schools where the student population is disproportionately skewed towards boys – in particular, White British and Black Caribbean – it might follow that based on the statistically lower attainment of these two groups, whole school outcomes might be impacted negatively. This has potential implications for curriculum design.

## Disadvantage gap: Inequitable outcomes

Judging by the GCSE outcomes in English and Mathematics; more than half (57 per cent) of students left school in 2019 without a strong Level 5 pass in English and Mathematics, with considerable variation in geographical/regional location and student groups.[4] In addition, many students made negative progress from their starting point. The persistent disadvantage gap has widened during 2011–2018 in GCSE Maths and English. The attainment gap between pupil groups demonstrates that the overall attainment gap between disadvantaged students and non-disadvantaged students is widening considerably across the secondary sector, with gender and ethnicity variations. Regional variations indicate the highest 25 per cent gaps are in the north west and north east – Blackpool, Peterborough, Rotherham, followed by Kent and Cornwall. 'If the recent five-year trend continues, it would take over 500 years for the disadvantage gap to close by the end of secondary school.'[5]

Most worrying of all is the absence of any progress in reducing the gap between special educational needs and disabilities (SEND) and their peers. SEND students comprise a national average of a sixth of the total school population. Students with an EHCP/statement are three years behind their peers when they leave school at 16 and students with SEND needs to achieve, on average, over half a grade lower than their non-SEND peers.[6]

OFSTED asserts that the curriculum should not be 'dumbed down' through 'a reduced curriculum' and the delivery of the EBacc continues to be the priority. Insufficiently detailed research exists on its impact, but we contend that this continues to be a major factor in inequitable outcomes for SEND students and others.

## The measure of curriculum success

The OFSTED expectation is that a 'broad and balanced' curriculum entails all students successfully achieving a strong academic core of subjects, through the EBacc suite and this, together with at least, three 'Open' subjects. The OFSTED framework's expectation is a curriculum, containing 'high academic/vocational/technical ambition for all pupils'.

The hard reality is that reconciling all these aspects within the curriculum and enabling all students, regardless of ability, to achieve their personal aspirations is a complex and tough juggling act. The vocational, technical and creative subjects do not feature in the EBacc target. For instance, overall entries in GCSEs arts and creative subjects have declined. Through exploring access to creative and cultural sectors, Huddleston and Ashton (2018) note that 'creative opportunities have been reduced ... the perverse consequences have been for schools to concentrate efforts on improving performance in (EBacc) subjects at the expense of others'.[7]

The intent of EBacc, with the single focus on knowledge-based outcomes, and pitching similar overall expectations for all students, is to create a level playing field. Ironically, by not taking sufficient account of different pupil groups' starting points, abilities and socio-economic factors, the intent appears out of kilter with the impact. The Progress 8 and Attainment 8 accountability measures indicate that schools with a high ability intake, such as selective schools, tend to achieve higher A8 scores, as it is easier for students to gain the high level 5, rather than the standard pass level 4. Arguably, this could be because the education curriculum is at risk of teaching rote method and recall. These are the easiest skills to measure, and certain pupil groups might be more adept than others. Moreover, moving towards a two-year GCSE might increase barriers for certain pupil groups, who require longer to successfully complete their GCSEs in line with their potential.

## Adapting the educational curriculum is timely

The convergence of these diverse factors is timely for us to consider our curriculum design. We are not alone in revisiting our secondary curriculum. Other countries are also responding to the same global challenges as we face. Japan, Singapore and Finland, all renowned for their high levels of achievement, have reduced the size of their knowledge curriculum in order to make space for schools to develop creativity skills and personal attributes.

Once we have a notion of what the intent of our curriculum is, and how we intend to shape our students and adequately prepare them for careers and/or further education, we find we are limited by a curriculum focused primarily on the acquisition of academic knowledge. With an increasing number of students wishing to opt for apprenticeships and work-based training,[8] we have to consider whether the principles of a solely knowledge-based curriculum are really serving the needs of every student. To seriously pursue education's 'levelling up' agenda within the 11–16 curriculum, a renewed focus on genuine choices between academic, technical, creative and vocational training is an excellent place to start.

## Summary

Returning to our example of Henry Ford's famous black Ford car: it diversified rapidly from the late 1920s, and delivered a more bespoke and increasingly sophisticated model in different colours that catered for all tastes worldwide and served the needs of a fast-changing global economy. Can we do the same with our curriculum?

We are now at a crossroads, aiming towards the destination of successful outcomes for all our students. To borrow from the title of Robert Frost's famous poem 'The Road Less Travelled', may we dare to venture off the beaten path of the knowledge curriculum and blaze a new trail? We must explore the road less well travelled if we are to make the difference for all our students' life chances![9]

At this crossroads, we educationalists, along with politicians and the leaders of our country, must make a paradigm shift. There is now a compelling case for a stronger balance of skills and knowledge within the English secondary 11–19 curriculum, thus moving away from the broadly knowledge-based curricula, developed over thirty years ago. The priority must be to ensure equitable and inclusive outcomes for all our students through relevant curriculum pathways.

The Edge Foundation reports that a 'knowledge rich' curriculum learned by rote for end-point examinations, 'fails to give all young people the skills that employers have clearly asked for in their workforce for the future'.[10]

We must not lose sight of the relevance for all our students as they are not simply vessels to be filled with data and a sequence of facts! The intense spotlight on the study of the EBacc academic subjects, with an end-point assessment and exam grades as a prime measure of success, arguably risks becoming elitist in its ambitions. We might churn out students, at one extreme, who like the students in Charles Dickens's *Hard Times*, attending Mr Gradgrind's model school, are trained to become the perfect utilitarians![11]

At the same time, creating a rote-learning culture is not congruent with twenty-first-century skills and jobs, needed in the age of the Fourth Industrial Revolution. While technology has rendered many jobs that existed in the 1990s obsolete, it has also led to the creation of new possibilities and avenues that never before existed. From making a living off selling artisanal candles, to managing social media, through to the creation of an app that delivers health and social care for the elderly, the career options available today are nothing like they were 20 years ago.

## Notes

1   OFSTED (2019) *The Education Inspection Framework,* 1st edn. www.gov.uk/government/publications/education-inspection-framework. London: OFSTED.

2   A. Powell (2018) NEET: *Young People Not in Education, Employment or Training.* London: The House of Commons.

3   Department for Education (2019) GCSE results ('Attainment 8'). Available at: www.ethnicity-facts-figures.service.gov.uk/education-skills-and-training/11-to-16-years-old/gcse-results-attainment-8-for-children-aged-14-to-16-key-stage-4/latest (Accessed: 25 November 2019).

4   Department for Education (2020) Statistics: GCSEs (key stage 4). Available at: www.gov.uk/government/collections/statistics-gcses-key-stage-4 (Accessed: 3 February 2020).

5   Education Policy Institute, J. Hutchinson et al. (2019) Education in England: Annual Report 2019, https://epi.org.uk/publications-and-research/annual-report-2019/. London: EPI.

6   Department for Education (2019) *Special Educational Needs: An Analysis and Summary of Data.* London: Department for Education.

7   P. Huddleston and H. Ashton (2019) *Essays on Employer Engagement in Education,* 1st edn. Abingdon: Routledge.

8   Department for Education (2020) Apprenticeships and Traineeships, England: January 2020. Available at: https://assets.publishing.service.gov.uk/government/uploads/system/uploads/attachment_data/file/861944/Apprenticeships-and-traineeships-commentary.pdf (Accessed: 1 March 2020).

9   R. Frost (1916) *The Road Not Taken.* Available at: www.poetryfoundation.org/poems/44272/the-road-not-taken London: Macmillan (Accessed: 2 October 2019).

10  The Edge Foundation (2018) Towards a twenty-first century education system: Edge Future Learning. Available at: www.edge.co.uk/news/edge-news/towards-a-twenty-first-century-education-system-edge-future-learning (Accessed: 19 November 2019).

11  C. Dickens (1854) *Hard Times,* 1st edn. London: Cignet Classics.

PART

# The students' voice: An inclusive and equitable curriculum

# 4

# A curriculum for SEND and vulnerable students

## Introduction

The curriculum intent should be flexible for meeting the diverse needs of all students, and especially those with SEND (special educational needs and disabilities); so that we ensure true equity and equality of opportunity. Aiming for high standards and aspirations enables students to optimise their progress and achieve successful outcomes. The quality and impact of teaching on learning for SEND students, as opposed to 'additional support/intervention', frequently receives less attention in a school. Yet, increasingly, SEND students are expected to achieve the very same qualifications as their non-SEND peers over the same period of time.

The government's EBacc equality impact analysis[1] recommended successful outcomes in EBacc subjects through 'differentiated and personalised' provision, including additional teacher support, and effective use of pupil premium funding. The intent would be appropriately planned lessons, without barriers to every student achieving.

> students without EHC plans, need appropriate curriculum models and pathways ...in view of further destinations, training and jobs.[1]

As the EBacc may not be entirely suitable for some of these students, schools must review 'alternative options'. Pathways that include Wave 2 and 3 interventions are more likely to support students in progressing to a broader range of options post-16.[2] Gordon School's provision map illustrates these diverse and differentiated approaches very well.

In this chapter, we explore various ways that schools within their own curriculum intent facilitate access to the mainstream curriculum through high-quality teaching and support for SEND students.

## Evaluating need within curriculum

Developing the right pathway required insights into the reasons behind students' negative behaviours. Students' insecurities and frustrations are often because they

| GL Assessment (PASS) Attitudinal factor | What it measures |
|---|---|
| 1. Feelings about school | Explores whether a pupil feels secure, confident and included in their learning community. |
| 2. Perceived learning capability | Offers an insight into a pupil's level of self-respect, determination and openness to learning. |
| 3. Self-regard | Equivalent to self-worth, focused specifically on self-awareness as a learner, highlighting levels of motivation and determination. |
| 4. Preparedness for learning | Study skills, attentiveness and concentration, looking at the pupil's determination and openness to learning. |
| 5. Attitudes to teachers | Young person's perceptions of the relationships they have with adults in school. A low score can flag a lack of respect. |
| 6. General work ethic | Highlights pupil's aspirations and motivation to succeed in life; focuses on purpose and direction, not just at school, but beyond. |
| 7. Confidence in learning | Identifies a pupil's ability to think independently; to persevere when faced with a challenge. |
| 8. Attitudes to attendance | Correlating very highly with actual attendance 12 months later; teachers intercede earlier with strategies to reduce the likelihood of truancy. |
| 9. Response to curriculum demands | Focuses more narrowly on school-based motivation to undertake and complete curriculum-based tasks; highlighting the pupil's approach to communication and collaboration. |

**FIGURE 4.1** A description of 'attitudinal factors' used by GL Assessment

cannot express themselves. Knowing the reasons can usefully inform the strategies for learning. Widely used assessments include the Boxall Profile,[3] an assessment of social, emotional and behavioural development. Other assessments listed in Appendix 4.1 (available at www.routledge.com/9780367900878) identify the cognitive and non-verbal abilities, working memory, reasoning and auditory processing skills and dyslexia.

The *PASS* factors that determine self-efficacy for academic success and self-regulation

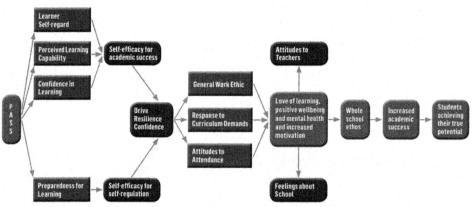

**FIGURE 4.2** Pupils' Attitude to Self and School (PASS) factors and how they lead to success

The GL Assessment's psychometric measure, Pupil Attitudes to Self and School (PASS),[4] helpfully act as an academic barometer, through identifying the barriers to learning (Figure 4.1). Evaluating student attitudes to learning and school are compounded by external factors over which the school has no control. These include family, friends, social media, economic and social circumstances and perceptions of self. Whilst these factors do not relate directly to learning, they are key influencers and contribute to students' wellbeing; ultimately, having an impact on attitudes to learning and outcomes.

It is worth investing in an assessment for all students so that a school can build a profile of each student; in particular, to self-regard, preparedness for learning, general work ethics and response to curriculum demands.

The case study below evidences how the nine attitudinal factors in the PASS assessments can influence interventions. Figure 4.2 identifies the interrelationship between these factors, culminating in students achieving their full academic potential.

### SHEVINGTON HIGH SCHOOL

All students at the school underwent the PASS, along with the Cognitive Abilities Test® (CAT4). A group of Year 10 students with negative PASS scores were identified and their Cognitive Abilities Test® (CAT4)[5] results, and current attainment data reviewed. Maths, Science and Humanities were identified for intervention. Mentors supporting the students worked closely with the subject teachers.

The school's headline findings were:

80 per cent of students improved their mean PASS score; the pilot had had a highly positive impact on improving attitudes. 30 per cent of students had improved total progress through comparing target total points against current total points. The Self-Regard factor was most improved in three students; the mentoring had had a positive effect on this element of PASS.

In the case of All Saints Catholic College, the students' 'high needs' were assessed and best met through an accredited alternative curriculum.

### ALL SAINTS CATHOLIC COLLEGE – WESTMINSTER LONDON

The Alternative ASDAN curriculum, provides students with a range of life, social, literacy and numeracy functional skills in touch-typing, cooking, travel training, money handling and gardening. A high teaching assistant to student results in students receiving a scheme of learning tailored to their learning needs.[6]

## Making learning accessible

Wave 1 teaching that carefully takes into account differentiated/personalised teaching strategies by the teacher and/or teaching assistant will have the greatest impact. These include strategies outlined below.

*Varying the content* can include changing font size, coloured overlays, reducing length, reading age of text (covering curriculum content from a different key stage), a multi-sensory approach, such as adding pictures.

*The pace and model of delivery* is prime: presenting information (spoken and written) in a way that all students follow; appropriate vocabulary, chunking information, rephrasing tasks and instructions for clarity, examples/modelling of what is expected, scaffolding learning, students given sufficient time to think and to respond. The accelerated pace of lessons – while well-intentioned, results in allocating all students the same time, for instance, 5–10 minutes on average to complete a task. This can be non-productive, cause anxiety and potentially a sense of failure for those who need longer.

*Differentiated learning objectives or outcomes* can usefully guide learning tasks and activities with students completing different objectives and/or targets, still within the overall class objectives, but most importantly, relevant to their level and pace of learning.

*Allowing students flexibility* to move up or across to a different objective and a different task or activity increases motivation.

*Opportunities to evidence learning* using a wide range of methods means students can choose how best to complete a task, such as storyboard, presentation, or by digitally researching information that need compilation and sequencing.

What is especially helpful is outlining *subject specific strategies* that are proven effective for the student, such as writing frames, types of questioning, use of worked examples, self-checking techniques. Where appropriate, short periods of time can be spent on improving specific aspects spelling, reading, handwriting, revision and study skills and literacy, outside the classroom. Group work on social skills, often with external agencies, can only be effective, if regularly monitored for impact in relation to attitudes to learning in class.

As an example, the student in the case study below usually exhibited low levels of concentration, but felt comfortable with this learning method in English classes; the notes he produced were relevant and concise. The same student however lost focus in Maths as there were no identifiable strategies to guide him.

## CASE STUDY: SECONDARY LONDON ACADEMY

In an English lesson, while the English subject teacher talked through the character and social analysis in the J. B. Priestley play *An Inspector Calls*, a Year 9 student with ADHD used his Chromebook, to independently make Cornell style notes. When questioned by the reviewer he responded that this way of working assisted his revision and extended writing skills. The *'assess, plan, do, and review' cycle passport* provided by the school was helpful in providing practical strategies to teachers on behaviours and seating arrangements in lessons.

## Motivating students with SEND

Students with SEND often have low internal motivation for different reasons; such as, negative previous experiences of completion of academic tasks, or simply failing to see the relevance to their lives, or being unable to sustain the focus on task to see it through.[7] It is understandable for teachers in these situations to provide an external motivation, either a reward, or a sanction such as the threat of a detention, for the completion of the task to take place. Whilst both forms of external motivation may result in the completion of the task, what is less secure is the depth of knowledge learnt.

What needs prioritising is students' capacity to develop the 'invisible', but essential metacognitive skills. They can then develop a greater awareness of the need to learn, how to learn best and can revisit gaps in their learning. However, this is a consistently undervalued and underinvested aspect in schools. A SEND student's learning plan may only contain the 'Assess, Plan, Do and Review' cycle of tutoring that outlines 'visible' strategies and these may include behaviour techniques, seating plan, additional support and so on. Importantly most plans do not prioritise *learning to learn skills*.

One of the greatest challenges facing SEND students relates to generalised learning skills, or 'thinking skills': attention, working memory and processing difficulties, specifically within a subject context. Students with ADHD and moderate learning difficulties find varying levels of success accessing aspects of subjects; as this is highly dependent on motivation and resilience in learning. They will need to focus on the task at hand, inhibit inappropriate responses, hold and transfer information to long-term memory, make decisions on the basis of the information and finally, plan how best to organise their response.

We must also consider the dynamics of teacher/student relationship, quality of teaching assessment, including teacher feedback. These are the constant variables in each lesson for each student each day and will affect the quality of their educational experience in the school, turning it into a game of snakes and ladders … with winners and losers! Students experience frustration, disappointment, brief glimpses of success in their achievements and so on.

Precious time is potentially wasted in the classroom when teachers are confronted with students' aptitudes, attitudes and skills-set, influenced by a matrix of factors over which, they sometimes have no control. Precisely because of this fact, the degree to which a student then effectively interacts with his/her learning in any subject and takes responsibility for own learning may fluctuate. There are students who may move from subject lesson to subject lesson over the course of a day, five days a week, with a precarious degree of uncertainty as to what they are actually learning.

If questioned on the knowledge or skills they have acquired or are acquiring, they may not know, or give bare monosyllabic responses. There is little sign of actual progress in learning in their work books, or indeed in assessments they undergo. Breaking this dysfunctional cycle of superficial learning so that we re-enthuse and inspire these students is paramount. We cannot risk marginalising a significant group of young people, through no fault of their own, only because they are not well served by teaching in the mainstream curriculum.

Once, we accept the prime importance of metacognition skills, motivation and resilience in learning, we can influence this. SEND students must be offered opportunities to be trained in these disciplines. At this point, successful outcomes for students cease to become dependent on an amalgam of random factors that can turn the quality of students' educational experiences into a lottery!

## Overcoming barriers

Acquiring metacognition skills, within a subject context, is key for impactful retention and manipulation of knowledge. This is about seeking out a combination of what works for different students and in different contexts.

There are physical factors that interfere with effective learning, particularly, for students with attention deficit and distraction tendencies. Sensory (hearing, looking and sensation) systems provide a constant source of competing input, disrupting sustained focus and concentration. This in turn, will have an impact on short-term memory. Considering that most adults can hold approximately seven items in mind at once, for children, especially those with learning difficulties, this might be more like three or four items. A further note at the task planning stage is that students with SEND find it challenging to understand how to mentally sequence activities and to complete a complex task; therefore, thoroughly checking students' understanding is key. One of the most important challenges facing students with dyslexia is poor auditory short-term memory and retention of written information, long enough for it to transfer to long-term memory.

In relation to self-regulation of own behaviours, the student must first recognise the off-task behaviour – for instance, daydreaming, doodling, chatting – and then make positive changes to modify that behaviour. One way of overcoming this is to time activities against achievable targets or to set a sequence of short tasks. Critically, the students must time themselves and set the levels of their targets. In many cases, the element of competing against self rather than peers is highly motivational and leads to students experiencing a sense of achieving baby steps!

The EEF report[8] evaluated metacognition and self-regulation as the second highest impact with very low cost; students gained seven months of learning through this method. Teacher feedback to students being the most successful in gaining eight months of learning at very low cost.

## Out of class interventions

Interventions can often result in silo learning with no reference to subject aspects. Thus, the sequencing of knowledge and skills gets lost, even distorted for SEND students, with misconceptions being reinforced. What is paramount is that interventions are consistent with, and extend learning inside the classroom. No assumptions should be made that students can consistently identify and make sense of these links on their own.

The example below illustrates how a teaching assistant can work with a teacher on an individual learning plan, through *feedback on subject aspects*. The teaching assistant can subsequently assist students on a 1:1, or in small groups, in developing their metacognition and motivational skills, *outside the classroom*. Activities and tasks taken from a subject's Knowledge Organiser, or scheme of learning can help those students who are less confident, who have misconceptions, or who have not acquired basic concepts or skills. The focus of the teaching assistant is on training students to self-regulate (meta-cognition skills).

(a) Each task is taken from a menu, populated with the individual student's gaps in knowledge and skills, in that subject.

(b) In using a KO rather like a checklist, learning becomes purposeful; by actively asking students to sequence the order in which they wish to work confers a degree of autonomy.

(c) This helps them in setting their goals or selecting the materials to use, (graphic organisers and so on), and further consolidates ownership and responsibility for learning.

(d) Soliciting feedback from students on what works and what does not work for them, at end of each session, helps them develop self-awareness and start the process of self-regulation and consequently the skills they need to recall, transfer and apply.

(e) Linking this to a personal log or diary, students note the strategies that work best for them.

(f) Consolidating the gaps in their knowledge and skills will help them progress once they are in the classroom setting.

The advantage is that as tasks are subject-based; what is highlighted is the intrinsic value of developing the '*recall, transfer and apply*' techniques for learning the subject, rather than focusing on exam results, or external rewards. This further reinforces motivation and challenges negative attitudes to learning and education. Different techniques, modelled by the teaching assistant, give students insights they can relate to in different ways. Overcoming the student's fear of failure and building resilience in learning has a knock-on positive impact once they return to the classroom. Developing a 'growth mind-set' is important so students' mistakes are presented as learning opportunities rather than failures.[9]

In any well-designed curriculum, with a clear intent and implementation plan– leaders must ensure that there is positive impact for all students. Creating *out of class curriculum opportunities* should be part of the intent of developing students as *leaders of own learning*. This would result in time and funding well deployed on training TAs and teachers, in developing resources, so that students can actively practise effective metacognition strategies at their own pace, within the context of the core subject.[10]

## Deploying teaching assistants and learning support assistants (TAs)

Where schools have assigned a teaching assistant[11] or a learning support assistant, the two weaker areas are usually:

1. the monitoring of the impact on students' academic progress and standards of attainment within the subject;

2. a school investing in a partnership model of the teacher working proactively with the TA/LSA.

The EEF report judged the model of the teaching assistant working with students as ineffective and the most expensive; low impact with high costs.[12] The report iterates concerns that TAs can encourage dependency as they prioritise task completion over enabling opportunities for students to think and act for themselves.

> TAs tended to close talk down and 'spoon-feed' answers ... as students 'outsource' their learning to TAs, they develop a 'learned helplessness' ... in terms of interference with ownership, responsibility for learning, and separation from classmates.

It is highly debatable whether the 1:1 approach to learning in lessons allows students the independence they require for the cognitive processes to be effective; 'weakening students' sense of control over their learning'. For students to make meaningful progress, a TA's contribution to tutoring a student should be integrated into curriculum planning. A reactive 'here and now' process in the lesson, between TA and student, is not conducive to deeper learning. In many instances, especially where a student has an EHCP or individual plan, the TA's knowledge of that student is key to informing the overall planning of learning with the teacher. In principle, this should provide differentiated tasks and activities and increase student engagement.

However, there is a very real risk that in reality, without built in curriculum planning time and with the TA unclear on his/her role or learning aim, the student's *independent learning skills* becomes variable. This is because of the high probability that the TA completes or partially completes tasks on the students' behalf. Additionally, SEND students may have less input from the teacher and possibly, less peer inter-action. Another factor is potentially TAs going into lessons 'blind' and having to 'tune into' vital subject knowledge, tasks and instructions, followed by insufficient evaluation of the impact of the student's learning.

The EEF model[12] provides a useful scaffolded approach for TA–student inter-action. It ranges from self-scaffolding to prompting, clueing, modelling and correcting. This model needs to be used in tandem with the monitoring of impact on students' progress and outcomes.[13] Other practical resources are listed in the appendix for further reading.[14] These include a useful Appendix 4: Questions and Key Words for Critical Thinking and an Appendix 5: Prompts for Facilitating Learning and Thinking.

Helpful recommendations that emerge from the report are useful guidelines for teachers/TAs working with a diverse range of students (low ability, EAL and so on):

- training TAs to avoid prioritising task completion, instead, concentrating on students developing ownership of tasks;
- TAs allowing adequate time, so the student can attempt each stage of a task independently;
- TAs intervening appropriately, once the student demonstrates that he/she is unable to proceed, or not understood the task at all;
- allowing a student attempting a task, to make frequent errors, using these for learning through questioning;
- confirming that a student partially but independently completing the task, has greater value than completion of whole task.

## An inclusive curriculum model: SEND students are leaders of own learning

We propose that leadership has clear intent for the role and activities expected of the TA. In addition, there should be structured opportunities for quality planning time with teachers and evaluation of the student's academic progress. These maybe captured through the Student Passport, Raising Achievement Plan, Individual Learning Plan. The essential point is that equal focus is given to individual curriculum outlines and techniques for assisting the 'special educational needs' and these are contextualised and evaluated within each subject. Students log how well they work in and out of lessons, this helps them reflect and lead on their learning.

Teachers require allocated planning or feedback time with the TAs they work with, and training in relation to managing and organising their work with TAs. We suggest that an inclusive mindset shift in how staff work together effectively is key. This shifts the responsibility to teachers having greater ownership of students' learning. A different methodology and terminology is proposed. Instead of 'teaching/learning support', 'facilitation of independent learning' is more productive and 'teaching facilitator' can replace 'teaching assistant'. This moves away from dependency to autonomous and self-regulating learners.

All students at start of lesson benefit from clear objectives and achievable targets, including an assessment of their prior learning. This is especially good practice for SEND students, but sometimes overlooked in the 'traditional support model'. Both for the TA and the student, an end of lesson evaluation looks forward to preparation for the next lesson; identifying any gaps in the knowledge and skills of the student, and possibly, for the TA. This would avoid the learning of disjointed silo information; enabling the student to see the bigger picture and develop continuity in his/her learning. For the TA, this enables a professional dialogue with the teacher in relation to the student's longitudinal sequencing of knowledge and skills.

TAs have the potential to deliver structured, evidence-based interventions effectively to individuals or small groups, in or out, of the classroom. To achieve this, they require professional updating of the curriculum and adequate time to prepare and record their teaching. Additionally they require a thorough knowledge of a student's strengths, common misconceptions and the areas that need further consolidation. Where there are sufficient TAs, linking some TAs to curriculum strands (subject-based or within faculties) works exceptionally well, as the TA can focus on building resources and materials and approaches for specific subjects. These can be shared with other teachers and TAs.

## Case studies of good practice

A number of factors for whole school approaches to improving SEND education for students can usefully inform curriculum implementation. A selection of case studies providing good insights into the 'SEND offer' of schools and colleges are profiled in a DfE report.[15] The examples include transition to a new setting or to adulthood; non-taught times (providing safe spaces and homework clubs); varied curriculum offer (vocational and different level courses) and resource bases.

## Drop in resource centre

**CASE STUDY**

Myerscough College's study centre is staffed with specialist support tutors (SST). SEND students drop in and receive catch up support and guidance on aspects covered in the day's lesson, with a SST or their Inclusive Pupil or Student Mentor (TA).
Additional input includes:

■ pre-teaching: vocabulary, topics and concepts are introduced to students before being covered in class;

■ catch up activities: additional time making sure students have mastered what has been covered in lessons;

■ transferable study skills sessions: students are supported to help them independently access learning and complete tasks set, (essay writing; understanding what a question is asking; exam revision, time management and organisational skills).

These three examples below illustrate practical strategies that develop *leaders of own learning.*

## Case study of engaging students in their learning

1.  *Post-it notes* are a useful technique for creative/practical subjects such as a student's Art portfolio or a Design and Technology resistant materials project.
    Figures 4.3 and 4.4 represent an example of the assessment of artwork. It has been submitted by a Year 11 GCSE student who is dyslexic. The artwork in Figure 4.4 is of a good calibre, but the student's writing needs further drafting.

|  | AO1 | AO2 | AO3 | AO4 |
|---|---|---|---|---|
| Marks | Develop ideas through investigations, demonstrating critical understanding of sources. | Refine work by exploring ideas, selecting and experimenting with appropriate media, materials, techniques and processes. | Record ideas, observations and insights relevant to intentions as work progresses. | Present a personal and meaningful response that realises intentions and demonstrates understanding of visual language. |
|  | You need to clarify how examples have influenced your practice | Wide range is evidenced with good evidence of process | Good range of pix and use of multi media | Connection needs clarifying so that the 'journey' is visible to the reader |

FIGURE 4.3 An example of how the artwork in Figure 4.4 is assessed using Post-it notes against marking criteria

**FIGURE 4.4** The Year 11 student's artwork to be assessed

*Post-it notes* can also be used for essay prompts and discursive writing. Students are required to provide extra explanation for key grammatical features, spellings, openers and connectives for a narrative.

2. In the example below, '*blank questions*' are graded to increase levels of skills difficulty for assignments and exams. Levels are based on students predicted performance level and metacognition skills are enhanced gradually. The student is guided through prompts until arriving at *Level 4*.

**CASE STUDY: ST JAMES CATHOLIC SCHOOL**

*Level 1: factual questions*; naming or simple requests for information.

*Level 2: information or a picture*; requiring a selection on colour, function, who, what, where questions; identifying or explaining differences – 'how is a square different from a triangle?'

*Level 3: language of instruction* (not graphic); requiring recall and re-order of information such as 'sequencing of pictures/information … retell a story … assume the role of another person … state how a character might feel … summarise the picture sequence in one sentence'.

*Level 4: reasoning skills beyond what is said, heard or seen*; drawing on prior knowledge, make linkages, draw parallels, compare/contrast, examine causes and effects, justify decisions. Complex skills are demanded such as prediction or definition of words/concepts, even using computational skills by creating a set of directions or instructions. Examples include, making an inference from an observation; justifying a prediction/hypothesis/explaining logic behind process.[16]

3.  The third example, based on the highly structured and *predictable nature* of LEGO®
    Education, helps students with autism spectrum disorders and related social commu-
    nication difficulties. The potential exists for increasingly complex tasks and roles, for
    instance, a marketing/branding role. Not only will students use a variety of key skills
    in this task, but also develop entrepreneurial skills.

**CASE STUDY: ST JAMES CATHOLIC SCHOOL**

A TA's one-hour intervention comprises three students at a time, whilst other students
participate in a library reading session. The students are assigned to one of three roles –
Supplier, Builder or Engineer – and the purpose is for the team to assemble an agreed
structure. They 'develop verbal and non-verbal communication, joint attention and task focus,
collaborative problem-solving, sharing and turn-taking'. These invaluable communication
skills lead to self-confidence, lateral thinking skills and resilience on task. Students gain
versatility as they switch roles to work on another structure.[17]

## Building on strengths: Dyslexic students

For most students with dyslexia, their abilities in conveying thoughts and conceptual
ideas in writing is markedly different to articulating information verbally. However,
there may be issues of self-worth and lack of confidence affecting the verbal communication skills: 'dyslexic children could become talented and gifted … if we worked
with their specific areas of difficulty, but also their specific areas of strengths … oral
skills, comprehension, good visual spatial awareness/artistic abilities'.[18]

There are excellent examples of assistive learning; use of iPads and audio recordings
of teacher's input; invaluable for the student absorbing key information, working at
his or her own pace. For the sequence of learning to continue, the student must know
and understand what he or she has learnt. Therefore, the use of graphic organisers,
Cornel notes and so on, deployed by a skilled TA facilitates students with dyslexia and
those with poor concentration to develop their conceptual thinking skills.

The examples below (A and B) illustrate the use of blended technologies and
assistive learning and how these lead to overcoming barriers, facilitate independent
learning skills and accelerate progress.

(A) relevant and creative real life/social media contexts for reading and writing;

(B) greater accuracy and self-checking.

(A) *Springwell Learning Community, Special Academy Barnsley*
EdTech has 'transformed the learning environments of Springwell from four walled classrooms
to no walled classroom'. Tracking of achievement indicates the progress of disadvantaged
students is improving in line with their peers, particularly with reading and writing. iPad 1:1
programme and blogging highlights the real differences in the quality of students' writing and
learning through a writing platform for a real audience. Imaginative use of social media (e.g.

'Honey I Shrunk the Pupils' on YouTube) means there is a 'buzz' about the place; attainment is up, negative behaviour incidents are down, morale is high as 'we continue to redefine learning and promote creativity'. Staff have noticed a 'massive rise in the confidence' of autistic students.[19,20]

(B) *Millfield Secondary School* [21,22]
Millfield Secondary School uses the IDL programme; a specialist literacy/dyslexia programme, with a multi-sensory approach (sight, hearing, touch and voice). The programme provides structured, sequential, cumulative learning and importantly, integrates repetition and overlearning opportunities. Students are guided through a series of graded typed lessons based on a story format interspersed with comprehension, grammar and spelling rules exercises. These teach them to work independently and to self-check their work.

## Dyscalculia

Patricia Hodge[23] identifies practical strategies for literacy in Mathematics, stressing the importance of Tier 3 Maths vocabulary being understood at a deeper level before application can be effective. She argues that 'add, plus, sum of, increase and total all describe a single mathematical process … related difficulties could be with visual/perceptual skills, directional confusion, sequencing, word skills and memory.'

She outlines that 'aspects of Mathematics that place a heavy load on the short-term memory, e.g. long division or algebra' need particularly careful handling, as students may have difficulty counting backwards, or remembering basic facts, despite rote learning. In GCSE Mathematics examinations, one-third of the paper is devoted to problem-solving questions and students may struggle, unless they understand the sequencing and meaning of the language. Therefore, being aware of the range of activities that trains students in the language of Mathematics is intrinsic to successful outcomes. A range of activities exist that enable reinforcement on process.[24]

## Mathematical skills cross curriculum

Dowker (2009)[25] highlights three types of mathematical knowledge: factual knowledge (knowledge of number facts, such as number bonds and times tables); procedural knowledge (knowledge of how to carry out mathematical operations); and conceptual knowledge (understanding arithmetic operations and principles).[26] Perhaps more than any other area of the curriculum, Maths can be associated with anxiety and negative beliefs, for students who perceive that they 'can't do' Maths or are 'no good'. They are unable to improve, usually encountering obstacles accessing procedural and conceptual knowledge. This self-inflicted stigma hinders the student's progress across other subjects that require these skills, certainly, in Geography, Science, Design and Food Technology.

All teachers and TAs working with SEND students can reinforce mathematical skills through mapping structured opportunities across curriculum. In the survey below, teachers were asked to comment on the subject specific numeracy skills, aside from the routine Maths lessons.[27] Every subject demonstrates real life application of mathematical skills.

**Table 4.1** Examples of how mathematics can be embedded into other subjects

| | Tasks in class, homework and assessment | Written examples |
|---|---|---|
| Science | Solving equations, measurements and handling data | 'Microscopy in Science, homework activities, standard form in Science and calculations in Science all related to GCSE and careers in Science.' (Science teacher, East of England). |
| PSHE | Finance, budgeting and enterprise activities | 'In PSHE students might work out the number of units of alcohol consumed.' (Citizenship curriculum leader, London). |
| Modern Foreign Languages (MFL) | Surveys and mathematical equations | 'Students can be encouraged to read a longer text in French which may contain statistical information, e.g. a survey conducted amongst young people may reveal the issues that young people feel strongly about.' (MFL curriculum leader, North West). |
| Computing | Coding, data analysis and working with graphs | 'Certain other subject such as Science and ICT/Computing will provide opportunities where Numeracy skills are required.' (Computing teacher, East Midlands). |
| Design and technology | Working with graphs and measurements | 'DT has 15% examined numeracy skills so new curriculum reflects this do much more numeracy in situ used.' (DT curriculum leader, London). |
| Geography | Statistics, graphs and measurements | 'Geography has huge Maths content, skills are practised most lessons through reading and creating graphs and doing statistics.' (Geography teacher, South West). |
| Business Studies | Finance, budgeting and enterprise activities | "Business requires mathematical skills be applied to real life scenarios.' (Business studies teacher, London). |
| Art | Working with graphs and measurements | "Scaling up, drawing in proportion, photographing composition.' (Art curriculum leader, London). |
| Citizenship | Statistics and enterprise activities | 'When we look at Maths or representation of ethnic minorities in power/in prison.' (Citizenship teacher, London). |
| English | Reading and drawing graphs | 'Cross curricular skills (designing scatter and bar graphs to show rise and fall of Macbeth and Lady Macbeth.' (English teacher and careers advisor, South East). |

## Looking ahead: The engagement model

The engagement model[28] replaces P scales 1 to 4 and will become statutory from 2020/21. 'Engagement,' through 'regular observational assessment and reflective pedagogy' can assist schools in reflecting on the curriculum's effectiveness in helping students to progress. It will not replace a school's existing plans, assessments and reporting systems, but add value by helping schools assess students' progress from a different angle. The model's five strands of *exploration, realisation, anticipation, persistence* and *initiation* assess why students who are currently working below the level of the National Curriculum may have begun to plateau or regress in their anticipated outcomes.

## Summary

First and foremost, the teacher is best placed to equip SEND students with the necessary skills and knowledge through clearly differentiated strategies. Leaders defining curriculum intent for SEND should ensure that scheduled time allows teachers and TAs to plan, deliver and evaluate the teaching. Where there is no TA, subject departments can helpfully focus on creating, or locating commercial resources that differentiate schemes of learning by tasks, activities and learning outcomes.

A strong focus on developing cognitive and metacognition skills for all students is highly desirable. For students with SEND, ensuring out of class provision for developing these skills is paramount. Subject specialists or trained TAs, can reinforce the skills of recall, transfer and apply, in a subject–specific context. Achieving the green shoots of success in a non–threatening environment, with a clear focus on the learning of skills, develops confidence, motivation and resilience and, in turn, promotes independent learning. We must take account of the primacy of these skills within the learning process.

SEND students, along with others, must become confident readers who can successfully access the curriculum and develop Tier 3 vocabulary. In particular, they along with their peers must become fluent in the language of Mathematics, so they understand how to problem solve, develop basic skills and sequence information that will help them access other subjects. In Part VII, we explore literacy strategies.

The curriculum pathways for those at risk of disengaging from education, should be carefully designed with an intent and implementation that is in line with the mainstream curriculum and is not in danger of 'dumbing down' the knowledge and skills that students require for GCSE examinations. Unless we break down the barriers in accessing the curriculum, we cannot provide an equitable education; 'a level playing field', for our most vulnerable SEND students. We must remind ourselves that these young people are the most susceptible to becoming NEETs.[29]

## Notes

1    Department for Education (2017) *English Baccalaureate Equality Analysis*. London: The Department for Education.

2    Wave 2 (targeted at a group of students with similar needs) Wave 3 (highly tailored intervention for a minority of students to accelerate progress) www.gordons.school/page/?title=Provision+Map+%2D+Wave+2+%26amp%3B+Wave+3+Interventions&pid=140

3    NurtureUK (2019) Boxall Profile website. Available at: https://boxallprofile.org/ (Accessed: 30 September 2019).

4    N. Lambros (2019) PASS interventions. Available at: www.gl-assessment.co.uk/content-pages/pass-interventions/ (Accessed: 11 October 2019).

5    GL Assessment (2019) Childrens' wellbeing report. Available at: www.gl-assessment.co.uk/content-pages/children-s-wellbeing-pupil-attitudes-to-self-and-school-report-2018/ (Accessed: 22 December 2019).

6    www.allsaintscc.org.uk/

7    A. Skipp and V. Hopwood (2017) SEN support: Case studies from schools and colleges, https://assets.publishing.service.gov.uk. London: Department for Education: ASK Research.

8   Education Endowment Foundation (2019) Teaching and learning toolkit. Available at: https://educationendowmentfoundation.org.uk/evidence-summaries/teaching-learning-toolkit (Accessed: 11 November 2019).

9   C. Dweck (2000) *Self-theories: Their Role in Motivation, Personality, and Development (Essays in Social Psychology)*, 1st edn. London: Psychology Press.

10  We can look at this model in Chapter 4 under working with hard to reach students. Engage and Achieve setting deploying funding to engage qualified teachers Maths, English, Humanities and Science to work with so that all students in lessons can begin to work more meaningfully and are better motivated.

11  'TA' means 'Teaching Assistant' or Learning Support Assistant.

12  Education Endowment Foundation (2019) Teaching and learning toolkit. Available at: https://educationendowmentfoundation.org.uk/evidence-summaries/teaching-learning-toolkit (Accessed: 11 November 2019).

13  Education Endowment Foundation (2018) Teaching assistants: EEF publishes updated guidance to support schools achieve greater impact. Available at: https://education endowmentfoundation.org.uk/news/teaching-assistants-eef-publishes-updated-guidance/ (Accessed: 22 November 2019).

14  R. Webster (2016) *Maximising the Impact of Teaching Assistants*. 2nd edn. Abingdon: Routledge.

15  A. Skipp and V. Hopwood (2017) SEN support: Case studies from schools and colleges, https://assets.publishing.service.gov.uk: London: Department for Education: ASK Research.

16  Ibid.

17  Ibid.

18  P. Hodge (2000) A dyslexic child in the classroom. Available at: www.dyslexia.com/about-dyslexia/understanding-dyslexia/guide-for-classroom-teachers/ (Accessed: 2 October 2019).

19  Springwell Learning Community website (2019). Available at: https://springwelllearning community.co.uk/ (Accessed: 14 November 2019)

20  T. Goddard et al. (2019) The Ed Tech 50 Schools, www.ednfoundation.org/wp-content/uploads/EDTECH-50-SCHOOLS-2019.pdf: London: The Education Foundation.

21  Millfield School (2020) Millfield School. Available at: www.millfieldschool.com/ (Accessed: 21 February 2020).

22  T. Goddard et al. (2019) The Ed Tech 50 Schools. www.ednfoundation.org/wp-content/uploads/EDTECH-50-SCHOOLS-2019.pdf: London: The Education Foundation.

23  P. Hodge (2000) A dyslexic child in the classroom. Available at: www.dyslexia.com/about-dyslexia/understanding-dyslexia/guide-for-classroom-teachers/ (Accessed: 2 October 2019).

24  J. Hornigold (2019) 6 magical maths activities to keep children engaged. Available at: https://mathsnoproblem.com/creative-magical-maths-activities/ (Accessed: 21 October 2019).

25  A. Dowker (2009) What works for children with mathematical difficulties? Available at: www.catchup.org/resources/735/what_works_for_children_with_mathematical_diffi-culties.pdf (Accessed: 17 December 2019).

26  J. Dabell (2019) 8 ways to deliver effective maths interventions. Available at: https://mathsnoproblem.com/deliver-effective-maths-interventions/ (Accessed: 21 October 2019).

27  E. Kashefpakdel et al. (2018) Joint dialogue: How are schools developing real employability skills. Available at: www.educationandemployers.org/research/joint-dialogue/ (Accessed: 14 October 2019).

28  Department for Education (2020) *The Engagement Model*. London: Department for Education.

29  See S. Goldman-Mellor et al. (2016) Committed to work but vulnerable: Self-perceptions and mental health in NEET 18-year-olds from a contemporary British cohort. *J Child Psychol Psychiatry* 57(2), 196–203. This article examines the characteristics of young people

who are NEET (Not in Education, Employment or Training). Individuals with a history of behavioural difficulties, attention deficit hyperactivity disorder (ADHD) or depression in childhood are much more likely to be NEET at age 18, even after accounting for socio-economic background, cognitive abilities and reading skills. Therefore, those who are particularly vulnerable to becoming NEET should be carefully supported through CEIAG and a well-structured curriculum that prepares them for their future destinations.

# 5

# Engage and Achieve: Reducing exclusions

## Introduction

An increasing focus on a knowledge-based curriculum, dealing primarily with 'sequential learning,' begs the question as to what opportunities are afforded to students who miss chunks of these sequences, either through absence, or because of exclusion? Between 2012/13 and 2018, there has been an unacceptable 70 per cent increase in the number of permanent school exclusions, and a 54 per cent increase in fixed term exclusions.[1] On average, 2000 pupils are excluded for a fixed period each day. 'Every extra day of school missed can affect a child's chances of achieving good GCSEs, which can have a lasting effect on their life chances.'[2]

A headteacher's duty of care towards staff, so they can teach and work in a safe environment, extends to ensuring a productive learning experience for all students. A key priority is re-engaging those who are disrespectful of other students and adults within the school community and those who resort to anti-social, disruptive, bullying, and violent behaviours.

Schools strive hard to ensure that all staff implement and sustain high expectations of behaviours, academic achievement and aspiration. A whole school approach means that all curriculum and pastoral staff have a common understanding of how to respond to individual students, so they are supported to meet those expectations. If students are at risk of underachieving, this is identified early on and addressed, thereby, avoiding the need to exclude, either through formal channels or through 'unexplained exits'[3],[4]. Our case studies illustrate good practice that prioritises reformative behaviours and students' learning through an appropriate curriculum.

## Impact on the most susceptible student cohorts

In relation to the life chances of the children, less than 2 per cent of excluded pupils finish school with the qualifications they need in Maths and English; half of all those who are excluded are not in education, employment or training post-16 and enter the NEET category.[5] According to *Education Datalab*,[6] four-fifths of those attending

PRUs have a statement of special education needs or an Education Health and Care Plan. Only around 1 per cent of young people in state alternative provision receive five good GCSEs.

The Timpson report[7] found that vulnerable groups of children are more likely to be excluded, with 78 per cent of permanent exclusions issued to children who had special educational needs (SEN), classified 'in need', eligible for free school meals or supported by social care. While some ethnic groups – Bangladeshi, Black African, Pakistani and Indian – have significantly lower exclusion rates than the national average in 2016/17; others are excluded at a higher rate, including Irish, Black Caribbean, Gypsy and Roma students. Unsurprisingly, boys have an exclusion rate more than three times higher than that of girls.[8]

In addition, a recent report[9] confirmed the endemic nature of 'unexplained exits' draws attention to how more vulnerable learners are far more likely to experience these unexplained moves. In 2017, around 80 per cent of students experiencing an unexplained move were vulnerable. Patterns of Year 11 exits suggest 'deliberate gaming of the school accountability system'. The EPI report's conclusion is 'a systemic problem of too much mobility under the assumption that moving a child is a "solution" to educational challenges'.[9]

## The 'invisible' students; the lost potential of excluded and off rolled students

We can see from this case study below that Kwesi (not his real name) failed to be successful 'academically' and entered a downward spiral of exclusions that eventually resulted in a permanent exclusion. However, he is one of the luckier ones! Despite not being able to access the curriculum and not receiving effective support to sustain him in his studies, he managed to stay on in education at 16. This is the true story of one young man who acted in a play entitled 'Excluded' with the Intermission Theatre Company (see Appendix 5.1, available at www.routledge.com/9780367900878).

### INTERMISSION THEATRE – CASE STUDY OF STUDENT

### MEET KWESI

*Age: 18, studying for a Diploma in Performing Arts in a sixth form college.*
I hated school. I struggled to learn. I'm not smart academically. English and Maths were hard. The only things I found easy were Science, Construction and Technology. I wanted to be an architect but it involves Maths. I failed my Maths and English GCSEs. I was 14 when I was diagnosed with dyslexia. I didn't tell anyone I was dyslexic because dyslexia meant you were stupid and dumb. I got extra tuition to help me, but it didn't work out. I had to find my own way of solving things, my own way to remember stuff. I created my own techniques. I can't count numbers in my head, so I visualise numbers on my fingers. That's how I do big calculations. I learn my lines (for the play) by marking them through the actions and movements.

I got excluded from school for dumb reasons. I broke a chair, got into some fights. I was excluded for two to three days at a time, although once, it was for a whole week. It was

> boring. I just sat at home playing games and walking in the park because all my friends were at school.
>
> When I returned to school, they put me in an isolation room for two weeks. I wasn't allowed to see anyone all day. My lunch was brought to me. I had to leave school at a different time to anyone else.

The national data presents a bleak picture of which Kwesi is a typical example. The target group are those students at risk of disaffection with learning, especially the rising numbers of students diagnosed with ADHD. They should be at the heart of the curriculum and not marginalised. Appropriate resources and curriculum choices for these students could create an inclusive 'wrap round' model, keeping students in learning, and not on the streets.

Only in rare or exceptional circumstances, would a student start the school day, contriving to disrupt lessons, misbehaving repeatedly, so he or she could actually be excluded! Evidence suggests that repeated exclusions by schools do not lead to reformed behaviours. There has been an exponential increase; with the fixed period exclusion rate almost three times higher over a six year period 2012–2018.[10] The typical pattern in those schools where internal isolation and fixed term exclusions are high suggests that there are rising numbers of repeat offenders. Many of the same students who are relegated to an internal inclusion unit or behaviour unit appear daily in the room and suffer that fate through re-offending behaviours, becoming square pegs in the round hole of education! What they do in the units for these hours/days is highly variable and usually, but not always, the responsibility of pastoral staff.

## Trigger factors leading to exclusion

For our purposes, we will focus on the pattern of student disengagement from learning and resultant poor behaviours. These we present as a consequence of the curriculum design and delivery, the student's profile and the school parental engagement. We have identified five broad areas by way of explanation for exclusion trends.

1.  Literacy, language and numeracy barriers prevent students from accessing the secondary curriculum. The curriculum for Years 7/8 may not effectively bridge the gap between primary and secondary, nor cater for students with special educational needs across the spectrum, those with social, emotional, behavioural difficulties, other contextual factors, or complex family circumstances. As we saw, vulnerable students, including those with SEND, are most affected. This is often because of insufficiently well-monitored KS2/3 transition and learning support in school.

2.  The secondary curriculum can be deemed neither 'broad nor balanced', unless it recognises students' actual capability and future aspirations through design. By Years 8 or 9, students are making curricular choices that will affect their destinations post-16. In reality, how informed these are will largely depend on the effectiveness of CEIAG and the relevance of the choices on offer in KS4

for individual students. A standard model of decision making at end of Year 8 or 9 might involve students choosing from the curriculum options available, rather than students engaging in meaningful discussions about future aspirations/ destinations in relation to subject choices. Understandably, schools cannot always provide an exact match to students' wishes as the curriculum is designed in advance. However, collating this information year on year and using it to inform future curriculum planning is an intelligent use of the data. This at least creates curricular pathways that enable the student to move seamlessly from KS4 to post-16 academic or vocational education, training or apprenticeship. The fact remains that far too many students are not able to follow the subjects they want, or need for their chosen post-16 destination. It is hardly surprising that owing to the potentially narrow choices, a number of these students can become disaffected in subjects, which they may not have ideally chosen.

If, for example, a school's curriculum intent is focused on increasing the number of EBacc entries, this pre-supposes that all students want to study either Geography or History with a foreign language. In this example, we can see the negative impact result from an inappropriate GCSE curriculum.

### CASE STUDY: SECONDARY ACADEMY, LONDON

Selma, a Year 9 student, is adept at Computer Science, Design and Technology. Along with English, Maths and Science at GCSE, she wants to study both of these subjects as her long-term ambition is to study to be an architectural engineer.

Had both these subjects been offered as part of the eight choices, she would be more engaged and motivated in her learning. However, she can only choose one of the two desired subjects, alongside the EBacc subjects that she must study. Selma chooses Computer Science.

On-going internal assessments and scrutiny of her outcomes indicate that she is not progressing, as she should in French, and will not achieve the 'Progress 8' outcomes she was predicted across the eight subjects. As she is disinterested in French, and does not see the relevance to her future ambitions, Selma's attitudes to learning are affected. She believes that she will easily gain a Level 4, and begins to exhibit occasional disruptive behaviours in lessons, such as off-task chatter. Eventually, she is removed for more than one lesson to the internal inclusion unit. She is disinclined to catch up on work missed, and the teacher does not consistently follow up to ensure that she does.

3. Whole school inconsistency in applying the behaviour policy has dire consequences for managing students' behaviours. This is especially the case if the interpretation of the policy has an emphasis on a culture of punitive sanctions, or is not perceived as 'fair' by students. Little is known about  the effectiveness of various behaviour policies in  preventing poor behaviours and reintegrating students successfully into school, so that they do not fall into the vicious cycle of reoffending. The roots of challenging behaviour have been researched by educa-tional experts, and much written regarding the causes. Most commonly, the debate is focused on the student and can be polarised. Challenging behaviour is either a student's choice, or the inevitable consequence of a lack of boundaries, either

at home, or in school. In these cases, behaviour policies led by senior leaders and behaviour management training for staff are implemented. Others may perceive negative behaviours as the communication of unmet needs; contextualised as pastoral, relating to the student's mental health, learning difficulties or background.

At present, there is insufficiently conclusive national research on the underlying causes of disrespectful and poor behaviours and the actual causes of positive and negative attitudes to learning; and even less, on the importance of the curriculum in fostering these attitudes.

## The Three Rs of the behaviour curriculum[11]

i.   **Routines:** classroom routines; high expectation, a community vision of optimal habits and behaviour.
ii.  **Responses:** strategies and interventions for de-escalating confrontation, resolving conflict in a productive and proportional way. Formal interventions (consequences described by the school behaviour policy); informal responses (verbal/non-verbal cues, body language).
iii. **Relationships**: regulating teacher's own emotional state; understanding personal triggers in own behaviour, expectations or reactions; understanding how special educational needs and disability affect behaviour (ADHD, autism, dyslexia, Asperger's; motivation; long/short-term memory; cognitive load, spacing and interleaving; group dynamics).

We propose a fourth area essential for closing the loop of poor behaviours; minimising re-offending through re-integration of the student into the classroom.

iv.  **Rehabilitation**: as part of a whole school strategy on academic outcomes and culture; it is key that students 'catch up' on learning missed; monitored by teachers and middle leaders. In line with the school community's values, students should understand the reason for their exclusion as do their parents/carers.

4.   The role of home background and parental engagement in reforming behaviours is less well researched. However, parental background and cultural factors, upbringing and so on, must in part, account for this; *nurture*, rather than nature. A range of examples showcase strategies deployed to re-engage students through their families within the Timpson report.[12] Proactive approaches break the spiral of 'repeat offenders' leading to exclusion. Investment in staff time and meticulous follow up in reaching out to families and external agencies speak volumes about a provision's vision, ethos and curriculum intent that genuinely values each student. Part VI profiles further good practice.

(a)  An all-through academy operates a regular behaviour panel where children at risk of exclusion and their parents/carers meet with the head for a constructive discussion about how to get them on track. Parents and student receive a full summary of the impact that the behaviour has had on the student's progress and others' welfare. A problem-solving approach involves the student, parents and professionals. A regularly reviewed plan focuses on addressing the key issues through positive reinforcement.

(b) An alternative provision specialises in short-term placements for students with complex needs and behavioural difficulties, offering professional therapeutic support for children and their families. Parents attend weekly and are supported to work with their child to get them ready to return to mainstream. Parents describe this as 'consistent positive reinforcement' as opposed to 'inconsistent negative reinforcement' they had previously experienced inmainstream schools. There they were contacted only once their child had breached the rules.

(c) A local authority described taking a 'Think Family' approach to working with children. SEND district practitioners work alongside the family, acknowledging the importance of co-production and the wealth of knowledge that parents have about how best their children's needs can be met. Parents also give feedback on service design and delivery.

5. The quality of the teaching is without doubt the prime factor that affects learning and motivation; but less is said about what happens in schools where recruitment of staffing, or long-term absence cause problems with continuity. Staffing absence coupled with weak teaching and assessment will have a negative impact on students' sequencing of knowledge and skills. More often than not, all students, but especially SEND students, suffer with significant gaps in their learning. This in turn, can result in behavioural issues and demotivated students. In the absence of the substantive subject teacher, lessons taught must take sufficient account of students' abilities, prior learning, knowledge and skills in the planning of tasks and activities.

The gaps in students' knowledge and skills, accruing over time, owing to removal from lessons, or through a succession of cover staff, can constitute one of the biggest causes of poor behaviours and low achievement. It is widely underestimated in its impact by senior and middle leaders. In one school with staffing turbulence, a Year 11 Science class endured successive supply staff over a period of eight weeks. One student in response to a question on making copper sulphate crystals, wrote in his December practice Science paper: 'I don't know this as every time we get to this, my teacher gets mysteriously ill and I have a cover teacher so I feel like an idiot!'

All it takes is for a toxic mix of any of these pre-determined factors, in addition to the student's mental well-being, resilience and focus in lessons for the student to become the 'square peg in the round hole'! Light the touch paper of the exclusions cycle and stand well back while students slip into a vortex of missed lessons and unsafe behaviours. This can lead to erratic attendance in school and, possibly, persistent absence, as the student finally decides that school has little or nothing to offer him/her. Worse-case scenario, the school decides for the student, believing that there is no choice but to move the student to a permanent exclusion or an 'unexplained exit'.

## Reducing exclusions: A values-led curriculum

In the case study below, senior leaders made a business case for deploying funding streams more effectively. This led to significantly reducing fixed-term exclusions and re-offending behaviours over three months. Rather than struggling on their own, in an isolation unit, students were supported in completing their work, with support from a subject specialist, in a quiet environment that the vast majority valued. The most important point being that this allowed for continuity in learning and facilitated a more effective reintegration into lessons. This was because students had usually completed the work satisfactorily, during the period of removal from the lesson. The sanctions system differentiated between *unsafe behaviours* and *disruptive behaviours* in a lesson or subject and, as far as possible, removal time was proportionate and ensured students did not miss more lessons than needed.

Looking through the students' books it was clear that this was an invaluable way of avoiding the gaps in learning. Previous deployment of teaching assistants or pastoral staff in supervising the centre had not had the same impact as deploying subject teachers. The former did not have the subject expertise required to help students with the work set, whereas the latter did, despite some of the subjects lying outside their range.

### CASE STUDY OF THE ENGAGE AND ACHIEVE UNIT (EAU): WHOLE SCHOOL APPROACH

In a secondary academy with a track record of exceptionally high levels of fixed-term exclusions and repeat offenders, involving disproportionate numbers of SEND and disadvantaged students; the overriding priority of reducing exclusions and improving attitudes to learning became a mission for the school and its local community.

Senior leaders developed a whole school culture of three key values; *respect, tolerance and resilience*, reinforced through assemblies, displays and tutor groups, focusing on why and how students should embody the values. The concept of this was explained in assembly as 'seva' the act of serving – one of the major tenets of the Sikh religion – echoed in other religions, Christianity, Buddhism, Islam. Students also learnt of the Vedic scriptures' symbiotic link between repeat behaviours morphing into character (Appendix 5.5, available at www.routledge.com/9780367900878).

The headteacher established monthly parental forums for parents as a two- way process on soliciting their feedback and providing an update on strategies in place. The mantra adopted was that the school's values-based culture informed the partnership between parent, student and school (Appendix 5.2, available at www.routledge.com/9780367900878). The 'Engage and Achieve' behaviour strategy was launched; the ethos and intent envisioned students as *leaders of their learning and leaders of their behaviours.*

The 'removal room' was renamed EAU (Engage and Achieve unit). Far from being a location, where students sat in cubicles, facing the wall, subject teachers (English, Maths and Science) supervised and assisted completion of the lessons' work. Teachers and students had access to KS3 and 4 Schemes of learning, resources and text books and SAM learning (see www.samlearning.com). Knowledge Organisers could be used by students to indicate what they found difficult to learn, or what they had missed. This was helpful for both the student and the teacher to see at a glance what had been taught and where gaps lay, if students were in the unit for longer. The student's report card was completed by the

EAU teacher and included reference to the work completed, gaps in understanding and the attitudes to learning.

Restorative justice approaches included an apology letter based on the values of *respect, resilience and tolerance* to the subject teacher/adult or student, and community service, if that was appropriate. These included litter picking; cleaning graffiti, clearing weeds in the garden beds, helping the librarian, putting up displays, acting as reading buddy with younger students and so on.

The underlying concept of this was that if a student disrupted others' learning or had committed anti-social behaviours of any description; they needed to put back something into the school's learning community. The apology letter (Appendix 5.3, available at www. routledge.com/9780367900878) was key as it meant the student had to reflect on their actions and the impact for others and identify what they would change in their behaviours.

Students in the spiral of poor behaviours signed a supportive home school contract (Appendix 5.4, available at www.routledge.com/9780367900878) with targets for the student, parent and the school to fulfil. The vast majority of parents' feedback indicated that they were satisfied with the reforming nature of the strategies.

Students who had reformed behaviours, were nominated Ambassadors of Behaviour and encouraged to model positive attitudes with others around the school. All staff were encouraged to adopt calm, respectful behaviours with students; this percolated through to students as the school moved towards a 'mutual respect' model. Year 11 and sixth-form student prefects worked with younger students as mentors during tutor time; assisting with aspects of English or Maths. In some cases, mentors received training as a 'talk buddy' or 'listening ear', so that students could share concerns.

Students logged this valued work in a passport, signed off by the head of year and accredited through the ASDAN volunteering certificate. Credits contributed towards a work experience log; a CV and potential UCAS statement.

## Three key points: How the EAU successfully lowered the percentage of 'repeat offenders'

Firstly, in prioritising students' academic needs, a strong connection exists between students' learning, their behaviours and the curriculum.

Secondly, this is framed within a reformative behaviour policy linked to a values-based culture with strong parental buy-in.

Thirdly, the curriculum model deployed ring fenced funds for disadvantaged and SEND students in recruiting professional English, Maths and Science subject teachers. They were used in workshop delivery for catch up learning (1:1 and small groupwork).

Value frameworks can be underpinned with a notion of *ubuntu*. Desmond Tutu defined *ubuntu* as referring to 'compassion, hospitality, openness to others, to be available to others and to know that you are bound up with them in a bundle'.[13] These values were translated into the school mission and reflected in school policies, as they underpinned the sense of a school community.

Rather than draconian, punitive measures, students respond to stability within a culture of respect and most will take responsibility for own behaviours, if trusted to do so by staff. The motivation for developing a different set of positive behaviours has to come from within the students themselves and not from fear of punishment.

Creating the right culture within a school setting is challenging if staff and students have only ever worked within a culture of rewards and sanctions. Changing the cycle of behaviours and mindsets is necessary, but the long-term rewards are considerable.

## In house units

In-school units offer 'a halfway point between excluding a pupil and keeping them in the mainstream classroom'.[14] Understandably, there will always be a tiny minority of students who, for any number of reasons, are not willing to engage with staff. In some cases, they pose a real safety risk or create a disruption for other students and require isolation in school. A well-managed fixed period exclusion can be a positive intervention, especially if there is rigorous follow-up on ensuring students do not miss out on the 'sequence of knowledge and skills'. However, a repeated pattern of fixed period exclusion is not likely to be addressing the underlying issues facing both the school and the students.

This is especially the case if the exclusions are disproportionately affecting the most vulnerable, like those with special educational needs and learning difficulties, and particular ethnic groups. If a student is receiving multiple exclusions, schools must ask themselves what they should be doing differently to break the cycle. Additionally, excluding a student out of lessons with little focus on the continuity of learning can have a negative impact on the quality of learning for peers at the point of reintegration into the lessons. This potentially disrupts valuable learning time for all students. The academy below successfully broke this negative cycle.

### EXCLUSION IN SCHOOL, NOT FROM SCHOOL – ALL-THROUGH ACADEMY SCHOOL, NORTH EAST LONDON

Students with a fixed period exclusion were habitually left at home alone and unsupervised. Children were seen on the streets. On their return, a period of education had been lost, with little evidence of benefit when faced with re-admission.[15]

Fixed period exclusion was a decreasing deterrent for poor behaviour. This was leading to disengagement and rising rates of repeat exclusion, which had a negative impact on the pupils concerned, as well as workload implications for staff, administering the exclusions.

The academy minimised exclusion by using reprimand or detention for a first offence, through keeping excluded students on site, during a fixed period exclusion. Students were excluded from lessons and taught separately under supervision. Procedurally, there was no change, but the headteacher described the message changing from 'we cannot manage your behaviour so we are sending you home' to 'your behaviour was unacceptable, you have to show that you can behave in school before you return to lessons'.

This has reduced fixed period exclusions dramatically; enabling parents and carers to engage with the school in addressing the child's behaviour, rather than concerns over their child's safety when their child is excluded from school.

## Promoting inclusion and limiting exclusion

Schools retaining the most challenging students by finding ways of including them in the school community helps break the negative spiral of exclusions.[16] There is a compelling case for students receiving structured learning, so they do not fall behind in their knowledge and skills and are reintegrated effectively into lessons. An inclusive and equitable curriculum needs to focus on genuine learning, balancing this alongside the nurture aspect, whilst addressing behavioural issues. This is a challenge for all schools and clearly has resource implications.

Systemic changes to behaviour policies involve a process of changing a school culture, staff mindsets and how students learn. A zero-tolerance policy needs to be proportionate and fair. This student reports 'I would get excluded and sent home more often, for unnecessary reasons, like not wearing a blazer, my socks not coming up to my knees. Just silly things like that. It is encouraging kids to go out and do what they want because you are not giving them an education.'[17]

Six references to curriculum linked to outcomes exist in the OFSTED EIF,[18] including evidence of studying effectively, students resilient to setbacks and taking pride in their achievements. Regardless of inspection, each school should be judging itself against the benchmarks of an inclusive curriculum. Schools will be hard pressed to justify that the curriculum they offer is 'broad and balanced', should they not evidence reforming behaviours, or 'off roll', repeatedly exclude, and, one way or another, remove the offending 'square pegs' from the classroom and/or school.

## Exclusions and wider community response

> Exclusion is a marker for being at higher risk of becoming a victim or perpetrator of crime …[19]

We must consider that a young person is motivated to get involved in criminal activity for different reasons, and for some young people, these may well have resulted in being excluded from school.

'Since they kicked me out, I've got time on my hands to do more crime, commit more crime … in Croydon with my friends who have also been kicked out who are also doing wrong things, who are also selling drugs, who are also carrying knives.'[20] Alongside the importance of schools in the lives of the children, it is clear from the APPG report on Knife Crime (2019)[20] that the areas suffering the largest cuts to youth spending have seen bigger increases in knife crime. The APPG identified the number of youth centres supported by local authorities had fallen by half since 2011, with significant losses in youth service staff over this period.[21] 'Young people need a place to go where they belong, where they have the opportunity to come together with peers outside of school and develop their personal growth. If they fall into the wrong group, they are unfortunately likely to stay there' (Denise Hatton, chief executive of YMCA England and Wales). Young people – and the practitioners working with them – have noticed the effects of funding cuts, in particular citing the negative impact on the availability of youth clubs:

I think they should re-open a lot of youth clubs … because I've seen the youth club close and then gang violence increase, literally the next day …

(Peer Outreach Worker)[20]

## Summary

Schools and multi-academy trusts owe their students a curriculum that leads to successful outcomes, within the context of a values-based culture. We have prioritised staffing an Engage and Achieve Unit, a reformative behaviour policy and the deployment of ring-fenced funds for 'catch-up learning'. These in themselves are not a silver bullet for avoiding poor behaviours and reducing exclusions. But working strategically with governors, trustees, staff and parents in these key areas and sustaining these initiatives over time reaps dividends.

The leadership of curriculum and teaching is symbiotically linked to leadership of behaviour. The only way that schools can fully meet the needs and aspirations of students at risk of disruptive behaviours and exclusion is to ensure that the two leadership roles strongly interact. Both academic and pastoral 'leaders', including the staff they line manage, are undeniably accountable for students' attitudes to learning, behaviours and academic progress. Where schools create leadership silos in relation to roles and responsibilities, this is precisely when students slip through the net of learning, seriously affecting their life chances.

As a priority, it is incumbent for school leaders to ensure that all students consistently access the curriculum. If excluded or absent, the golden rule of thumb must be to 'catch up' on the learning missed, a safety net that seeks to avoid the downward spiral of academic failure, along with consistent monitoring of their academic progress by subject leaders and teachers. A staff cover policy's intent, at its heart ensures subject and curriculum leaders are ultimately responsible for the quality assurance of lessons taught by supply/temporary staff, so that the relevance and quality in learning does not suffer (Appendix 5.5, available at www.routledge. com/9780367900878).

Curriculum design must re-engage disaffected students and those with learning difficulties. Fixed Term Exclusions and 'repeat withdrawals' for students from lessons (to an 'isolation unit') must therefore be contextualised around meaningful discussions about how to avoid recidivism, academic catch up and proactive reflection with students and parents on future strategies.

The pernicious cycle of exclusions currently continues unabated. This has a massive impact on the life chances of the affected students who are marginalised, with tragic, social and economic consequences for our society – knife crime, gangs, grooming and so on. Local authorities can support schools through re-instating youth provision and helping to ensure good quality alternative provision.

We propose a framework for all schools that effectively creates checks and balances in the academic progress, mental well-being and pastoral care of excluded students. This would fit in with the intended focus by OFSTED on the 'experience of each student', exclusions and gaming (off rolling) and would extend to point of transition, if the student exits to alternative provision. In the academic interests of the excluded students, schools should always share assessment data on students' progress and standards with the alternative provision, for continuity in learning. Fairness and accountability for all mainstream schools would be assured, as all would be subject to the same scrutiny of their educational processes. Integrating an inclusive and relevant curriculum with a values-based school culture can reform challenging behaviours, and those schools that are successful will be recognised for their leadership strengths.

Schools and academy trusts must respect and value all their children equally, including the 'square peg' students, the 'Pinball Kids'.[22] In the long run, the initial 'startup costs' of transforming aspects of the curriculum so that schools retain students at risk of exclusions, far outweigh the potential loss of students' life chances. Not giving all students, like Kwesi, the opportunity to fulfil their educational aspirations is counter-intuitive. It is difficult to justify why a school, or an academy trust, would not invest its resources wisely in this.

# Notes

1   All-Party Parliamentary Group (2019) All-Party Parliamentary Group on Knife Crime. Available at: www.preventknifecrime.co.uk/wp-content/uploads/2019/10/APPG-on-Knife-Crime-Back-to-School-exclusions-report-FINAL.pdf (Accessed: 17 January 2020).

2   E. Timpson et al. (2018) *The Timpson Review of School Exclusion*. London: Department for Education, Crown Copyright 2019 [Online]. Available at: https://assets.publishing.service.gov.uk/government/uploads/system/uploads/attachment_data/file/807862/Timpson_review.pdf (Accessed: 1 December 2019).

3   We mean exits from a school to either another school, alternative provision or an unknown destination, where those exits do not appear to be driven by families or a formal exclusion

4   Education Policy Institute, J. Hutchinson et al. (2019) Education in England: Annual Report 2019, https://epi.org.uk/publications-and-research/annual-report-2019/: EPI.

5   The DIFFERENCE (2019) The DIFFERENCE Website. Available at: www.the-difference.com/included (Accessed: 22 December 2019).

6   D. Thompson (2017) Who are the pupils in alternative provision?. Available at: https://ffteducationdatalab.org.uk/2017/10/who-are-the-pupils-in-alternative-provision/ (Accessed: 14 December 2019).

7   . E. Timson et al. (2018) The Timpson Review of School Exclusion. London: Department for Education, Crown Copyright 2019 [Online]. Available at: https://assets.publishing.service.gov.uk/government/uploads/system/uploads/attachment_data/file/807862/Timpson_review.pdf (Accessed: 1 December 2019).

8   Department for Education (2019) *Special Educational Needs: An Analysis and Summary of Data*. London: Department for Education; Department for Education (2019) Statistics: Exclusions. Available at: www.gov.uk/government/collections/statistics-exclusions (Accessed: 5 December 2020).

9   Education Policy Institute, J. Hutchinson et al. (2019) Education in England: Annual Report 2019, https://epi.org.uk/publications-and-research/annual-report-2019/: EPI.

10  Department for Education (2019) Statistics: exclusions. Available at: www.gov.uk/government/collections/statistics-exclusions (Accessed: 5 December 2020).

11  A. Carter, OBE (2015) *Carter Review of Initial Teacher Training (ITT)*. London: Department for Education.

12  E. Timpson et al. (2018) *The Timpson Review of School Exclusion*. London: Department for Education, Crown Copyright 2019 [Online]. Available at: https://assets.publishing.service.gov.uk/government/uploads/system/uploads/attachment_data/file/807862/Timpson_review.pdf (Accessed: 1 December 2019).

13  D. Tutu (2000) *No Future without Forgiveness*, 1st edn. London: Rider.

14    Department for Education (2018) *Investigative Research into Alternative Provision*. London: Department for Education.

15    E. Timpson et al. (2018) *The Timpson Review of School Exclusion*. London: Department for Education, Crown Copyright 2019 [Online]. Available at: https://assets.publishing.service. gov.uk/government/uploads/system/uploads/attachment_data/file/807862/Timpson_ review.pdf (Accessed: 1 December 2019).

16    P. Garner (2011) *Promoting the Conditions for Positive Behaviour, to Help Every Child Succeed: Review of the Landscape*, 1st edn. Nottingham: National College for School Leadership.

17    All-Party Parliamentary Group (2019) All-Party Parliamentary Group on Knife Crime. Available at: www.preventknifecrime.co.uk/wp-content/uploads/2019/10/APPG-on-Knife-Crime-Back-to-School-exclusions-report-FINAL.pdf (Accessed: 17 January 2020).

18    OFSTED (2019) *The Education Inspection Framework*, 1st edn. www.gov.uk/government/ publications/education-inspection-framework. London: OFSTED.

19    E. Timpson et al. (2018) *The Timpson Review of School Exclusion*. London: Department for Education, Crown Copyright 2019 [Online]. Available at: https://assets.publishing.service. gov.uk/government/uploads/system/uploads/attachment_data/file/807862/Timpson_ review.pdf (Accessed: 1 December 2019).

20    All Party Parliamentary Group (2019) All-Party Parliamentary Group on Knife Crime. Available at: www.preventknifecrime.co.uk/wp-content/uploads/2019/10/APPG-on-Knife-Crime-Back-to-School-exclusions-report-FINAL.pdf (Accessed: 17 January 2020).

21    M. Bulman (2019) Youth services 'decimated by 69 per cent' in less than a decade amid surge in knife crime, figures show, *The Independent*, 24 September.

22    The RSA (2019) Pinball kids. Available at: www.thersa.org/action-and-research/rsa-projects/creative-learning-and-development-folder/pinball-kids (Accessed: 29 December 2019).

# Phenomenal learning

# 6

# Knowledge through skills

## Introduction

> Learning does not make one learned: there are those who have knowledge and those who have understanding. The first requires memory and the second philosophy.
>
> (Alexandre Dumas, *The Count of Monte Cristo*, 1844–1846)[1]

OFSTED defines a 'knowledge-rich' approach as one in which curriculum leaders are clear on the 'invaluable knowledge they want their pupils to know'. The intention and hall mark of the knowledge-rich curriculum would be sequenced information, with students recalling successfully what they have been taught. Importantly, the knowledge concepts need understanding, so that students effectively transfer and apply these to the relevant contexts. The principles of this are sound, but the practice in schools, significantly variable, owing to a range of factors.

The academic curriculum, comprises knowledge strands. Like the pieces of a mosaic, these start to make sense only once the individual pieces are pieced together. It is only then the previously disconnected colours and shapes resident in the pattern, provide us with a vibrant narrative. Historians and archaeologists, through these connections unearth so much detail about ancient civilisations; society, language, religious practice, economy, culture and day to day life. To pursue this analogy of acquiring knowledge as in a mosaic; students acquire isolated strands of knowledge in lessons, in each subject on a daily basis. These are interpreted, only once, students are able to glue together the pieces and conceptualise the broader picture through the cognitive lens. We explore here the cycle of *recall, transfer and apply* through the synergy between, cognition, (understanding knowledge) metacognition (self-regulation and learning to learn skills) and self-motivation.

## Knowledge underpinned by conceptual thinking skills

In 1597 Frances Bacon, arguably, the father of scientific methods of inquiry, asserted, 'Knowledge is power' ('*Scientia potentiaest*').[2] Much has been written regarding knowledge organisers and many schools, strongly advocate their use.

Knowledge Organisers (KOs) can be much like the pieces of the mosaic that remain in separate pieces, until these pieces are sequenced. Making the connections and providing the glue are the key to the successful use of KOs. '....understand those facts in the context of a conceptual framework and organise knowledge in order to facilitate retrieval and application'(Bransford et al., 2000).[3]

Digesting and memorising knowledge, however, risk being prioritised over the importance of activities and tasks that seek to develop the skills. If we need reminding of this, the OFSTED framework specifically refers to 'Developing understanding, not memorising disconnected facts....pupils connect new knowledge with existing knowledge.... unconsciously apply their knowledge as skills ... not be reduced to, or confused with, simply memorising facts'.[4]

Myatt rightly maintains that students require key dates, quotes, technical vocabulary, concepts, key figures and timelines, contained in knowledge organisers.[5] Memorising facts has value as the information, once mastered, creates 'resilience and confidence'. Yet, at first glance, this may now appear to be in direct contrast to what inspectors would perceive as 'deepening understanding' at the expense of 'prompting *pupils to learn glossaries or long lists of disconnected facts'*.

'Knowing more, remembering more and being able to do more' according to the EIF, requires the presentation of knowledge to be meaningful to all students. The KO must be more than a list of tenuous or decontextualised facts. Otherwise, it risks becoming another aide-memoire that is certainly kept and well used by conscientious students, but not valued and potentially lost, by those who are more random in their approaches to learning.

The American poet James Russell Lowell likened books to 'bees which carry the quickening pollen from one to another mind.'[6] KOs are predicated on the assumption that students, like the bees that carry the quickening pollen, *know how to* make the 'connections'. Myatt's beliefs are based on those expounded by Ed Hirsch; that 'knowledge builds on knowledge.... because you have a lot of analogies...for connecting the knowledge to what you already know .... Our students become more intelligent when they know more ...'[7]

According to this theory, our students, living in an age where they are data and knowledge rich, with easy 24/7 access to the internet and social media, should all be increasingly '*more intelligent*'! It is highly debatable whether a causal link exists between *accessing* the information and knowing *how to use it* meaningfully. The intelligence grows, once, the student is open to absorbing the information and has the key skills that he/she needs to manipulate this knowledge and consequently, to transfer and apply to the appropriate context.

Consider this. A young boy explained to his friend that he had taught his dog to whistle and his friend, expressing excitement, asked the boy to demonstrate this with the dog. His friend turned to him with a bemused expression and replied, 'I said that I had *taught* him to whistle ... I didn't say that he had *learnt* it!' Therefore, 'learnt' not taught!

Therefore, before KOs or any other methods of imparting knowledge can be *learnt* effectively, students and teachers need to evaluate and identify gaps in the sequence of knowledge, as well as identify key skills for retention and application. The essential point is students' ability to conceptualise information. Before starting any process of revising 'knowledge', students must acquire a deeper understanding of what they are learning. Only then will they be able to successfully transfer and apply the knowledge they acquire to any relevant context.

## Cognitive learning theory of knowledge memorisation

Our short-term working memory capacity is limited, so by storing more in our long-term memory, we can free up working memory capacity (Paas et al., 2004). Knowledge organisers in lessons, it is argued, can assist students in storing knowledge in the long-term memory, with a view to recall, as and when necessary (Paas et al., 2004).[8] Cognitive science research indicates that the best way to revise is to repeatedly test oneself; a method that may work for the majority of students. In principle, frequently isolating the piece of knowledge from memory increases the likelihood that it will be remembered the next time. Each time it becomes increasingly harder to recall this knowledge, the more accurately it will be remembered.

Prime to this theory of successful transfer are three underlying assumptions that students

1. are interested in what is being taught and are therefore motivated;
2. will engage proactively with their learning;
3. are alert during the memorisation process.

The key point, less well researched, *is the degree of effectiveness of the transfer process within a typical classroom contextor during online learning.* Full transfer of information will be uniquely dependent on each student's profile. In each subject, there are thirty students in a class where transfer of knowledge is potentially subject to a number of variables on a spectrum.

Sleep deprivation, distraction will impact negatively on the quality of transfer during memorisation. The low frequency of exposure to the knowledge being learnt is a main factor because checks and balances may not be in place to ensure effective recall. This has implications for timetabling and also for home-learning tasks. Out-of-school/home life distractions might take precedence over the learning in lessons, as students perceive the learning to be irrelevant and become unmotivated. This will affect outcomes. In addition, students who have missed school, or lessons, owing to exclusion and or sporadic absence, illness and so on, will be asked to revise information that may be incomplete or poorly presented, or taught at a point when they were absent. Students with ASC, ADHD, dyslexia or other special educational need will face other challenges during the transfer process.

## Case studies of 'hard to reach' students in the classroom

Let us consider a typical scenario for teachers with a range of vulnerable students, who arrive on a daily basis, with 'chaotic' lives and, or extraneous factors that affect their lives and attitudes towards learning. These students present themselves in a Year 9 Science lesson with a learning objective to revise 'Mitosis and the cell cycle' (AQA GCSE Biology) using a KO. Observing the students in their learning and questioning them reveals their 'take aways' from the lesson and demonstrates the impact of a 'well-taught' lesson.

Joe has arrived late in school. He is sleep deprived, from too much exposure to social media and 'gaming', late into the night. He cannot focus at all, keeps yawning, but keeps his head down to look like he is revising. *He confuses cytoplasm with cell membrane and has not fully understood the concept that when a cell divides, each new cell has the same genetic information.*

Meera is vulnerable on account of a non-supportive family; her parents' violent quarrel meant that she did not eat any supper and missed breakfast. She is upset, suffering from hunger pangs and withdrawn. She looks at the KO, attempts the 'look, cover and check' revision technique and then starts chatting intermittently to her friend, as she cannot focus for long periods. *She has limited understanding; this includes new 'daughter' cells containing genetic information, identical to the parent cell.*

Mike, a 'looked after' student is unhappy living in his foster parent's home, wishing to return to his biological mother, whilst social services maintain he cannot. He is frequently absent from school. He doodles in his book, when he should be revising from the KO. *He knows simply that mitosis is a type of cell division.*

Kane is frequently unable to concentrate on learning, owing to his undiagnosed ADHD. In this subject, he has missed key facts and knowledge, owing to repeat exclusions. Without understanding the context, Kane struggles to make sense of the information being presented in the KO. After a while, he loses interest and ends up once more being removed from the lesson for poor behaviours and disturbing others. He is sent to an inclusion unit to complete the revision on his own. *All he learns is cells divide when an organism becomes damaged and needs to produce new cells.*

If we look into the exercise books of each student, across this subject and then across all their subjects, we might see evidence of fragmented knowledge learnt in class, unfinished pieces of work, gaps, where the student was 'absent' (physically or mentally) for a topic or an aspect of a topic, practical investigation or creative activity. Teachers' feedback comments will encourage 'catch up' on the sequencing of the knowledge and skills. This may, or may not be carried out by the student. The pattern across the curriculum along with each subject teacher's perseverance in following up to ensure the work has been learnt, recalled and successfully applied will dictate the quality of each student's learning and progress. Hence, the critical importance of students *acting on teacher feedback* as part of the metacognition 'recall, transfer, apply' cycle.

Working with each of these students so that they meaningfully access the information will require different strategies. If the purpose of the class activity is students testing themselves, or being assessed on knowledge from the KOs, the odds of successfully developing memorable networks of powerful knowledge, are stacked against them. Circumstances beyond the teacher's control, in all probability, are not sufficiently conducive for each student to process information from the short-term memory into the long-term memory; the only way that ensures successful transfer.

Just as an architect should pay heed to the rules of physics when designing a flying buttress or a pointed arch, teachers can benefit from understanding how our minds and memories work.

(Robbie Coleman EEF Blog: Education and architecture – a cognitive science analogy, 5 December 2018)[9]

We can extend Coleman's analogy to include attitudes to learning. In the same way, that an architect would sum up the fitness for purpose of specific types of materials; metal, alloy, stone or wood for producing the best results, a teacher must consider how fit for purpose is the student for the activity of memorisation and most importantly, which learning strategy would work best.

## Metacognition and self-regulation

The EEF report found that metacognition and self-regulation approaches have 'consistently high levels of impact, with an average of seven months' additional progress'.[10] Despite the potential high impact, the complication is students needing to 'take greater responsibility for their learning and develop their understanding of what is required to succeed'. Research indicates that overtly teaching metacognition and self-regulation to students, 'can be particularly effective for low achieving and older pupils'. The EEF report's 7 stage guide in how to implement metacognition and self-regulated learning is highly informative. Self-regulated learning contains three essential components.[11]

Firstly, *cognitive skills;* fundamental to acquiring knowledge and completing learning tasks. Examples include 'memorisation techniques. Subject-specific strategies ....making different marks with a brush, using different methods to solve Maths equations'. We add here; accurately differentiating between the immediate future and the conditional tense in French, when describing forthcoming weekend activities; correct use of English language devices in creating suspense in creative writing; deciding whether to organise statistical information in a graph, or pie chart for a business studies presentation; knowing how to accurately present the write-up of a practical investigation in Science with a hypothesis, method and conclusion.

Secondly, *metacognition strategies* are paramount for students reflecting on the effectiveness of their task; evaluating how successful their choice of cognitive or learning strategy has been, and importantly, whether they need to make radical, or nuanced changes, based on the outcomes. As students get older and move into the post-16 phase, these skills become the requisite higher order skills, as there is greater need for independent learning, self-reliance, critical and analytical thinking skills during the learning process.

Thirdly, students' personal *motivation* is essential as is students' willingness to engage 'cognition, metacognition, and motivation interact in complex ways during the learning process'.

## Fragile knowledge: Learning to learn

The importance of reinforcing metacognition; the 'learning to learn' skills are exemplified through 'fragile knowledge'.[12] Through an insightful scenario of a student's Shakespeare essay, we see how even the most carefully sequenced curricula may not be well understood by some students, despite once again, the teacher's best efforts. Perkins' fragility is linked to the term 'metacognition'; how we think and use our knowledge, as follows.

- *Missing knowledge.* Alex forgets that Macbeth was written with the audience of James I in mind.

- *Inert knowledge.* Knowledge lets the student pass the quiz, but Alex doesn't mention the 'divine right of kings', which his teacher implicitly wants him to focus on.
- *Naïve knowledge.* Knowledge as naïve theories and stereotypes, even after considerable instruction; with the notion Lady Macbeth is solely to blame for her husband's behaviour.
- *Ritual knowledge.* Knowledge acquires a ritual character, useful for certain academic tasks. Alex pleases his teacher by mentioning the rare rhetorical device 'anadiplosis'.

## Leaders of own learning

In the EEF example, Figure 6.1, John has some knowledge (*word problems in Maths are solved by expressing them as equations*) and strategies (*how to turn sentences into an equation*). His knowledge develops as the word problem translates into a simultaneous equation. He has strategies for solving simultaneous equations that he evaluates through substituting his answers into the word problem and checking they are correct. If proved wrong, and assuming he is resilient and motivated, he attempts other strategies and then re-evaluates once more.

Zimmerman's definition of self-regulated learners stresses their awareness 'of strengths and limitations … guided by personally set goals and task-related strategies … self-reflecting on their increasing effectiveness.'[13] The key point is that this 'self-fulfilling positive' cycle increases self-satisfaction and motivation, which in turn, has an impact on continuous improvements in learning methods.

Simply put, the process of acquiring knowledge and applying it in context is about planning how to undertake a task, cognitively undertaking that activity, while monitoring the strategy to check one's own progress, and then knowing how to

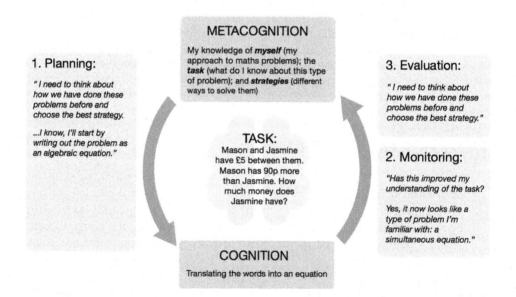

**FIGURE 6.1** Planning for metacognition around a specific task

evaluate the overall success. All of these prime skills come under the umbrella term of Executive Function (EF). EF has impact on both emotional and thinking processes[14] and is indicative of an individual's mental capacity for planning, organisation, efficient decision making and action.

Reverting back to our students in the case study, what is apparent is that for the students who are not engaging with their learning, their capacity to reach the meta-cognition stage is significantly lessened without motivation, tenacity and resilience. They should want to actively tackle the 'cognitive process', become aware of the strategies for overcoming the barriers to learning and develop motivation to learn; all this, before they can meaningfully address the tasks set.

So, it is not simply a case of 'recall, transfer and apply'. Metacognition is a corollary of cognition and without a *clear understanding* of the knowledge that is being learnt, a student's evaluation of how well it is applied cannot be effective, even with the best will and motivation. Therefore, providing a student with a checklist of skills that requires them to simply tick the skills-led activity they have accomplished, may not lead to recall. However, giving them the opportunity to *evidence* what underpins the assessment allows them to evaluate and self-regulate.

The criteria list as in Figure 6.2 requires students to evaluate the skill along the lines of WWW (what went well), EBI (even better if) and Next steps.

Actively encouraging students to articulate what has been successful or less effective and what they need to do to achieve the next stage promotes reflection on their learning. This we know is essential with assessment and feedback processes; 'activating students as owners of their own learning'(William et al., 2005)[15]

## Learning styles: How we retain information

Transforming students into leaders of own learning means training each to know what works best. This cannot be left to chance or to individual subject teachers. Students vary in how they learn and retain knowledge so that it can be stored in the long-term memory.[16]

1.  Visual photographic memory; re-read the material, recall the information as patterns and concepts emerge; note take, construct concept maps, diagrams and charts.

2.  Recording information, e.g. quotations, timelines on flash cards; process of writing helps retain information; with annotated questions that students answer. Actively thinking about the words, helps when struggling to retain a particular concept or fact. Using a look cover check approach is useful.

3.  Creating tests; writing questions as students re-read their notes/course materials; reflecting on questions featuring in exams. Reviewing answers against model answers allows students to identify their own gaps in learning, leading to revision strategy.

4.  Applying a concept identifies students' own areas of weakness; trying to explain the concept to someone else; helps consolidate how much they have learnt and recall. This works well as a peered activity in class.

| | I can | I can | I can | I can |
|---|---|---|---|---|
| *Research & analysis* | Research limited selection of high street bags producing a basic collage | Research and identify a basic range of high street bags to create a collage that will influence design ideas | Research and identify a good range of high street and high end bags | Research and identify a detailed wide range of high street and high end bags |
| *Reflecting on my work* | WWW: my collage showed the quality of the bags in my sample<br><br>EBI: my sample of high street bags was not broad enough – only 3<br><br>Next steps: I need to research 8 bags so that I get a good idea of range of designs so that I have greater influences on my designs. | | | |
| | I can | I can | I can | I can |
| *Production of a textured handbag using a range of techniques* | Carry out simple practical tasks, with help | Plan and organize basic activities | Plan and organize sound activities | Plan and organize complex activities |
| | Select and use equipment safely with limited competence | Select and use equipment safely mostly appropriate | Select and use equipment safely consistently appropriate | Select a range of equipment safely consistently appropriate |
| | Prepare, print, cut, machine sew to assemble basic bag construction | Prepare, print, cut and machine sew, assemble sound product to show good quality construction | | Skilfully prepare and cut with precision to show a range of techniques: dye sublimation, machine sewing, applique, hand embroidery and a recycled feature to assemble high quality outcome |
| *Reflecting on my work* | WWW: I chose appropriate equipment. I considered safety aspects especially with the sewing machine.<br><br>EBI: didn't show a wide enough range of techniques, I could have included hand embroidery for example<br><br>Next steps: To consider how I build in hand embroidery or a recycled feature could be built into the final design to improve it aesthetically. | | | |

**FIGURE 6.2** An example of feedback influencing metacognition in Design Technology: 'What went well', 'Even better if' and 'Next steps'

5.  Producing Cornell notes requires confident and literate note-takers who actively
    listen and translate what they hear into coherent and legible notes, summarising
    key points.[17] Of the five stages, Record and Reduce are the most helpful for
    students to retain and recall and enhance reflection. Students' summary of the
    ideas and facts use key words as *cue words*, explaining relationships of ideas and
    reinforcing continuity.

## Learning to learn skills

Introspection on one's own learning does not come naturally to all students and
need modelling with some, so that they know how best to capture associated ideas
or linkages. A mind map can helpfully indicate how previous knowledge can be
extended to encompass new knowledge. The dual process of reviewing the Cornell
notes along with the mind map creates additional challenge for students and enhances
retention of old material, while adding new material to memory.

Reflection skills steer students to think about their opinions and ideas, while they
read over the notes; actively adding further information to the notes, through regular
review. Deploying digital research skills and identifying useful websites are invaluable as an element of independent learning and creativity, especially when answering
assessment questions, or in classroom discussions.

## 'Learning to Learn Skills' diary

All students should make the progress of which they are capable. One of the ways
is for schools to require all students, or targeted students to complete a 'Learning
to Learn Skills' (L2L) diary (see Appendix 6.1, available at www.routledge.com/
9780367900878). The principle behind this is that through students taking increasing
responsibility and ownership of their studying, they become more motivated. The
pathways to acquiring motivation and self-regulation are necessarily different for Joe,
than for Meera, Mike or Kane. Additionally, in our students' case study, there will of
course be external negative circumstances that require the school to provide appropriate pastoral, special educational needs and other types of support.

Nevertheless, the first significant step is for students to reflect on what motivates
them, helps them learn, as well as the barriers that are stopping them from learning.
The key headlines in the diaries are shared with teachers, to be used in their lesson
planning. The students retain the diaries in their personal school planner. What is
especially helpful in this diary is that students are responsible for updating it and
they can post images of teacher feedback and their responses (taken from their work
books) that they identify as helpful in their learning. They meet half-termly with
their form tutor to discuss their learning strategies.

This process contributes to reflection on learning and develops the necessary
metacognition and motivational strategies students need across the curriculum. The
example of the L2L diary can be adapted for KS3–5. As we can see from the example
for Joe Davies (Appendix 6.1, available at www.routledge.com/9780367900878),
strategies are discussed with the tutor and his parents for limiting the time of

exposure to media during the evenings. Once this discipline in learning is gradually introduced and adhered to, Joe starts to focus on more positive examples of work in his books with motivational teacher feedback. This discipline in learning and acquiring the L2L skills becomes more essential as all students increasingly resort to online learning.

## Raising teachers' awareness of students' metacognition skills

The valuable information taken from the diaries along with the teacher's evaluation of the students' ability to 'recall, transfer and apply' knowledge will inform the Metacognition Zonal Learning graph (Figure 6.3) for a class. This can be compiled by the form tutor in discussion with students on their L2L diary. The aim is for a class teacher to review the Metacognition Zonal Learning graph for his/her subject and to think through the additional strategies that might genuinely assist individual students in 'recall, transfer and apply' of knowledge.

KOs work as long as students have a sound conceptual understanding of what they are being requested to recall. The degree of accuracy is highly dependent on the effectiveness of the revision and transference of the information from short- to long-term memory (see Figure 6.1). This brings us back to the Metacognition Zonal Learning graph that posits students on high to low impact, in relation to their learning to learn skills (Figure 6.3). The profile will vary from subject to subject, dependent

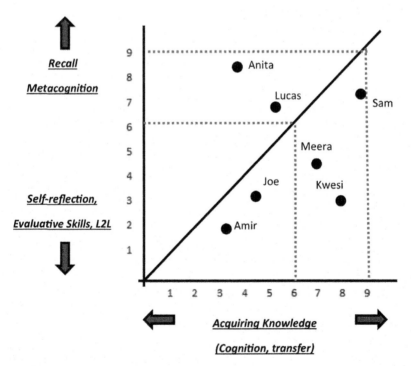

**FIGURE 6.3** Metacognition Zonal Learning graph: comparing students' acquisition of knowledge with their ability to self-reflect

Copyright Meena Kumari Wood and Nick Haddon.

on the motivation and interest that a student demonstrates. The levels are broadly designed to be in line with the GCSE levels. In this diagram, in Biology, Anita and Lucas have high metacognition abilities and recall facility. Lucas acquires knowledge slightly faster than Anita. All those below the diagonal axis have varying abilities of retaining and transferring knowledge from their short-term memory to their long-term memory, as they lack metacognition, self-reflection skills and, possibly, motivation. Teachers can use this information about their students for lesson planning and adopt targeted learning and assessment strategies.

## Summary

The greatest challenge facing curriculum leaders and teachers is how we define what the 'knowledge-rich curriculum' is, and sequence this so that students can access, store and create the mosaic of learning into the bigger picture. This is especially the case with students who are vulnerable, persistently absent, frequently excluded or simply will not engage with the subject for a variety of reasons. Most importantly, teachers require effective strategies with those who present with SEND – ADHD, autism, emotional, behavioural and communication difficulties. These are precisely the students who are at risk of potentially opting out from their learning. The risk is exacerbated if the feedback students receive from the teacher does not properly address the barriers they face.

We can better understand the facilitators and barriers through how significantly the Metacognition Zonal Learning curve affects each of our students, albeit positively or negatively. At first sight, reviewing students' metacognition skills will appear a luxury and is not intended as a precise science. It can feel like a time-consuming exercise for a busy subject teacher, who is understandably anxious to complete the scheme of learning. However, the importance of spending some time periodically revisiting how well students recall, transfer and apply their cognitive and metacognition skills can influence teaching activities.

Schools invest time in reviewing data on students' progress and attainment measures to ensure they are on track to achieve their potential. Surely investing quality time in boosting that academic potential is key for transforming a student's learning and outcomes. OFSTED inspectors do not request internal data from the school on students' progress according to the EIF (2019). This methodology may change over time with successive inspection frameworks. However, with the focus on curriculum, one of the central questions that needs addressing is that 'pupils embed key concepts in their long-term memory and apply them fluently' (EIF, 2019).

Teachers must think through deploying motivational strategies for students who are frustrated when they perceive they may not be achieving as well as their peers. Ensuring that teacher feedback to students is coupled with encouraging self-regulation skills through the L2L Diary model (Appendix 6.1, available at www.routledge.com/9780367900878) strengthens students' motivation and resilience. This hooks in the most vulnerable students so they appreciate how best they learn, and builds in challenge for more able students.

A *whole school curriculum intent* that creates opportunities for developing metacognitive skills will facilitate learning, retaining and applying. Returning to Dumas' contention; we identify knowledge that requires memory; however, first and foremost, we must always check the corollary of this, that students have acquired deeper understanding or 'philosophy'.

## Notes

1    A. Dumas (2008) *The Count of Monte Cristo*. Gutenberg [Online]. Available at: www. gutenberg.org/files/1184/1184-h/1184-h.htm (Accessed: 15 November 2019).

2    D. Fo (2004) Knowledge like challenge to every form of powers. repubblica.it (in Italian).

3    J. Bransford, A. Brown and R. Cocking (2000) *How People Learn*, 1st edn, Washington: National Academy Press.

4    OFSTED (2019) *The Education Inspection Framework*, 1st edn. www.gov.uk/government/ publications/education-inspection-framework: London: OFSTED.

5    M. Myatt (2018) *The Curriculum: Gallimaufry to Coherence*, 1st edn. Woodbridge: John Catt Educational Ltd.

6    BrainyQuote: Russell Lowell (2019) James Russell Lowell quotes. Available at: www. brainyquote.com/authors/james-russell-lowell-quotes (Accessed: 27 December 2020).

7    E. D. Hirsch (1999) *The Schools We Need: And Why We Don't Have Them*, 1st edn. New York: Anchor Books.

8    F. Paas and A. Renkl (2004) Cognitive load theory: Instructional implications of the interaction between information structures and cognitive architecture, *Instructional Science*, 32(1): 1–8.

9    R. Coleman (2018) Education and architecture – a cognitive science analogy. Available at: https:// educationendowmentfoundation.org.uk/news/eef-blog-education-and-architecture- a-cognitive-science-analogy/ (Accessed: 1 December 2019).

10   Education Endowment Foundation (2019) Teaching and Learning Toolkit. Available at: https://educationendowmentfoundation.org.uk/evidence-summaries/teaching-learning- toolkit (Accessed: 11 November 2019).

11   Education Endowment Foundation (2019) *Teaching and Learning Toolkit*. Available at: https:// educationendowmentfoundation.org.uk/evidence-summaries/teaching-learning-toolkit (Accessed: 11 November 2019).

12   D. Perkins (1995) *Smart Schools: Better Thinking and Learning for Every Child*, 1st edn. New York: Free Press.

13   B. Zimmerman (2002) Becoming a self-regulated learner: An overview, *Theory into Practice*, 41(2).

14   T. Otero, L. Barker and J. Nagliera (2014) Executive function treatment and intervention in schools, *Appl Neuropsychol Child*, 3(3), 205–14 [Online]. Available at: www.ncbi.nlm.nih. gov/pubmed/25010086 (Accessed: 2 December 2019).

15   D. William (2011) *Embedded Formative Assessment*, 1st edn. Bloomington, IN: Solution Tree Press.

16   K. Roell (2019) The visual learning style. Available at: www.thoughtco.com/visual-learning- style-3212062 (Accessed: 11 November 2019).

17   W. Pauk and R. J. Q. Owens (2005) *How to Study in College*, 8th edn. New York: Houghton Mifflin Company.

# 7

# Consolidating and assessing knowledge and skills

## Introduction

The GCSE specifications' greater focus on the application and evaluation skills means that where graphic organisers of knowledge are used their impact needs evaluating. Here we review the usefulness of Knowledge Organisers (KOs) and their potential in improving knowledge retention. Secondly, we focus on the prime value of teacher feedback to students on their learning. Only by undertaking evaluative processes might we identify the teaching and assessment strategies that best organise knowledge effectively and develop students' *learning to learn* (metacognition) skills. We propose assessment practice that interlace teaching and learning, helping students address misunderstandings and embed key concepts in their long-term memory. The impact is they apply key concepts with confidence. Students know more, remember more and do more!

## Deploying graphic organisers

Graphic organisers have a variety of formats in which to capture the KO information, thereby providing the additional challenge of reordering or reorganising that aids retention.[1] Devising writing frames, graphic organisers, mind maps, can help students with individual learning styles, so that each finds the best way of retaining and recalling knowledge.

The EEF's model of a *fishbone organiser*[2] (Figure 7.1) as a worked example using seven steps provides a visual graphic that benefits students by introducing them to the *process* of planning, monitoring and evaluating. The importance of locating strategies *within the subject specific task cannot be underestimated.*

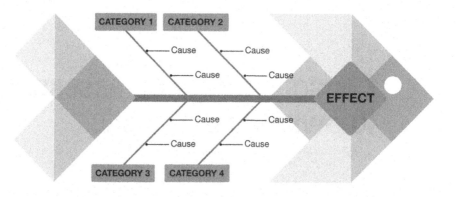

FIGURE 7.1 Education Endowment Foundation – Fishbone Organiser. A graphical way to support students in planning a response

1. *Activating prior knowledge.* The teacher discusses with pupils the different causes that led to World War I while making notes on the whiteboard.
2. *Explicit strategy instruction.* The teacher then explains how the fishbone diagram will help organise their ideas, with the emphasis on the cognitive strategy of using a 'cause and effect model' in History that will help them to organise and plan a better written response.
3. *Modelling of learned strategy.* The teacher uses the initial notes on the causes of the war to model one part of the fishbone diagram.
4. *Memorisation of learned strategy.* The teacher tests if pupils have understood and memorised the key aspects of the fishbone strategy, and its main purpose, through questions and discussion.
5. *Guided practice.* The teacher models one further fishbone cause with the whole group, with pupils verbally contributing their ideas.

Most students will participate and learn interactively, contributing to question and answer, but the case study students in Chapter 6 are likely to show a different pattern of learning. This will *not be sequential* but a zigzag of dipping in and out of the five stages above. How well these students lead their own learning will be a determinant of the eventual quality and impact of outcomes. Equally importantly, their potentially distracting and disruptive behaviours and attitudes in the class will affect the learning of their peers.

The learning and focus of all students may then be interrupted and take place in fits and starts. At the point of 'Independent practice' is when a teacher can then request the class to work on different activities. The teacher may need to provide further practice for some of the students who lack motivation, or those are struggling to populate the diagram with accurate knowledge. It may well be that the teacher changes the activity for some, as they are not ready for the fishbone organiser and, in the first instance, need to produce a mind map brainstorming the knowledge they already know, whilst identifying the gaps. Only then can they begin the process of transferring the information to the fishbone diagram, with any meaningful analysis.

Once the diagram is complete with analysis, the final stage of 'Structured reflection' is 'where students reflect on how appropriate the model was, how successfully they applied it, and how they might use it in the future'.

This scaffolded approach in the classroom needs to take into account the different profiles of students in the lesson, with the aim of accessing the knowledge and increasing independent practice. These include, for instance, those students who have a lower reading and writing age than their chronological age, as well as students who have English as an Additional Language (Advanced Bilingual Learners); whose spoken language is better than their written language.

## Advantages and disadvantages of KOs

A proliferation of good examples of KOs can be accessed.[3] Some are more fulsome or versatile than others. Commercially bought revision guides can, in many instances, dependent on the model, easily substitute for KOs, if used by students at the start of the GCSE course in Year 9 or 10 (see Twinkl).[4] Therefore, KOs should have a USP (unique selling point) that works for all students.

In the simplest and possibly less useful knowledge organisers, the information is presented in a list format of facts and dates, including a timeline where appropriate. In others, there are references to key formulae, for instance, solving quadratics or expanding binomials. This may not be the best way to assist students in terms of showing links between ideas or most importantly, *concepts.* All Year 11 students are taught to make the link between expand and simplify to factorisation of quadratics and then to expanding binomials. The challenge for Maths teachers will be those students who do not understand the interrelationship of formulae, as they have not internalised the *essential conceptual links.*

Providing students with opportunities to deduce the conceptual link between factorisation and its use in everyday life aids understanding. For instance, illustrating real-life application of factorisation within the KO is useful; with problem-solving examples such as exchanging money, comparing prices and making calculations during travel. Students can engage more with the concept once they understand the relevance of this skill and knowledge to their everyday life. In addition, they realise that factorising successfully allows them to navigate number relationships in the real world without relying on their calculator or phone to do the sums for them.

This is illustrated through the example of this Year 8, 13 year-old student. In a Maths lesson she used a calculator for simple percentages, subsequently self-checking against 'text book answers'. She was asked to problem solve, without a calculator and to find the original price of a 35 per cent reduction on a dress in the sale. Unable to rely on other strategies, and not having understood the basic concept, she was distraught! During a 'mechanical exercise' of this nature, what is key in testing understanding and cognitive skills are reflective challenges. So adding in problem-solving stimulates metacognition skills and enables meaningful application.

## Evaluating effectiveness of KOs

In better thought out KOs, the information is organised in such a way as to encourage or facilitate further independent research by the student. *Malling School*[5] for instance, provides students with the knowledge and opportunities for application and transfer through further links to established sites.[6]

A number of schools have posted KOs and/or Curriculum Outlines[7] on their websites for access by students, their parents/carers, and the wider school community. This can have the dual effect of creating independence in student learning and encouraging parents/carers to get involved in their children's learning. Parents actually understand what their children need to learn and can help by testing for retrieval of information when students are asked to revise information from the KO. Learning starts to take a greater prominence in the life of students and has the potential of creating a whole school learning community.

Techniques for *recall* vary amongst students, as we saw in previous chapters. We must not fall into the trap of assuming that one size fits all. As retrieval of information is key, material should be presented in such a way that it can be easily tested, to maximise the opportunity for retention in the long-term memory. Students with, for instance, ADHD, dyslexia or dyspraxia face barriers accessing the relevant knowledge.[8] For the successful retention of information to take place, the knowledge organiser needs to be designed differently for students with different abilities and capabilities across the subjects. Testing understanding could be through free recall, where students write down everything that they can remember on the topic before checking the KO, or perhaps filling in a blank (or partially blank) knowledge organiser. Other techniques include quizzes, writing down key dates or formulae in Science or Maths as aspects of meta language, such as dramatic irony in English.

*Toot Hill School*[9] has helpfully provided five different techniques filmed on YouTube on its website that aim to help students make good use of their KOs. These range from Look Cover Check, Word Up, Map Your Mind, Test your Mind and Flash Cards. The techniques are presented in a student friendly style, aimed to deepen students' understanding about how they retain information. This is linked to the importance of regular revision being key.

At *Durrington School*,[10] knowledge organisers are used as a focused curriculum guide for teachers and a revision tool for students. They also lie at the heart of the school's literacy strategy: departments use them to list the relevant Tier 2 and Tier 3 vocabulary taught in the lessons.

*Meridien School's*[11] website states that students receive a KO containing relevant key facts and information related to the topic. The content of the KOs are variable ranging from glossaries, for instance, for Ancient History and Sociology, to highly detailed information in Geography, Spanish and Maths. In Maths, students are given a 'have a go' opportunities, with signposted questions. In one example, the sine and rule equation is posited in an everyday context and provides good opportunities for students to transfer their learnt knowledge and to see whether in doing so, they have understood the application.

With this variance in the quality of KOs within a school, closer scrutiny of the documents to ensure that they all provide students with equally high quality information may be helpful. Appendix 7.1 (available at www.routledge.com/9780367900878) provides a suggested checklist for moderating the quality and impact of knowledge organisers.

## The importance of elaborative interrogation

Elaborative interrogation was coined by Willingham (2014)[12] in reference to retaining information. He identified that students had to engage in 'active understanding and meaningful consideration of what is being learnt', through, for instance, the 'how' and 'why' questions. Rather like Socratic questioning, based on the practice of disciplined thoughtful dialogue, this questioning encourages connectivity between concepts.

The Socratic approach poses six types of questions:

- clarifying concepts;
- probing assumptions;
- probing rationale, reasons and evidence;
- questioning viewpoints and perspectives;
- probing implications and consequences;
- questioning the question.

The short extract in the Intel link below is interesting because it illustrates through a teacher/student classroom dialogue, how questioning is deployed to probe and deepen knowledge.[13]

Asking questions that require more than just monosyllabic answers guide students to make important connections. In this case, students are learning about climate change and the link to global warming and pollution. The teacher building on students' prior knowledge at the start of the session, questions students about how they learnt of global warming from newscasters. However, the questioning also touches on the veracity of the information in the media. This skill is key if we wish to encourage critical thinking in students, so that they can distinguish between false news and what is authentic.

| |
|---|
| **Heidi:** The ice caps in the Arctic are melting. The animals are losing their homes. I think the newscasters hear it from the scientists that are studying the issue. |
| **Teacher:** If that is the case and the scientists are telling the newscasters, how do the scientists know? <br> **Chris:** They have instruments to measure climate. They conduct research that measures the Earth's temperature. |
| **Teacher:** So, looking at the last 100 year's climate on this graph, what can we say about the Earth's climate? |
| **Raja:** The twentieth century has become much warmer than previous centuries. |
| **Teacher:** Can we hypothesise why? |
| **Raja:** Pollution. |
| **Teacher:** What are you assuming when you say that pollution is the cause for the temperatures to rise? |
| **Heidi:** Carbon dioxide from cars causes pollution and chemicals from factories. |

How does this relate to use of KOs? We cannot make the assumption that all students know which relevant and interrogative questions to ask themselves when they begin the process of 'elaborative interrogation'. Therefore, these must be modelled for them in the lesson to ensure that the teacher is not simply *testing a list of unconnected facts.*

The downside of the KO is that in the quest to retain essential knowledge, the KO could become reductionist in approach. Making conceptual links therefore, becomes vital for students. In this school's KO for business, students are given topics regarding business growth.

---

Methods of business growth and their impact:
- Internal (organic) growth: new products (innovation, research and development), new markets (through changing the marketing mix or taking advantage of technology and/or expanding overseas).
- External (inorganic) growth: merger, takeover public limited company (PLC) Sources of finance.

---

Students would greatly benefit from some core elaborative interrogative questions posted beneath the topics. Through practising their conceptual thinking skills, they move away from the detail to the big picture. From the outset, they can start to gain a more secure grounding in the broader concepts of how internal organic internal growth relates to external inorganic growth. Moreover, students could be tasked at this initial stage to research, reflect and hypothesise on the advantages and disadvantages of both aspects to prepare them for writing case studies. Even if all students do not manage the whole task, some will rise to the challenge.

## Prime value of teacher feedback

Much debate in schools focuses on feedback/formative assessment and marking, regarding the rationale and nature of feedback, the frequency, the format and so on. We contend that feedback is an integral aspect of learning and with this cognitive and metacognitive processes happen – enabling students *to know more, remember more and do more.*

Simply put, there are three strands.

1. *Task level* feedback means that the student receives feedback about the content, facts, or surface information. (How well has she or he completed/degree of accuracy relevance and so on? To what extent does he/she successfully understood the task?)

2. *Process level* feedback indicates that the student receives feedback on how effectively he/she understood the task (the learning to learn strategies) and processed the information necessary for completion.

3. *Feedback at the level of self-regulation* means that the student receives feedback about how he /she completed the task in relation to the strategies used and where this could have been improved. At this point, the onus is on giving the student prompts on monitoring his/her choice of process strategies in the completion of task. In this way, he/she can develop self-evaluation and confidence.

Hattie on the power of the feedback[14] in the learning cycle asserts that effective feedback must address three major questions asked by a teacher and/or student: *Where am I going? (What are the goals?), How am I going? (What progress is being made toward the goal?),* and *Where to next? (What activities need to be undertaken to make better progress?).* Hattie rightly identifies addressing misconceptions (faulty interpretations) in feedback as key to helping students move forward. In general, the majority of feedback in classes is task feedback, followed by 'where to next' and the least effective is focus on self-regulation or constructive ways that improve learning to learning skills.

It is notable that central to OFSTED's methodology on gathering evidence on the quality of education is the emphasis on teacher feedback (in whatever format), in helping students make the progress they should in their learning over time. 'Teachers check pupils' understanding effectively, correct misunderstandings … use knowledge fluently and develop their understanding' (EIF OFSTED, 2019).[15] Feedback is a genuinely on-going, two-way dialogic process, once students themselves take responsibility for their learning through their metacognition skills.

Students are more likely to increase motivation and effort when their intended objective 'is clear … high commitment is secured for it, and when belief in eventual success is high'.[16] To sum up, teachers need to demonstrate that the goal is relevant and that they believe in the 'high eventual success of each student', so that the student believes this about himself/herself. To do this, teachers need to be familiar with how their students acquire a sequence of knowledge and skills and the strategies students use. Only then can teachers decide whether knowledge organisers and/or graphic organisers are indeed the best way for every student. As we have seen in Chapter 6, whichever methods are comfortable for students can be effective, along with a L2L Skills diary.

The most helpful strategy, as with any assessment process, is what the teacher does. Checking understanding is key to the process of learning during a lesson. Testing is a sounding board of what a student knows at a given point in time. By subsequently following up the gaps in the knowledge and skills, this increases the likelihood that the student will recall later. The best way for a teacher to encourage the learning is to build in a systematic evaluation of what has been learnt and, most importantly, what has not been learnt and by which students, and why. This source of information presents an excellent opportunity for teachers to influence future learning tasks and activities. By doing this, students get valuable feedback and then specific repeat opportunities either to extend, deepen or consolidate their knowledge.

## Iceberg Learning Model

The Iceberg Learning Model in Figure 7.2 illustrates a process that incorporates the three strands outlined above within the feedback process through the *active interlacing of learning and teaching*. This is a continuously fluid process triggered by teacher feedback (written and verbal). The quality of the feedback will facilitate the student's *conceptual thinking and metacognition*, thus enabling students to better retain knowledge and skills. Students are then able to apply the knowledge and skills in the relevant context; *Recall Transfer Apply (RTA)*. The *darker arrows* indicate the teacher's input and the *lighter arrows* show the students' responses at all points of the interaction.

Iceberg Learning Model

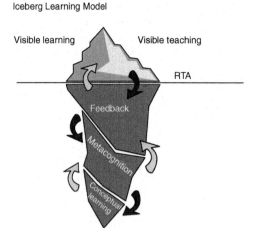

**FIGURE 7.2** The 'Iceberg Learning Model': feedback loop, interlacing teaching and metacognition (RTA)
RTA = Recall, Transfer, Apply
Copyright Meena Kumari Wood

The iceberg clearly denotes the key importance of what is happening *below* the surface. Two-thirds of the iceberg (the invisible learning) contains the active acquisition of knowledge and skills. This happens through the continuous process of teacher feedback followed by student reflection and actions. In the one-third of the iceberg above the surface, the knowledge and skills then re-surface as visible learning in students' responses during lessons and in their written work. Teacher feedback and the students' responses are key for embedding learning, and for students' to increase self-reflection through the 'learning to learn' skills (metacognition). In the section on 'powerful feedback', we illustrate the impact of teacher feedback as an *interlacing model*, through examples sourced from schools and an alternative provision.

## Different types of feedback

It is worth reminding ourselves of the types of feedback that are highly useful and most commonly deployed in schools.

- *Ipsative* assessment is against the student's own previous standards as it measures how well a particular task has been undertaken against the student's best work or against their most recent piece of work.
- Used with *dialogic feedback,* it focuses on the areas where a student needs to improve/consolidate/extend learning to the next level. The student compares the previous work and the amended work that has resulted from acting on feedback. This is motivational as the student is leading on his/her own learning.
- *Synoptic* assessment encourages students to combine elements of their learning from different parts of the programme of study and show their accumulated knowledge

and understanding of a subject or topic, along with their ability to integrate and apply their skills. A student's capability of applying the knowledge and understanding gained in one part of the programme helps to increase their understanding in other parts of the programme or across the programme as a whole. This is especially useful for linear subjects such as Maths, Science and Languages.

- *Formative* assessments at regular intervals enable teachers to know how well individual pupils are progressing.

Frequent *formative and synoptic* assessments help teachers identify what students remember from prior teaching and can usefully differentiate between who needs extra practice and who is ready to move on. This is especially important with a *Spiral Curriculum*, as students should be involved in active practice, consolidation and reflection, so they cement deep learning. For students to fully benefit from the Spiral Curriculum, commonly used in linear subjects such as Maths, Science and Languages, they require opportunities to produce their own work by applying the learned concepts. This is reviewed more fully in Chapter 13.

A good model of *dialogic teacher feedback* ensures all students respond to the *Next Steps/Do Now Action* and that these are checked by the teacher, either through verbal or written feedback. If a teacher has identified a misconception that needs addressing by the whole class, this could be through question level analysis, or error analysis.

Acquiring knowledge and skills is at its best when the assessment focuses on how students can apply their knowledge of the subject in progressively more challenging real-world situations, rather than testing only the knowledge itself. Students should be encouraged to reflect as they are assessed, so that they are better able to make links to past study and solve problems on their own.

We propose *formative* assessment across all subjects through the following steps using success criteria shared with students:

---

A. Mapping curriculum in each subject with the sequencing of knowledge and skills; linking this to success criteria (for an example of English success criteria see Figures 7.3 and 7.4).

B. The focus on the RAG (Red, Amber, Green) rating of students' learning against the success criteria gained through assessed work, results in a *spikey profile* and this enables the teacher to focus on the appropriate strategies for feedback. This means there will be some areas where the student has strengths and others where he/she needs to develop further.

C. Teachers know which concepts/skills they need to rehearse either, as whole class, or for individual students. They also know whether students are lacking challenge in their work and can address this through more specific actions.

D. Teachers ensure that fundamental 'concepts' essential for students to progress are identified through an effective *Next Step /Do Now Action*. This 'action' addresses misconceptions, or skills-based issues that either reinforce or challenge the student's learning to the next level.

E. Importantly, the information gained on their students' understanding, influences teachers' lesson planning and leads to reframing of activities, resources, or creating additional challenge.

## Illustrative examples of powerful feedback

The examples below illustrate the impact of effective teacher feedback that enables students to tackle misconceptions, or extend/deepen the knowledge or skill using the feedback techniques outlined. These students' assessed work illustrate that the most commonly effective assessments incorporate a combination of *ipsative and dialogic marking*, whilst *synoptic assessment and formative assessment are good measures of Recall, Transfer, Apply (RTA)*.

St Thomas More Language College has good examples in English of students in Years 7, 8 and 10 setting their own targets from the assessment criteria sheet – referred to by the teacher as 'reviewing assessment – learning enquiry'. Training students to reflect on their learning against the assessment criteria and to evaluate what they can do to improve is immensely powerful. The process strengthens their metacognition skills through making them self-reflective learners and motivated. They are actively engaged in their own learning through the *dialogic marking*. For more able students as in the examples, the process creates additional challenge. The teacher uses a combination of written and verbal feedback for the students and they are given 20 minutes at the start of the lesson to complete the *Do Now action*. This means learning is seen as an immediate cyclical (interlacing) process between teacher and student and as such, is greatly valued.

### CASE STUDY: ST THOMAS MORE LANGUAGE COLLEGE

Our English department's guiding principle is that feedback should be more work for the student than it is for the teacher. First, we believe that feedback should be measured against established assessment criteria which is shared with and understood by students. Secondly, feedback only has value if students engage with it, the best engagement being 'response'. Thus, making feedback 'active' provides students with the opportunity to act upon the feedback and make immediate improvements – a 'Now Do This' task serves this purpose well. From their feedback students should go on to generate their own targets. This is extremely powerful as targets are personal and students have ownership of them – they have that 'buy in'.

In this regard, our feedback system is as follows:

*Establish success criteria*: students use their flight path (based on GCSE target grades) and identify the skills they should demonstrate from the assessment matrix.

*Feedback*: work is reviewed and students are given a 'Now Do This' task to act upon – the design of this is to improve the work in some form.

*Green pen*: students respond to the 'Now Do This' task (in lesson time) and make improvements to the piece of work. SPaG is also corrected at this stage.

*Target setting*: students set their own targets based upon their feedback. Targets may be explicit in the teacher's comments or more nuanced, i.e. the student has to digest the feedback and formulate a target/s on the feedback received. Targets should then be logged in students' Assessment Log, on the back of their book.

**English Literature: 19th-century novel, Shakespeare, modern text, poetry**

| Skill | Simple | Supported | Relevant | Clear explanation | Thoughtful and developed | Critical explanation |
|---|---|---|---|---|---|---|
| **AQ1** | • Simple comments relevant to task and text<br>• Reference to relevant details | • Supported response to task and text<br>• Comments on references | • Some explained response to task and whole text<br>• References used to support a range of relevant comments | • Clear, explained response to task and whole text<br>• Clear comparison (poetry)<br>• Effective use of references to support explanation | • Thoughtful, developed response to task and whole text<br>• Apt references integrated into interpretations(s) | • Critical, exploratory, conceptualised response to task and whole text<br>• Judicious use of precise references to support interpretation(s) |
| **AQ2** | • Awareness of writer making deliberate choices<br>• Possible reference to subject terminology | • Indentification of writers methods<br>• Some references to subject terminology | • Explained/relevant comments on writer's methods with some relevant use of subject terminology<br>• Identification of effects of writer's methods on reader | • Clear explanation of writer's methods with appropriate use of relevant subject terminology<br>• Understanding of effects of writer's methods on reader | • Examination of writer's methods with subject terminology used effectively to support consideration of methods<br>• Examination of effects of writer's methods on reader | • Analysis of writer's methods with subject terminology used judiciously<br>• Exploration of effects of writer's methods on reader |
| **AQ3. (not unseen poetry)** | • Simple comment on explicit ideas, perspectives, contextual factors | • Some awareness of implicit ideas, perspectives, contextual factors | • Some understanding of implicit ideas, perspectives, contextual factors shown by links between context/text/task | • Clear understanding of ideas, perspectives, contextual factors shown by specific links between context/text/task | • Thoughtful consideration of ideas, perspectives, contextual factors shown by examination of detailed links between context/text/task | • Exploration of ideas, perspectives, contextual factors shown by specific, detailed links between context/text/task |
| **AQ4** | | | • SPag is frequently inaccurate and often hinders meaning. | • Spelling and punctuations are reasonably<br>• A reasonable range of vocabulary and sentences structures; any errors do not hinder meaning in the response | • Spelling and punctuations are accurate<br>• A considerable range of vocabulary and sentence structures to achieve general control of meaning. | • Spelling and punctuations are considerably accurate<br>• Vocabulary and sentence structure used to achieve effective control of meaning. |

**FIGURE 7.3** Writing assessment criteria: Year 8 English

**Year 8: English Reading Assessment**

| Skill | Beginning | Secure | Extending |
|---|---|---|---|
| **Understanding of the text as a whole** | *Some explained* response to the task and the text | Developed and consistent response to the task and the whole text | Thoughtful and exploratory response to the task and the whole text |
| **Use of textual references and quotations** | *A range of references* used to support comments | Relevant and consistent use of quotations, often *integrated* into interpretations(s) | Apt quotations integrated into response |
| **Comparisons** | *Supported* comparison | *Clear* comparison | *Critical, exploratory* comparison |
| **Understanding of the writer's craft** | *Relevant comments* of writer's methods | *Some developed* explanation of writer's methods and the language used | Focused examination of writer's methods and use of language |
| **Subject terminology** | *Relevant* use of subject terminology | Subject terminology *used effectively* | Subject terminology used consistently to *give insight* into writer's methods |
| **To effect on the reader** | *Comment* on the effects of writer's methods on the reader | *Some explanation* of the effect of the writer's methods on the reader | *Consistent examination* of effects of writer's methods on the reader (this might include *multiple integration*) |
| **Context** | Some understanding of implicit ideas, perspectives, contextual factors shown by *links between context/text/task* | *Some explanation* of ideas, perspectives, contextual factors shown by *relevant links* between context/text/task | *Thoughtful consideration* of implicit ideas, perspectives, contextual factors shown by *examination* of detailed links between context/text/task |
| **Spelling, punctuation and grammar** | Some level of accuracy, more frequently inaccurate with complex vocabulary | Mostly accurate spelling of a wide range of words increasingly complex sentence structures | Completely accurate SpaG including the use of complex vocabulary and sentence structures |

**FIGURE 7.4**  Reading assessment criteria: Year 8 English

The assessment sheets in Figures 7.3 and 7.4 illustrate the targets that students are working towards in the assessment objectives. This means they can self-assess against the criteria as well as receive the teachers' feedback. The interlacing impact of both, as in the Iceberg Model, means that students take control of their own learning.

The work below illustrates the combined importance of a teacher's guided prompts and the student's self-reflection on how he or she can improve. The green pen is used by the student through the redrafting process, so that the English success criteria for language and literature may be successfully met.

Figure 7.5 is a good example of the impact of verbal feedback from the teacher as captured by the student and used to redraft the writing (Figure 7.6).

Figures 7.7 and 7.8 provide an example of writing that illustrates the importance of the teacher feedback in extending the writing skills. The student who has already written a narrative that is of a good quality is then required to provide an additional paragraph.

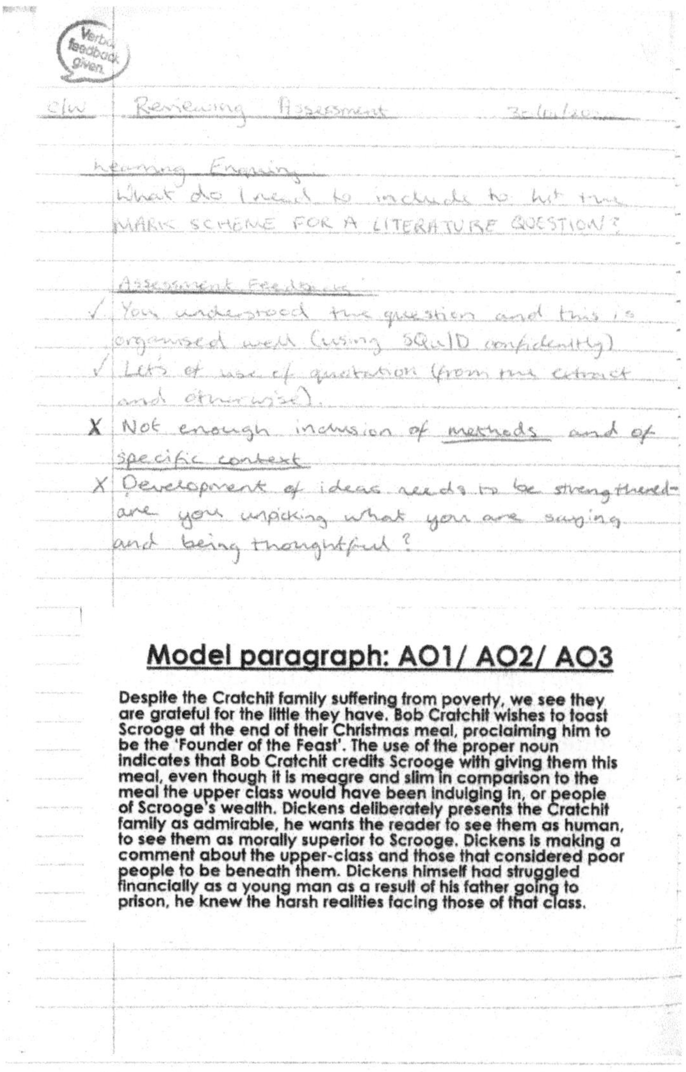

**FIGURE 7.5** The impact of teacher's verbal feedback

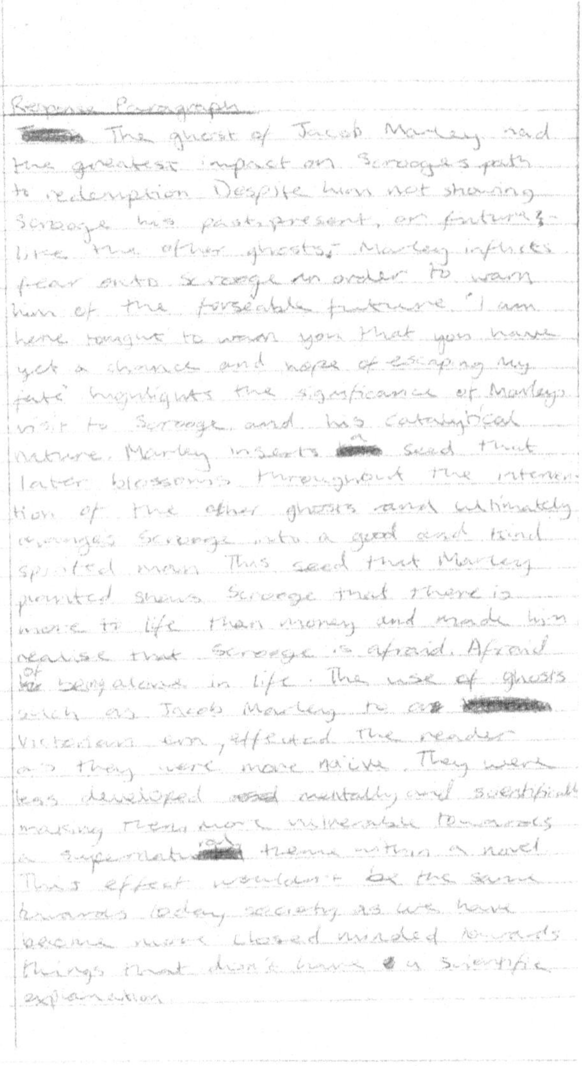

Response Paragraphs

The ghost of Jacob Marley had the greatest impact on Scrooge's path to redemption. Despite him not showing Scrooge his past, present, or future like the other ghosts, Marley inflicts fear onto Scrooge in order to warn him of the forseeable future. "I am here tonight to warn you that you have yet a chance and hope of escaping my fate" highlights the significance of Marley's visit to Scrooge and his catalysical nature. Marley inserts a seed that later blossoms throughout the interaction of the other ghosts and ultimately changes Scrooge into a good and kind spirited man. This seed that Marley planted shows Scrooge that there is more to life than money and made him realise that Scrooge is afraid. Afraid of being alone in life. The use of ghosts such as Jacob Marley to a Victorian even effected the reader as they were more naive. They were less developed mentally and superstitial causing them more vulnerable towards a supernatural theme within a novel. This effect wouldn't be the same towards today society as we have become more closed minded towards things that don't have a scientific explanation.

**FIGURE 7.6**  Feedback provided in Figure 7.5 used by student to redraft writing

Further feedback examples appear in the Appendices 19.5–19.13 (available at www.routledge.com/9780367900878) and feature in the original colour with teacher red feedback and green student response. Please also note that Figures 7.9–7.15 may be found in the Appendices, as follows:

Figure 7.9 *see* Appendix 19.5

Figure 7.10 *see* Appendix 19.6

Figure 7.11 *see* Appendix 19.7

Figure 7.12 *see* Appendix 19.8

Figure 7.13 *see* Appendix 19.9

Figure 7.14 *see* Appendix 19.10

Figure 7.15 *see* Appendix 19.11

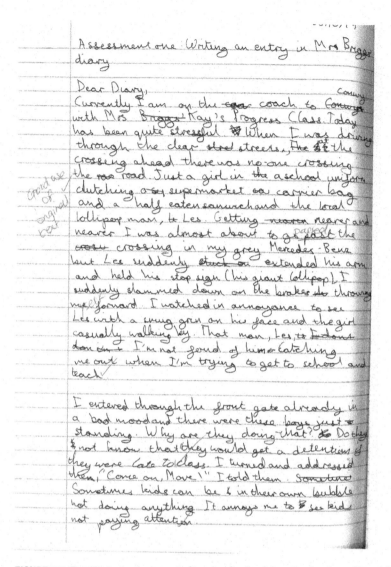

FIGURE 7.7   Text illustrates the impact of teacher feedback in extending the writing skills, continued on p. 96

## Feedback examples – Beachcroft TBAP Academy

The assessment aim in this Alternative Provision is to ensure that Year 11 students' responses are structured and link to the gaps in their previous learning, knowledge and skills that they accrued in the mainstream schools. Building up confidence through 'small wins' is key for these students. The level of literacy skills indicates significant shortfall.

1.   Year 11 learner, English Language, preparation for English Speaking and Listening exam, with a focus on structure. 'Statement/statistic/argument' is the student's response and the guidance given by class teacher is the red prompt questions. Response from learner is in green pen. Learner aged 15, at the academy for approximately 9 months (Appendix 19.5, available at www.routledge.com/9780367900878).

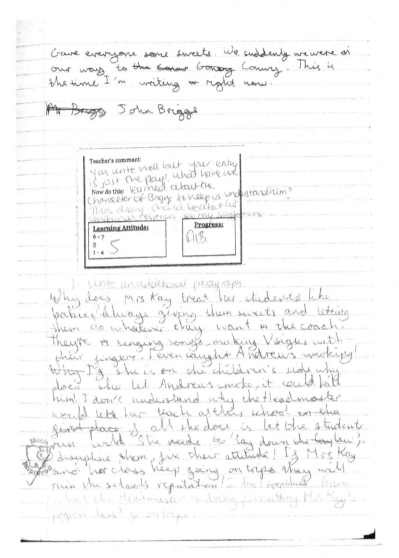

**FIGURE 7.8** Student's writing powerfully illustrates memorable learning

2. Year 11 Sociology. Learners focused on 'Education' unit, feedback during lesson given in green pen in the yellow box, recapping and consolidating learning from the lesson and ensuring there are no misconceptions around key words. Learner response is in red pen. Learner aged 15, at the academy for approximately 1 year (Appendix 19.6, available at www.routledge.com/9780367900878).

## All Saints College

Assessed work in *English Literature* on Jekyll and Hyde: teacher encourages students to make notes on how to improve from her *whole class verbal feedback.* The notes that the student made while the teacher was speaking are used for a second draft of the English essay below. This shows the impact of feedback in addressing the specific points in the student's essay (Appendix 19.7 and Appendix 19.8, available at www.routledge.com/9780367900878).

In *Maths*, students have a learning point or skill that need consolidation and they are required to practise this on green paper, so that they can identify the relevant information more effectively for recall and revision (Appendix 19.9, available at www.routledge.com/9780367900878).

In *Spanish,* redrafting is used by students as next step following teacher's written feedback. Clearly defined actions by the teacher result in a better written piece of work with the relevant tenses used appropriately. The impact is seen below between the first piece of work and the second (Appendix 19.10 and Appendix 19.11, available at www.routledge.com/9780367900878).

In this *Biology* example (Figure 7.16), the student's next steps are to respond to a specific action using the targeted feedback from the teacher. This is focused on the skill of making a scientific prediction. This is a low ability student. Therefore, the teacher, to help the student retain the information, is making *synoptic links* to previous work covered by her, as part of the 'science retrieval' strategy.

The *Chemistry* example (Figure 7.17) clearly shows links to previous learning and most importantly, requires the student to identify the information and use it to inform her next steps which she does effectively.

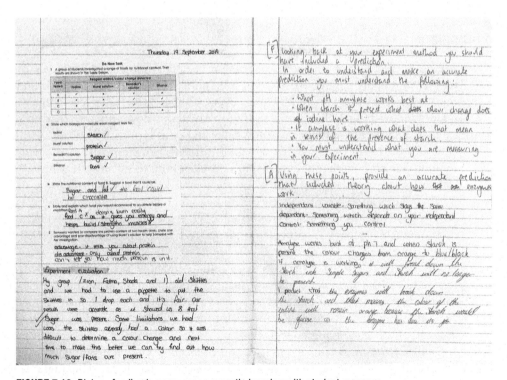

**FIGURE 7.16** Biology feedback: encourages synoptic learning with student response

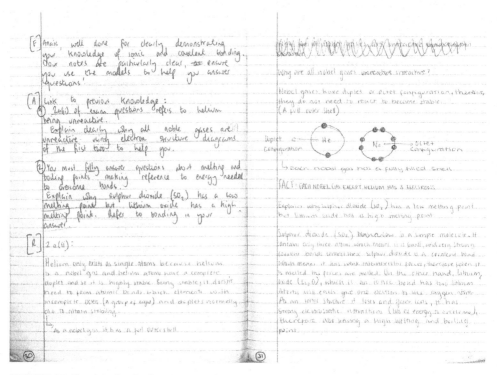

**FIGURE 7.17** Chemistry feedback: science retrieval strategy with student response

## Summary

Failing to address gaps in learning inhibits metacognition as the process of recall transfer and apply cannot operate without students gaining a full understanding of the sequence of knowledge and skills. Assessment is prime as is checking students' understanding before they are set on task. The most powerful way that ensures all students acquire the sequence of knowledge and skills is precise feedback actions that consolidate, extend, or deepen the learning. Students benefit greatly from quality time in the lesson to complete the next step actions, central to effective learning. Training students in peer and self-assessment, so they can identify accurate next step actions for themselves and each other, helps them become reflective leaders of own learning. As Hattie maintains, students 'develop effective error detection skills, which lead to their own self-feedback … provided students have some modicum of knowledge and understanding about the task.'[17]

Ultimately, the impact of KOs is measured by how successfully knowledge is retained over the KS3–KS4 journey; manipulated and transferred by students of all abilities into the relevant contexts, year on year. Simply sequencing the information and expecting students to revise and retain these will not necessarily lead to deeper learning of the underlying concepts.

Similarly, we must take account of prior learning/knowledge and skills brought by our students to the lessons. No student is a carte blanche or tabula rasa. Teachers must acknowledge this when planning KOs and consider the use of KOs post-16, extending to A-level or BTEC level 3. Nurturing an enquiring mind or a genuine interest in the subject extends learning. Teachers can acknowledge those students who have gone beyond the facts on the KO and probed into additional knowledge from talking with family/ friends/ internet sites. The best KOs will encourage students to use their prior learning, extend their knowledge and skills, sharing this with their peers.

There is no value in curtailing the knowledge and facts we want students to learn. Surely challenging students to develop curiosity and inquisitive minds is key to 'knowledge building on knowledge'. That is precisely where Socratic thinking (elaborative interrogation) comes in. KOs are not the golden panacea in themselves; but used effectively, along with timely and focused teacher feedback, they do have the potential to enable students to practise their metacognition skills and deepen knowledge.

# Notes

1    TeacherVision (2019) Top 10 most popular graphic organizers. Available at: www.teachervision.com/top-10-most-popular-graphic-organizers (Accessed: 18 November 2019).

2    Education Endowment Foundation (2019) Teaching and Learning Toolkit. Available at: https://educationendowmentfoundation.org.uk/evidence-summaries/teaching-learning-toolkit (Accessed: 11 November 2019).

3    J. Kirby (2015) Knowledge organisers. Available at: https://pragmaticreform.wordpress.com/2015/03/28/knowledge-organisers/ (Accessed: 14 November 2019).

4    www.twinkl.co.uk/resource/aqa-gcse-biology-knowledge-organisers-pack-t4-sc-1141

5    The Malling School (2020) The Malling School. Available at: www.themallingschool.kent.sch.uk/ (Accessed: 2 February 2020).

6    See https://hegartymaths.com/& https://corbettmaths.com/

7    Examples include The Chelsea Academy and Westminster Academy.

8    S. Nicolas, T. Collins, Y. Gounden and H. L. Roediger, III (2011) Natural suggestibility in children. Consciousness and Cognition: An International Journal, 20(2), 394–8.

9    Toothill School (2019) Toothill School website. Available at: https://toothillschool.co.uk/ (Accessed: 28 October 2019).

10   Durrington High School (2019) Durrington High School website. Available at: https://durringtonhighschool.co.uk/ (Accessed: 28 October 2019).

11   Meridian High London (2019) Meridian High School website. Available at: www.meridianhigh.london/ (Accessed: 15 March 2020).

12   D. Willingham (2014) Strategies that make learning last, Educational Leadership, 72(2), 10–15.

13   Intel Teach Program (2007) Designing effective projects: Questioning the Socratic questioning technique. Available at: www.intel.com/content/dam/www/program/education/us/en/documents/project-design/strategies/dep-question-socratic.pdf (Accessed: 21 October 2019).

14   J. Hattie and H. Timperley (2007) The power of feedback, https://doi.org/10.3102/003465430298487, 77(1), 81–112.

15   OFSTED (2019) The Education Inspection Framework, 1st edn. www.gov.uk/government/publications/education-inspection-framework. London: OFSTED.

16   A. N. Kluger and A. DeNisi (1996) The effects of feedback interventions on perform-
     ance: A historical review, a meta-analysis, and a preliminary feedback intervention theory,
     *Psychological Bulletin*, 119(2): 254–84.

17   J. Hattie and H. Timperley (2007) The power of feedback, *Review of Educational Research*,
     77(1), 81–112.

# 8

# Conceptual thinking skills

## Introduction

### Conceptualising thinking; underpinning knowledge

For curriculum to be successful, as we have seen, it must be designed with long-term learning in mind. At the heart of a curriculum is the principle of 'big ideas'. Dylan William[1] describes these as enabling teachers and students 'to see the connectedness of the whole curriculum – trunk and branches ... rather than a disorganised collection of twigs and pine needles'.

Here we look beyond cognitive theory and the presentation of knowledge through graphic organisers. We observed from the students' case studies in previous chapters, that cognitive, emotional and environmental influences, as well as prior experience, all played a key part in the quality of the learning to learn skills and the knowledge and skills they retained.

One strategy for helping students sustain the learning is through making it relevant and moving beyond the learning of facts and skills towards conceptual thinking: 'transferable ideas that transcend time, place, and situation'.[2]

Creating meaningful learning so that students can conceptualise their learning means that the examples should resonate as far as possible with individual students, drawing from their prior and/or current experiences. This has huge potential as *relevance* of knowledge is better retained. Cross curricular links assist students in understanding the transferability of learning in one subject to another and hooks them in. Students benefit from these signposts in their understanding of where the aspects of subjects sit, through the wider acquisitions of concepts; once again capturing the whole mosaic of knowledge, rather than its parts. We are encouraging students to experience phenomenal learning rather than to memorise silos of knowledge.

### Making connections

Let us consider this analogy: Learning knowledge is like standing in the middle of an unfamiliar city. We can get our immediate bearings by the signposting nearby but it is harder for us without a map or a Google App to orientate ourselves further afield. Details are easy to spot; we can of course hypothesise on what is up ahead and then get a sense of our bearings. For students to think conceptually in their learning, they need the opportunities to do the same, and to practise their predictive skills. Learning activities in which students navigate their way across factual and conceptual levels of thinking can help them construct understanding, facilitate transfer and meaningful application.[3] Through these, they can reflect on their hypothesis and navigate towards the broader picture – generalize, summarize and draw conclusions. In this way, students start to see their learning in a more connected and holistic way. This Singaporean school's curriculum is first and foremost, prioritising conceptual thinking as key for its students.

## CASE STUDY: CONCEPTUAL THINKING CURRICULUM

Singapore school UWCSEA's curriculum is specifically constructed around *teaching conceptual thinking*, so that students gain knowledge and skills through developing critical thinking and better recall, thereby transferring their understanding to new contexts and situations.[4]

Schools21's website uses the notion of 'zoom in zoom out', the idea of the particular versus the big idea to develop reflection and conceptual thinking.[5]

'Zoom in, zoom out' – encourages students (and teachers) to compare the skills needed for learning to the techniques used in the creation of films. Students ... balance the need for close-up analysis of material with a wide-angle view. Zooming in enables close analysis – identify, explaining, exploring and analysing. Zooming out is about seeing the big picture – evaluating and creating. www.learningspy.co.uk/english-gcse/zooming-in-and-out/

## Superficial to deep learning

To help students gravitate towards more meaningful learning, we must focus on three areas.

Firstly, from the facts or skills being taught, students must identify which concepts are at the heart of the learning. For instance, in a Geography unit on volcanoes, students gain from understanding the concept of how volcanoes relate to the Rock Cycle and how this affects the atmosphere.

Secondly, we focus on the concepts that are connected through the students' learning. For example, within a subject, such as in Mathematics, we may ask students to connect the concepts of fractions and ratio, or multiplication and division; they must understand the linkages of this to the substantive concepts of proportion and sharing – pie charts, graphs and so on. In Science, they may need to understand the links between photosynthesis and energy transformation and potentially the concept of renewable energies. In History, they may study industrialisation in the nineteenth century and then through cross-curricular links appreciate the linkages to Science and Geography. They start to conceptualise the full impact of global industrialisation on environmental changes, megacities and the push and pull factors of urbanisation, leading possibly to the rise of the BRIC economies (Brazil, Russia, India, China) – over two hundred years.

Thirdly, what opportunities for application and transfer exist to help students extend their learning further? For instance, students who have learned about the principles of marketing in business could create a case study that profiles how a company brands its product within three differentiated contexts: local, national and international customer bases. To make the learning memorable and harness knowledge from the students' other subjects, this could draw on their geographical, economic and cultural knowledge. Or, they could be required to extend their knowledge further by exploring an idea for an entrepreneurial startup company; detailing how they would establish it and attract venture capital.

## Threshold concepts: The epiphany/Eureka moment

Conceptual thinking involves 'threshold concepts'; the process of students on the journey of deeper learning within the subject. These concepts, once grasped, are referred to as 'light bulb moments'. Once students have understood the threshold concept, they encounter 'troublesome knowledge'; they need to reframe or reinterpret the subject aspect.[6] This may take time to fully accept as it may not be in line with what students had previously understood. Beyond this stage, students can begin to enjoy the learning and are motivated towards learning more.

---

**THRESHOLD CONCEPTS' CHARACTERISTICS**

*Transformative* – a change takes place through engaging with a new idea
*Irreversible* – knowledge is not perceived in the same way
*Integrative* – new concepts relate to and build upon other concepts
*Bounded* – concepts are limited and may run parallel or lie beside other (related) concepts
*Troublesome* – the new knowledge takes time to 'embed'; contradicting perceived wisdom

---

Self-motivation and resilience are the drivers for students. As within a jigsaw, they are required to connect ideas vertically and deepen their understanding, and horizontally, through sequencing knowledge and skills, across the key stages. As they become increasingly confident, working their way across *the threshold*, students develop the skills of recognising and understanding key concepts.

For the teacher, *threshold concepts* provide a unit structure upon which to design the scheme of learning, within a subject. This moves away from isolated pieces of knowledge to deeper understanding of overall concepts, and how these substantive concepts relate to one another. Some schools write a KS3 scheme of learning that selects English Literature texts (Shakespeare, Dickens, Modern Novel and anthology) around a theme such as 'power and conflict'. These are then revisited through the reading, writing, speaking and listening skills. This means that the texts act as a basis for interleaving core elements of the Key Stage 3 curriculum and the theme acts as a useful strand to weave everything together.

Conceptualising the wider picture transforms the learning into the mosaic pattern that makes sense. Without this process, students potentially face barriers in identifying patterns in their learning, as they progress deeper into the subject and learn potentially disjointed fragments of information.

Similarly, giving students time to deepen their understanding, helps them to transfer and apply their ideas to new projects, or other new contexts.

## Concepts organiser

A knowledge organiser compiles facts/data in sequence. A *concepts organiser* goes a step further. Students deploy a paradigm with simple prompts that guide them to use their research and critical thinking skills, so they can identify key concepts. This can prevent silo learning, with students arriving at a 'joined up transfer of the knowledge' to other contexts.

## Octowebgraphic organiser

We propose an *Octowebgraphic organiser*, based along the lines of the anatomy of an octopus. The octopus has eight tentacles and each of these has an autonomous brain; in addition, the octopus has a central brain that exerts influence on the brains in its tentacles.

Within the Octoweb's individual tentacles we detail the necessary knowledge – dates and information and each piece of information can stand alone. However, creating the *concepts and connections* between these is what makes an Octoweb significantly different from a mind map or a spider map.

As a graphic representation of a set of connected ideas, Mind mapping[7] can promote higher order synthetic and evaluative thinking. The combination of words and images aids recall and the process of creating the mind map supports metacognition.

The five usual characteristics of mind maps are:

1. The main idea, subject or focus is crystallised in a central image.

2. The main themes *radiate* from the central image as 'branches'.

3. The branches comprise a key image or key word on its associated line.

4. Topics of lesser importance are represented as 'twigs' of the relevant branch.

5. The branches form a connected nodal structure.

However, mind mapping does not automatically lead to conceptual thinking as there is usually a central idea/topic, that lies in the centre from which radiate the main themes. Conversely, the Octoweb starts with the different themes in the tentacles and through drilling into these themes; the main concepts emerge, crystallised *from the detail* and these are then lodged in the Octoweb's *'central brain'*.

The Octoweb is especially useful for *cross-curricular conceptual thinking*. The essential point of this graphic organiser is that the facts relating to each subject are in each of the tentacles and can be used individually. In addition, the interaction between the different curricular tentacles adds depth to the learning. In this way, students explore substantive concepts across a variety of multi-disciplinary contexts. It is a memorable way for students, especially in KS3, to retain the concepts.

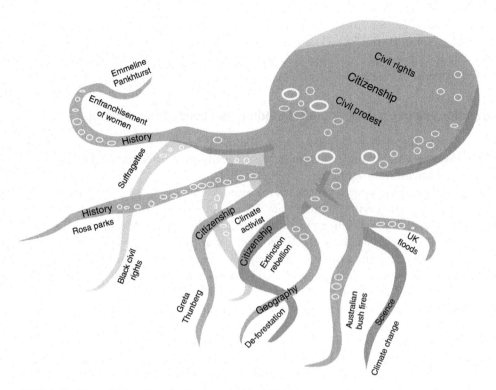

**FIGURE 8.1** 'Octoweb': Graphic organiser for conceptual thinking
Copyright Meena Kumari Wood

To illustrate in Figure 8.1, we propose the following context of radical environmental concerns and the impact of climate change; taught in Geography and Science. The Attenborough 'Blue Planet' effect,[8] coral reef destruction, bush fires, floods, plastic and air pollution, deforestation of the rainforests and wildlife habitat erosion continue to enter children's awareness daily and have high profile relevance globally. This was evidenced through the Climate Extinction Rebellion students' marches held worldwide during September–October 2019.

Through History lessons, students might study the women's suffragette movement as an example of civil rights, this can be extended to Rosa Parks, the American activist best known for her pivotal role in the Montgomery bus boycott, followed by Greta Thunberg for her key role in highlighting climate change protest (2019–2020). Thunberg inspired students worldwide to opt out of school for street marches.

The Climate Extinction Rebellion movement used similar strategies to the suffragettes through glueing/chaining themselves to railings and tubes. Similarities and differences across these three periods of history of the events will resonate with students and help them to make connections.

This sequence of events straddle *Citizenship, History, Science* and *Geography*. By drawing out connections between the twin concepts of *civil protest and civil rights*, students can refocus to grasp the bigger picture of their learning, 'the troublesome moment'. They begin to understand the universality of the concepts and the impact of these activities 'transcending space, time and situation.'

Drawing on these current events has potential for informed debate, outside of subject specific curriculum in broadening and deepening *cultural capital*. Not only would students deepen their understanding of the scientific and geographical concepts underpinning this knowledge, but also the global, political and economic aspects. The added advantage is preparing students for post-16 higher order reasoning, analysis and critical thinking skills.

## Transfer activities: Deeper understanding and conceptual thinking

Once students have formed the key relevant connections between concepts and demonstrate genuine understanding, they are ready to transfer and apply these concepts to new situations or contexts.

If we are staying with the civil protest/rights case study, we can give students a new case study with different data. This focuses on the disruption caused to civilians in central London, during the October 2019 Extinction Rebellion's demonstrations and 'boycott', preventing transport circulation. This is compared with the rights and wrongs of students worldwide missing school. In addition to other factual knowledge they may have, students analyse media coverage of these events. To assess the depth of knowledge and skills, we can pose the question:

'Civil rights create civil disorder and disruption!' How does society balance individuals' right to express their freedom to protest with upholding the rule of law?' This philosophical aspect will lead to students developing a different perspective and possibly revising their thinking from the previous study of the similarities and differences on 'protest' between the suffragette movement, Rosa Parks and Greta Thunberg.

The cross-curricular concepts linking climate change, deforestation, global warming and renewable energies give students a good opportunity to present a persuasive argument on a provocative statement, using their prior knowledge and understanding. For instance, 'Climate change is a myth, not a reality!'

This does not have to be an exercise conducted independently. If we would like to encourage *public speaking, persuasive reasoning* and *critical thinking skills*, then students can work in small groups with each of them presenting a concept-backed by empirical data; for instance, deforestation, effects of global warming, forest fires, plastics pollution, the economic interests of politicians and businesses. Another student can be tasked with seeking solutions to climate change; for instance, renewable energies, or changing human diets, and so on and presenting it to the UN!

## Cross-curricular connections

In English, through an analysis of the play *An Inspector Calls*, we see the characters act as cyphers for J.B. Priestley's socialist views; we encourage students to examine the concepts arising from the social and economic backgrounds of the characters, the position of women in society and workers' rights. The majority of English teachers do, in fact, elude to this as part of deepening students' understanding of the 1912 post-Edwardian context.

The correlation between the play's publication date and its impact on the theatre audience, watching it in 1946, identifies its ironic relevance to two world wars; illustrated in the Inspector's quote 'we are members of one body.... .responsible for each other...if men will not learn that lesson ... they will be taught it in fire and blood and anguish'.

Linking this key concept from *An Inspector Calls* to the study of both world wars in History has the potential for creating a *threshold concept*. The 'epiphany moment', is motivational and ensures relevance through deepening knowledge. Moving away from 'fragments' of knowledge in the English Literature text, to the rich mosaic of the historic picture, is brought alive through a play resonating with historical, social and ethical overtones.

Following clear lines of intent in each subject, mapping links across curriculum aspects is beneficial for students. Adjusting the sequencing of topics means that subject areas hold greater relevance for students through the connections made, resulting in the 'epiphany' moment. Building on links between English and History, many schools effectively dovetail aspects of the First World War during Year 8 with studying First World War poetry, making knowledge more memorable. Mapping across subjects, topics or aspects, when planning the sequence of knowledge and skills increases the likelihood of conceptual thinking, as students understand the bigger picture. A maximum of eight 'key strands' per topic in a year group produces an interconnected curriculum, similar to the one modelled by Turton School in Bolton (Figure 8.2).[9] This covers History, English, Classics and explores concepts of power, sovereignty, revolution conflict and resolution.

## How do we assess if students have learnt vital concepts, underpinned by knowledge?

End-of-year exams are intended to provide information about deeper understanding and changes in long-term memory. A focus on the specific detail is possibly less useful. What might be more helpful then is drilling down into students' awareness of underlying concepts. This evidences their ability to manipulate the information. In so doing, teachers, and the students themselves, gain key insights into the connections that they are making across their learning.

We can usefully ask students in Science to 'describe the conceptual differences between energy conservation and efficient energy use'; in Maths to explain 'when we require factorisation or negative numbers or sine and cosine rule in everyday life'; in English 'a common characteristic shared by three of Shakespeare's heroines or the role of fatalism in three of Shakespeare's heroes'.

By making connections across aspects of a subject or topics, students apply the higher order skills, plus the knowledge they have learned over the term or year, and they have to present a reasoned argument with examples. Assessment must be able to afford the teacher and importantly the student, valuable insights as to whether he or she has conceptualised the individual strands of knowledge they learn lesson by lesson, into a coherent whole, and where the gaps lie. This once again reminds us of the need to 'zoom in and zoom out' of the mosaic of knowledge.

## Summary

For teachers to fully develop conceptual thinking within a subject and across subjects requires a suspension of disbelief. The move away from uniquely teaching subject

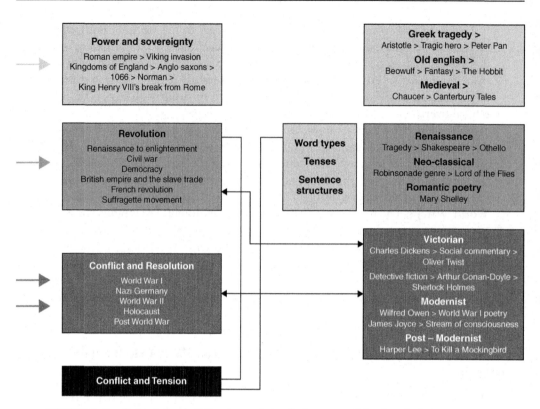

**FIGURE 8.2** How Turton School in Bolton demonstrates the interconnectivity of curriculum

knowledge within the scheme of learning feels naturally unsettling. This is understandable, given the pressures of impending examinations and the priority of deepening and revisiting that knowledge. Nevertheless, the advantages of teaching conceptually within the curriculum (albeit, as structured built-in learning and assessment opportunities) means that students have a greater chance of actually learning the knowledge, retaining and applying it. Surely this is the aim of phenomenal learning.[10]

Using a visual graphic organiser, such as an Octoweb, is memorable as it makes the connections within a subject and across subjects. This then allows for the concept to evolve through the stages of the threshold concept from 'transformative to integrative to troublesome'. Students engage with a new idea, build on other concepts, realise that each concept can stand alone, and eventually get their heads around the new knowledge, or concept; learning across subjects, across the years and making sense of the curriculum as a whole.

Despite the clarity of the connections for most students; for an even playing field, as with all learning activities, the teacher must take into account the varying levels of concentration and retentive powers that each student brings. A student with ADHD may take longer to understand whereas a more able student with higher cognitive skills may make rapid connections and decide that the activity lacks sufficient challenge and so risks becoming disinterested. A student who is dyslexic will require a different way of learning and retrieving information. So being cognisant of students' profiles is key to the successful impact of conceptualising the learning, and where needs be, providing additional challenge, or scaffolded support.

Whenever possible, learning should be a meaningful experience and one that arouses students' curiosity and hooks them in through relevance and the 'Eureka' moment. This can only happen if they are required to not simply list information that is interrelated, but to draw out the key concepts that go beyond the detail. This is reinforced by Foer's (Foer, 2012) TED Talk, in which he says 'We remember when we pay attention ... we are able to take a piece of information and experience, and figure out *why it is meaningful to us*'.[11]

## Notes

1   D. William (2013) *Principled Curriculum Design*. London: SSAT.
2   H. Erickson, L. Lanning and R. French (2017) *Concept-Based Curriculum and Instruction for the Thinking Classroom,* 2nd edn. Thousand Oaks, CA: Corwin.
3   C. Marschall (2019) 3 ways to boost students' conceptual thinking. Available at: www. edutopia.org/article/3-ways-boost-students-conceptual-thinking (Accessed: 25 October 2019).
4   C. Marschall (2019) Concept-based curriculum. Available at: http://stories.uwcsea.edu.sg/UWCSEA-s-Concept-Based-Curriculum/ (Accessed: 24 October 2019).
5   School21 (2019) Real world learning. Available at: www.school21.org.uk/rwlp (Accessed: 15 December 2019).
6   H. Fletcher-Wood (2018) *Responsive Teaching*, 1st edn. Abingdon: Routledge.
7   For more info see https://en.wikipedia.org/wiki/Mind_mapandhttp://popplet.com/andhttps://bubbl.us/and http://drichard.org/mindmaps/
8   BBC (2020) *Blue Planet II*. Available at: www.bbc.co.uk/programmes/p04tjbtx (Accessed: 21 December 2019).
9   S. Gorse (2019) A whole school Trivium curriculum for Turton School: An entitlement to knowledge and learning for everyone. Available at: https://leadinglearningtogether.wordpress.com/2019/06/28/a-whole-school-trivium-curriculum-for-turton-school-an-entitlement-to-knowledge-and-learning-for-everyone/ (Accessed: 3 January 2020).
10   https://phenomenallearning.fi/ (Accessed: 17 August 2020).
11   J. Foer (2012) Feats of memory anyone can do. Available at: www.ted.com/talks/joshua_foer_feats_of_memory_anyone_can_do (Accessed: 31 October 2019).

# Mandatory key skills: Leading to citizenship and employability skills

# 9

# Digitalisation permeating our lives

## Introduction

### Digitalisation: A core skill in the curriculum

Digitalisation through the internet, social media, apps and so on is a boon and provides a wealth of educational opportunities and upskilling benefits for our young people. Yet, in the worst-case scenario, digitalisation has the potential to become a poisoned chalice that disables and entraps young people. The curriculum must educate students with the skills they need to make intelligent choices, so they are better able to navigate their way through the digital maze. In this section, we present some topical examples of the benefits and the potential pitfalls of digitalisation and review coding languages and computational skills within the curriculum.

### Digitalised gaming or gambling – the Pandora's box?

In the UK, more than ever, schools need to be firmly in tune with their students' holistic abilities and capacity for learning outside of school. Let us consider gaming amongst young people – 'FIFA, Fortnite and Roblox'. With a focus on the impact of gaming on students in schools, a report by the Children's commissioner (2019)[1] cited that 93 per cent of children in the UK play video games and children as young as twelve were utilising gaming for as much as three hours daily – this at a key point in their lives. This exposure has increased in 2020. This is undoubtedly going to impact adversely on a student's learning outcomes during the school day, their school attendance, and absence from critical areas of the curriculum. The report provides evidence from children who expressed feeling out of control with their spending on online games. There are clearly worries that over-exposure to video game content may have a damaging effect on the mental development and socialisation of young people; along with the possible link between gaming and gambling, and the concurrent risk of addiction.

> I never get anything out of it [buying packs] but I still do it.
>
> (Lee, 14, FIFA player)

> You feel like it's a waste of money … and then you open more.
>
> (Nick, 16, FIFA player)

Other than through PSHE programmes, tutorial programmes and assemblies, schools have no mandatory curriculum strand that educates and upskills its students and their parents on the dual potential threats of gaming to students' mental well-being and their educational progress and attainment. Yet, given the significant numbers of young children participating, this arguably poses a challenge. There is a key missed opportunity in the statutory curriculum for students to learn financial literacy skills so that they become more aware of the value of money and the dangers of gambling.

## Digitalisation linked to financial literacy

How we are ranked in suitability for our credit fitness by AI is increasingly permeating our lives. Let us look at current 'disruptors'; for instance, 'open banking' that evaluates our credit rating from our financial transactions (indicator of lifestyle). In addition, AI online assessments of what potential claimants are owed in welfare benefits, do not allow recourse to human assessment. These global developments in countries, as diverse as Australia and India are referenced by Virginia Eubanks as 'the digital poorhouse, forged from databases, algorithms and risk models'.[2]

Currently nine million people in the UK are functionally illiterate. Together with illiteracy and lack of financial literacy skills, there are 1.5 million people in the UK with learning disabilities. Many of these people rely on a 'digital by default' welfare system. By implication, young people who are leaving school are subject to decisions created by an algorithm. They may not have the digital or financial literacy skills to even know or understand if mistakes are being made or if they are short-changed. They may be unable to challenge these errors.

The two examples of 'digital gaming' and being reliant on AI assessments indicate that the teaching of financial literacy is integral to becoming independent and informed citizens. In the case study below, the headteacher wished to move away from academic knowledge-led learning to offering a skills-based practical component as a subject. Although core PE and creative subjects were offered as alternatives, students overwhelmingly chose to learn about managing their finances. Therefore, the decision was made to run the Financial Capability course for students in KS4.

### CASE STUDY: FELPHAM COMMUNITY COLLEGE

Financial literacy[3] teaches students 'to become responsible borrowers, sensible savers and have an appreciation of the need for financial planning throughout their lives' through the Certificate in Financial Education (CeFE) Level 2, as a stand-alone subject, compulsory in KS4.

This certificate is included in the 14–16 Technical Awards Performance Tables and is accredited through the London Institute of Banking and Finance.[4] Through practical employability, enterprise and financial education programmes, Young Enterprise and Young Money aim to 'reduce youth unemployment, help young people realise their potential beyond education and empower a generation to learn, to work and to live'. Young Enterprise delivers activity-based programmes in schools, colleges and universities across the UK – providing young people with the opportunity to develop key skills and make the connection between school and the world of work. Young Money (formerly PFEG) provides resources and training to schools teaching money management skills. The two frameworks support the teaching of financial education through mapping in the delivery of financial education across the Citizenship, PSHE education, Maths curriculum.[5] We owe our students the opportunity to be accredited in these key skills.

## Digital literacy skills across the curriculum

The Royal Society[6] has identified three complementary strands within computing: Computer Science (CS), Information Technology (IT) and Digital Literacy (DL). Each component is essential in preparing students for the increasingly digital world.

1. Computer Science is the practical study of computation: what can be computed, how to compute it, and how computation may be applied to the solution of problems.

2. Information technology is how computers and telecommunications equipment work, and their application to the storage, retrieval, transmission and manipulation of data.

3. Digital literacy is the ability to safely and critically navigate, evaluate and create digital artefacts using a range of digital technologies, including digital film, computer programs, spreadsheets, 3D animations and apps. Felpham Community College's simple Year 9 scheme of learning provides a three year KS3 course in Computer Science, covering topics from coding using Python in Year 7 to constructing a mobile phone app by Year 9.[7]

Digital literacy is defined as being able to find, evaluate, create and communicate information, requiring both cognitive and technical skills.[8] These essential skills include reading online text that may contain embedded resources such as hyperlinks, audio clips, graphs or charts. These require students to make choices. They must be able to locate and understand digital information; to create digital content through blogs, podcasts, tweets, and finally, to communicate digital content safely. Therefore, at its simplest level, this is essentially navigating search engines, identifying pertinent information that is not plagiarised, but understood and transferred to the relevant context. Students receive training about cyber bullying, the use or abuse of social media; reflected in the DfE guidance 'Keeping Safe on Line'.[9,10]

However, the reality is students in Years 7–11 may not explicitly be taught digital literacy skills across the curriculum. We are all familiar with observing students relentlessly switching screens and clicking on a plethora of links, during research, as some lose focus on the academic task!

Surfing on a device and using it intelligently to access and manipulate knowledge are two markedly different skills. What many students lack are structured learning opportunities in developing their digital navigational skills. All students need to become digital savvy so they can identify and retrieve the relevant knowledge that they need. Knowledge is growing exponentially and our students need to make sense of increasing levels of complex data from diverse sources. When tasked with conducting research on a topic, theme or concept, students greatly benefit from knowing *how to* discern useful web links to follow, and *why these* are chosen, instead of others.

This analytical skill stimulates students' curiosity in learning and effectively increases their knowledge base, enhancing independent learning. Without this discipline, students are potentially distracted and suffer from 'digital link fatigue', once they are confronted with the plethora of bewildering information available to them. Given the increasing role of advertising and algorithms in the complex online news ecosystem, factual knowledge can easily be confused with news feeds and search results.

Digital literacy is one of the key skills that are likely to be underdeveloped across the curriculum. This is evidenced through a survey conducted by Joint Dialogue. About one fifth of teachers reported there were far fewer opportunities available for teaching this skill, since the introduction of the reformed GCSEs and A-levels.[11] The report identifies the importance of preparing young people with the skills and competencies demanded by the twenty-first-century labour market, so as to bridge the gap between what young people are actually taught and the skills and competencies demanded by employers.

As workplaces and society become more technologically advanced and digitalised, there is by inverse proportion, less focus on digital literacy and computing skills, with schools finding either less time to teach them or unable to recruit suitably qualified staff. This is evidenced by the continued reduction in take up in 2017 and 2018 in entries into the computer subjects at GCSE (JCQ Statistics, 2018), albeit with a hopeful marginal increase in 2019.[12]

As educationalists, we should be cognisant of the digital critical skills gap in the curriculum and ensure that all our students can function independently. If we uniquely rely on individual subject teachers to deliver this skill, students will have variable understanding and application across the subjects.

Although Computing Science is a statutory part of the KS3 and KS4 curriculum, it is still not considered as an essential component of the EBacc suite of qualifications,[13] which means that within an individual school's options block, a school's Year 8 or Year 9 students may not be able to choose this relevant subject for their future destination. Equipping our students for the world we live in means recognising the skills they need. Not structuring this into the curriculum or, at very least, not ensuring all students develop digital skills lies at variance with the curriculum intent of preparing students for the world of work and further training.

## The National Curriculum and coding skills

'Creativity is the goal. Creativity is in the front seat; technology is in the backseat. It is sort of the blend with both of these that you can do such powerful things now' (Tim

Cook, CEO Apple).[14] Looking to the future he asserted that coding was the language that everyone needs, and not just for the computer scientists.

Coding skills are part of twenty-first-century skills and students should leave school with a functioning understanding of at least one coding language. What is notable is that children as young as five today are increasingly familiar with coding skills; a significant departure from their parents' generation, as coding skills now appear within the primary curriculum.[15]

However, the OECD's director of education and skills,[16] Andreas Schleicher, speaking at the World Innovation Summit for Education (WISE) warned against coding education for precisely the same reasons that we see the obsolete nature of previous technologies. They flourish and wither over a short period of time. The question posed is whether coding languages is better replaced with data science and computational thinking, as these provide sustainable skills over the long term.

The TIOBE[17] index (2019) listed the coding practices on the market by popularity. Python was arguably the fastest growing code in the world in 2018, followed by Java as number 1 in 2019–2020. If each individual code has limitations, with new codes just around the corner, would rote learning one particular language produce an educational blind alley? Codes are unique and linked to specific employment opportunities. JavaScript is considered sound for mobile development and for coding websites, server-side applications to mobile apps and video games; Python is used for hacking, web apps and data analysis, Pixar for producing movies, and Spotify for songs. R and SAS are used for handling statistics and AutoCAD programmes by engineers. Minimising the over-reliance on specialist coding-language knowledge seems the way forward. Karen Panetta (Institute of Electrical and Electronics Engineers (IEEE)) believes that 'Programs will be built using coding blocks, like the wooden alphabet blocks … connecting the blocks to implement whatever functionality they need'.[18]

The reality is that much of the Python that primary school children learn today, could be redundant by the time they reach secondary school, let alone further/ higher education, or the world of work. In point of fact, we do not need to visit the future to see that even today, companies provide 'code- free' services. Bubble, a US-based company, invites its users to design and host web applications without having to write code, whilst accessing Sparkster enables a drag-and-drop platform for anyone to code, and Zeroqode have created a codeless creation service.

## Computational thinking skills across our curriculum

If learning to code is not about learning individual languages, then computational skills are necessary. Overtly developing students' fluency in computational thinking is a life skill, helping create a disciplined mindset, logical, analytical and reasoning skills. Students acquire the curiosity to be creative. They begin to recognise there are numerous ways to address an issue so promoting the language of coding as in computational skills, leads to independent problem solvers, capable of logical solutions to problems. The four essential elements of computational thinking are; decomposition, abstraction, pattern recognition and algorithmic design. Carl Wyatt,[19] has cited a wealth of inventive ways through which teachers already nurture; critical thinking, problem solving, creativity and reasoning skills. These include skills based activities, such as a storyboard sequence for an animation or filmed performance, choreographing a dance routine, creating a timeline of events in History, a water cycle diagram, a map route, composing music or a fitness training programme. These computational skills are especially relevant for students who may find accessing knowledge-based academic subjects challenging. This is because the practice of failing and giving it another go is valued, rather than marked down, as a right or wrong answer. Students with dyslexia may find computational skills more creative and easier to navigate in some instances.

Elizabeth Tweedale, founder of EdTech start-up Cypher, 'the coding company for kids', teaches computational skills to school children with the emphasis on creativity. Teaching links core computing concepts to real world creative themes, encouraging children to be curious, collaborative and problem-solving with confidence. Themes include relevant real-world subjects such as Architecture, Fashion, Art, Minecraft, Robotics and Entrepreneurship and children see their creations come to life via 3D printing and graphics.[20]

As an entrepreneur, she describes the 'entrepreneurial mindset' behaviours: 'we road-test ideas, we sometimes fail, and we try again. We develop resilience, present our ideas, pitch to investors, and we solve problems.' These qualities are not confined to success in business, but needed by 'young people to be successful in the future'.[21]

As we have seen, these skills are also key for the burgeoning start-up industry, as the skills of problem-solving and creativity are deemed necessary for finer tuning an entrepreneurial mindset. Yet, entrepreneurial skills are not specifically taught in our curriculum to all students. They may form part of an extra-curriculum activity, elective project, as part of work experience in KS4, or simply offered to those who opt to study business studies. Arguably this hit and miss approach will not help all our students. This core skill would open doors for many students to new possibilities. 'Passion, creativity, and resilience are the most crucial skills in business ... you are ready to embark on the journey' (Jo Malone, Founder of Jo Malone).[22]

## Summary

Skills shortages are developing so it is more important than ever that our education system creates structured opportunities for the skills, knowledge and competencies that young people need for their future life and work.

Schools that are at the forefront of innovative interactive and technological pedagogies should share more widely their excellent practice. Additionally, the best role that OFSTED can assume is to conduct a good practice survey that reports on the inclusion of digital technologies and computational skills within the curriculum. What is valuable is reporting on how a blend of technologies and more traditional teaching and assessment methods can transform the quality of education for all students, especially those who benefit from assistive technologies. This has become increasingly more relevant as a strategy, post-COVID pandemic, as schools come to rely more heavily on a curriculum model that potentially combines smaller face-to-face classes with online learning.

Curriculum design and delivery must prepare our young people for the dual onset of technologies and entrepreneurship. Developing young people's employability skills requires computational, creative and problem-solving skills. 'Learning to learn skills', learning through our experience and our mistakes, are akin to the computational skills. In both cases, adjusting what we do in the light of hindsight and improving as we go on are arguably the very skills that our students need for the process of learning itself across the curriculum. A core curriculum rethink makes a genuine commitment to optimising students' entry points into the labour market, enabling them to respond flexibly to its changing demands.[23]

We therefore strongly endorse the inclusion of Computing Science within the EBacc core and believe we make a strong case for the inclusion of digital and enterprise skills across KS3–4 in support of the National Ed-Tech strategy. Most importantly, students need to be equipped with these skills so that they optimise their learning, and are well prepared for their future training and employment destinations. We propose in Chapters 10,11 and 12 of this section that creating a Mandatory Skills Module that includes financial, digital literacy, oracy and critical literacy skills should be at the very heart of the curriculum.

## Notes

1   Children's Commisioner (2019) Changes to gambling laws needed as our report into online gaming reveals children's gambling fears. Available at: www.childrenscommissioner.gov.uk/2019/10/22/childrens-gambling-fears/ (Accessed: 24 November 2019).

2   V. Eubanks (2018) *Automating Inequality: How High-Tech Tools Profile, Police, and Punish the Poor*, 1st edn. New York: St Martin's Publishing Group.

3   L. Hamblin et al. (2019) Key Stage 4 Courses 2019–2021. Available at: fluencycontent2-schoolwebsite.netdna-ssl.com/FileCluster/Felpham/MainFolder/documents/WebDocs/WebDocs3/WEB-190128-1953-MA1.pdf (Accessed: 20 November 2019).

4   The LIBF (2020) Level 2 Certificate in Financial Education. Available at: www.libf.ac.uk/study/financial-capability/qualifications/certificate-in-financial-education-(cefe) (Accessed: 20 January 2020).

5   Young Enterprise (2019) What we do. Available at: www.young-enterprise.org.uk/what-we-do/ (Accessed: 23 January 2020).

6   S. Furber et al. (2012) Shut down or restart?, https://royalsociety.org/-/media/education/computing-in-schools/2012-01-12-computing-in-schools.pdf: The Royal Society.

7   Computer Science at Felpham Community College (2019) Available at: www.felpham.com/ICT (Accessed: 1 December 2019).

8   American Library Association (2019) Digital literacy. Available at: https://literacy.ala.org/digital-literacy/ (Accessed: 26 November 2019).

9   Department for Education (2019) *Teaching Online Safety in School*. London: Department for Education.

10   NSPCC (2019) Online safety. Available at: www.nspcc.org.uk/keeping-children-safe/online-safety/ (Accessed: 20 December 2020).

11   N. Chambers et al. (2019) *Joint Dialogue Final Report 2019*. Available at: www.educationandemployers.org/wp-content/uploads/2018/11/Joint-Dialogue-FINAL-REPORT-2019.pdf (Accessed: 10 December 2019).

12   D. Thompson and P. Nye (2019) GCSE results 2019: How entry numbers in EBacc and non-EBacc subjects have changed over time. Available at: https://ffteducationdatalab.org.uk/2019/08/gcse-results-2019-how-entry-numbers-in-ebacc-and-non-ebacc-subjects-have-changed-over-time/ (Accessed: 9 December 2019).

13   S. Peyton-Jones et al. (2014) Computing in the national curriculum: A guide for secondary teachers. Available at: www.computingatschool.org.uk/data/uploads/cas_secondary.pdf (Accessed: 23 November 2019).

14    T. Cook (2017) Apple CEO Tim Cook: Learn to code, it's more important than English as a second language. Available at: www.cnbc.com/2017/10/12/apple-ceo-tim-cook-learning-to-code-is-so-important.html (Accessed: 30 November 2019).

15    Department for Education (2019) EdTech Strategy marks 'new era' for schools. Available at: www.gov.uk/government/news/edtech-strategy-marks-new-era-for-schools (Accessed: 1 December 2019).

16    TESF (2019) TEDSF to grace 2019 World Innovation Summit for Education (WISE) in Paris. Available at: https://tedsf.org/tedsf-to-grace-2019-world-innovation-summit-for-education-wise-in-paris/ (Accessed: 18 January 2020).

17    TIOBE stands for *The Importance of Being Earnest*; the comedy by Oscar Wilde (1895). The index is calculated from the number of the search engine results for queries containing the language's name.

18    V. Daga (2019) The report: Is coding a 'waste of time?'. Available at: https://edtechnology.co.uk/Article/what-is-the-code-for-success/ (Accessed: 29 November 2019).

19    C. Wyatt (2017) How to teach students the language of coding. Available at: www.tes.com/news/how-teach-students-language-coding-sponsored-article (Accessed: 14 January 2020).

20    E. Tweedale (2019) How coding can hone an entrepreneurial mindset. Available at: https://edtechnology.co.uk/Blog/how-coding-can-hone-an-entrepreneurial-mindset/ (Accessed: 10 December 2019)

21    N. Fearne (2019) Diversity in tech starts in schools: an interview with Cycpher Coder's Elizabeth Tweedale. Availabe at: https://computing.co.uk/interview/4012280/women-in-tech-elizabeth-tweedale (Accessed: 11 November 2020)

22    K. Pande (2019) 51 entrepreneur quotes that'll get you out of bed in the morning. Available at: https://blog.hubspot.com/sales/motivational-quotes-from-some-of-the-world-most-successful-entrepreneurs (Accessed: 14 December 2019).

23    EdTechnology (2019) Two-thirds of UK business leaders say teaching children tech is more important than maths. Available at: https://edtechnology.co.uk/Article/two-thirds-of-uk-business-leaders-say-teaching-children-tech-is-more-important-than-maths/ (Accessed: 14 December 2019).

# 10

# Oracy skills

## Introduction

Oracy skills and self-expression are arguably part of cultural capital that distinguishes between those students who can deploy these successfully as a learning technique and those who can not. Oracy skills are a paramount indicator of successful learning which is why we advocate this as part of a Mandatory Key Skills unit in curriculum planning. We include within oracy skills, the importance of cultivating active listening skills. Whilst unable to control parental background and other home/background influencers, schools do have the potential for a 'green shoots' impact, through transforming students' communication skills.

## Human capital: Addressing the language disadvantage factor

Basil Bernstein, the sociologist, famously addressed the notion that 'class speech codes and controls' had the potential to stymy the education of the working classes.[1] He researched that working-class children had a more limited 'restricted code' with 'context dependent' vocabulary than their middle-class peers' 'dominating' vocabulary and elaborate code'. He concluded that the middle classes would gain the most from formal education, comparative to those with restricted codes.

Oracy skills are rarely mandatory, or an entitlement in the vast majority of schools' mainstream curricula. Speaking and debating skills aid enormously with extending self-expression, moving beyond basic vocabulary to more elaborate speech. Being articulate and succinct is necessary in day-to-day life, not to mention, job interviews, business and leadership roles. School21 'want every child to find their voice – metaphorically and literally' and profiles oracy skills within its curriculum, with a yearly 'Oracy Teach Meet Event'; assemblies for students to showcase and practise their presentation skills.[2] For a more detailed case study on how successfully the school integrates oracy and listening skills into every aspect of its curriculum, we refer you to Tom Sherrington's work.[3]

Now that the Spoken and Listening language assessments no longer count towards GCSE English Language outcomes, this can devalue the importance of speaking and listening skills within the curriculum. However, these skills as noted, are key to developing the persuasive and negotiating skills, much needed for today's jobs and increasingly so, for the jobs of tomorrow, as we saw in Chapter 2. Despite the obvious importance of public delivery skills (oracy and debating) within so many walks of life, this rarely features as an integral part of curriculum plans for all students, but may be an optional extracurricular lunchtime, or after-school activity.

A potential threat to developing oracy skills is ironically the impact of digital technologies, as all young people are subject to the pervasive influences of social media, iPads and so on from an early age. This could be a positive factor, because unlike previous generations they have unlimited access to 'knowledge and data'; in principle this should increase their self-expression. In reality with ever-increasing reliance on digital communication, there could be a gradual decrease in vocabulary. This is borne out by evidence in Early Years and the arrival at school of children who are unable to speak in anything other than monosyllabic language. Their parents may rely more heavily on the children interacting with television and iPads, and may not prioritise spending quality time talking and reading with their children. A recent article in the media demonstrated the impact of technology, when a toddler's first word was 'Alexa' as he had only ever had the Amazon's voice-activated virtual assistant read to him at bedtimes![4]

Cultivating oracy skills compensates for the possible deficit in the student's home and helps create a level playing field in accessing the curriculum. In lessons, encouraging students not to give monosyllabic answers and explanations, but fleshing these out with the how and why questions, *elaborative interrogation*, whilst time-consuming, pays dividends.

Promoting confidence in oracy skills is especially important for students on the whole spectrum of learning difficulties; from those who are diagnosed with ADHD/ASD, those with emotional, social and behavioural traits, and dyslexia. Vulnerable students with disruptive family backgrounds, those who lack confidence and those for whom English is an Additional Language greatly benefit. Structuring opportunities within the mainstream curriculum for practice and confidence building has never been more important. Stimulating interest in those students who are genuinely not engaged by the subject and do not see it as relevant to their lives is made through links with their life experiences, as in the case study below.

Students used their critical literacy thinking skills to evaluate media articles and through the process they discovered the 'Threshold Concept', as they interpreted the knowledge they had previously acquired in a different way. This helped with the process of 'recall, transfer and apply'. Learning became memorable through the interactive process of speaking and listening skills.

### CASE STUDY: ACADEMY IN NORFOLK

Year 9 students in Geography were learning about the historical evolution of the European Union from the Economic European Countries, prior to the 2016 Brexit Referendum. Views about the leave or remain vote reflected students' pre-conceived ideas learnt from families and friends. The vast majority saw no value in the EEC/EU. A show of hands at the start of lesson demonstrated that they would vote leave. Their understanding and ability to articulate 'why' was highly variable and patchy, based on hearsay.

One student when asked his view responded that 'his grandfathers had fought in the wars to free Britain of Europe and now they wanted their country back!'

Much of what they said reflected media reporting; but they were unable to articulate cogent arguments for either side. The teacher set up a debate with the pros and cons of 'leaving' and 'remaining' with the European Union. She divided the class into two camps and each had simple data regarding UK immigration patterns and impact on the local economy; EU subsidies for fishing, industry and fruit farming – major employment sectors in Norfolk and so on.

To avoid bias or subjectivity, students had media articles, illustrating both sides of the argument. Students reflected on the facts, before each side put forward a point of view, backed up with tangible evidence. Those who were less secure or confident in speaking had a partial script they could refer to, with a range of openers and connectives.

The debate was an opportunity for students to rehearse knowledge, practise persuasive skills., Importantly, they practised their metacognition skills through transfer of what they had learnt into a different context. They had to argue for a differing point of view to the one they had presented at the start. This meant manipulating the information and making it plausible to the audience in a presentation, using a visualiser.

The evaluation at the end of the lesson demonstrated students had changed their viewpoints with more evenly balanced outcomes. Three prime outcomes resulted: increasing students' knowledge base, distinguishing between false news and authentic fact and developing confidence in oracy and presentation skills.

Students evaluated the lesson as enjoyable and could articulate something each had learnt, but not known before!

## Accredited oracy skills

It is clear that disadvantaged children are the ones most in need of public speaking skills, especially those from homes, where there is not much talk. As we have seen in a world where entrepreneurial skills and communication skills are paramount, all our students must have the confidence and the ability to articulate their opinions; these are attributes that last a lifetime. Public speaking and debating helps students extend their vocabulary, structure their thoughts and think on their feet.

Oracy leads to reducing the attainment gap of the most disadvantaged students. Central to this is the role of school staff in helping to gain a broad repertoire of talk (Alexander, 2017).[5] Alexander (2012, p. 4) provides the following examples: 'narrate, explain, speculate, imagine, hypothesise, explore, evaluate, discuss, argue, reason and justify'.[6] Evidence shows that for the children who persistently experience poverty, three-quarters arrive at school below average in language development. As Mercer asserts during a media interview, 'if they are not getting it in school, they are not getting it'[7] (Severs, 2018) and Vygotsky (1962)[8] both stressed the links between language, thought and interaction, arguing that the use of language is key to new ways of thinking. All this well- researched evidence underpins the importance of the mandatory inclusion of this key skill within the curriculum.

Offering accredited opportunities is greatly beneficial for all students as a motivator.

---

*The English Speaking Board*[9] focuses on communication skills mapped to the relevant National Core Curriculum requirements through Pathways in Spoken English at Key Stages 3 and 4 leading to ESB Level 2 Certificate in Speech (Grade 4). A Pathways Project saw a dramatic increase in learners achieving the KS3 criteria: discussing language and meaning, expressing own ideas and high competency in using Standard English competently.

The 'Connect, Inform, Perform and Employability' Pathways contain specific oracy skills for each context. 'Connect' allows students to develop their literacy and analytical skills, through a biographical talk, a chosen poem or drama piece and includes being able to respond to audience questions. 'Inform' can be focused on a KS3 topic in any subject. Students may give a personal interest talk, review a news piece and give a persuasive speech, within a political, economic, environmental or social context. 'Perform' allows students to unlock their creativity through the performance of a self-composition or performance of an established work. 'Employability' supports those who wish to deepen their understanding of a career and to prepare for the job market.

---

## Developing vocabulary

Given that students arrive in secondary school with varying degrees of social and cultural capital nurtured from childhood; they may have a complex vocabulary or increasingly are able to acquire this and adapt through self-regulation. Other students will require a school environment that strongly encourages them to use Tier 2 (common usage vocabulary) and access Tier 3 (subject-specific glossary) with confidence.

David Didau (2014)[10] shares an interesting anecdote regarding a GCSE English examination. He cites that he was convinced his students would have easily answered 'a real gift of a question' on Steinbeck's *Of Mice and Men*. However, as students did not know the word 'futility' in the question, they could not! As Didau concedes 'poor vocabulary is a huge barrier to academic success'; stymying students' potential progress and subsequently their outcomes.

Neil Mercer's 'Thinking Together Project'[11] provides a useful compendium of classroom resources for a range of communication contexts. The toolkit within an Oracy Skills Framework assesses how well Years 6–7 use spoken English for different purposes through peer/teacher assessment-for-learning (AFL) tasks, accompanied by exemplar videos of students in classrooms undergoing these tasks. The tasks used for initial, formative and summative assessment build in feedback for students. The intent is that the materials showcase students demonstrating deeper understanding, articulating their reasoning and identifying substantive concepts; good preparation for accessing the secondary curriculum.

## Summary

In conclusion, the importance of students developing oracy skills and expanding vocabulary through the curriculum is central to the notion of engaging with cultural capital, and should lie at the heart of a curriculum's intent. We must include it as one of the mandatory core skills underpinning the curriculum's intent and implementation; profiling its importance on a school's website for students and their parents to share.

Without oracy skills, we are in danger of creating a glass ceiling for a significant number of our students, who are left behind and cannot access the cultural and academic curriculum we provide, owing to the paucity of their language skills. Addressing social disadvantage through increasing students' confidence in speaking, self-presentation and debating, undoubtedly helps them become *leaders of their own learning* and develop the interpersonal skills they will need for further training and employment.

## Notes

1    B. Bernstein (1970) Education cannot compensate for society. *New Society*, 38: 344–7.
2    School21 (2019) School21 website. Available at: www.schoo.l21.org.uk/ (Accessed: 17 December 2019).
3    T. Sherrington (2019) *The Learning Rainforest Fieldbook*. Woodbridge: John Catt.
4    T. Herbert (2018) Mum stunned after baby's first word is 'Alexa', *The Metro*, 4 June.
5    R. J. Alexander (2017) *Towards Dialogic Teaching: Rethinking Classroom Talk*, 5th edn. Thirsk: Dialogos.
6    R. J. Alexander (2012) Improving oracy and classroom talk in English schools: Achievements and challenges. In: *Department for Education Seminar on Oracy, the National Curriculum and Educational Standards*, London, Department for Education, 12 February 2012.
7    J. Severs (2018) How much of your lesson should be teacher talk? Available at: www.tes.com/news/how-much-your-lesson-should-be-teacher-talk (Accessed: 24 November 2019).
8    L. S. Vygotsky (1962) *Thought and Language*. Cambridge, MA: MIT.
9    ESB (2019) ESB launches new speech pathways. Available at: https://esbuk.org/web/esb-launches-new-speech-pathways/ (Accessed: 20 November 2019).
10   D. Didau (2014) Closing the language gap: Building vocabulary. Available at: https://learningspy.co.uk/literacy/closing-language-gap-building-vocabulary/ (Accessed: 24 November 2019).
11   University of Cambridge (2019) Thinking together. Available at: https://thinkingtogether.educ.cam.ac.uk/ (Accessed: 27 November 2019).

# 11

# Creativity skills across curriculum

## Introduction

The National Curriculum (Department for Education, 2014) defines creativity as 'the best that has been thought and said; helps engender an appreciation of human creativity and achievement'.[1] For students to better develop this 'appreciation', they require creative thinking skills. A third of teachers interviewed, in a recent survey,[2] believed that syllabus changes created a bigger focus on rote learning rather than developing appropriate attitudes for work, with two-thirds stating that creativity skills were not given space in the curriculum, whereas a half of teachers stated that as a consequence, their students were not developing self-confidence.

A common definition of creativity outlines two strands of creative thinking; convergent (identifying one good idea) and divergent (generating multiple solutions) (Guilford, 1950)[3]. Of these, divergent thinking lies at the heart of creativity and comprises three components: fluency (quickly finding multiple solutions to a problem), flexibility (simultaneously considering a variety of alternatives) and originality (selecting ideas that differ from those of other people). These are the skills necessary for deeper learning and also the skills set sought by employers. The Brookings Institution in its study has shown that the term 'creativity' comprises universal skills, mentioned in government education documents (alongside communication, critical thinking, problem-solving and communication) from more than 50 countries (Horton et al., 2017).[4] We contend firstly, that creative thinking skills are necessary within the taught curriculum, and secondly, that creative arts must gain a higher profile and value within a school curriculum's intent.

## International trajectory

The Organisation for Economic Co-operation and Development (OECD)'s research[5] explored the ways in which creative and critical thinking can be taught and assessed in schools (OECD, 2015). Creative Thinking is defined as 'engage productively in an iterative process involving the generation, evaluation and improvement of ideas, that result in novel and effective solutions'. Interesting to note is that the Programme for International Student Assessment (PISA), from 2021[6] is assessing the concept of creativity in schools, in a test of 'Creative Thinking'. The model of creativity developed at the University of Winchester in 2013 has five dimensions: being imaginative, inquisitive, persistent, collaborative and disciplined. It is currently in use in 27 countries from Norway to Chile. Interestingly, the Welsh Government's new curriculum (2019) aims to develop students as 'enterprising creative contributors'.

## Threading creative thinking across curriculum

Schools such as Thomas Tallis School in London[7] showcase a well-designed and thought-through model that assumes creativity exists across every discipline and is translated in diverse forms depending on the subject context in which it is located. Their website contains a useful catalogue of the most common pedagogical and assessment strategies that fall neatly within the Tallis Habits and sub-habits and a helpful Pedagogy Toolkit, used by teachers in schemes of learning. The Tallis Habits are a framework upon which each subject hangs its scheme of learning and threads creativity skills into the knowledge-based curriculum. Additionally, a rich plethora of links exist for students/staff and local community, such as aspects of London culture, learning resources, progression opportunities post-16 and staff blogs.

### CASE STUDY: THOMAS TALLIS SCHOOL, SOUTH EAST LONDON

The school[8] prides itself on developing creativity through the Tallis Wheel and Tallis Habits and states that 'The three cornerstones of our approach to teaching and learning are: Threshold Concepts, Powerful Knowledge and Habits of Mind. The Wheel (Figure 11.1) provides an aide memoire for implementing Habits-related strategies in the classroom … this features on the cover of staff planners and … as a poster in curriculum work areas. The wheel is divided into segments, building out from the centre, and beginning with the types of learning, explicitly supported by each of the Habits. The Wheel projects creativity's importance at a micro and macro level. Figures 11.2 and 11.3 illustrate the five core traits.

A model of creativity commonly used by schools contains five interconnected pedagogies of particular relevance to the cultivation of creative thinkers. These include problem-based learning, the idea of the classroom as a learning community, playful experimentation, growth mindset and deliberate practice (Lucas and Spencer, 2017).[9]

Schools can lead students towards 'an unshakeable sense of possibility thinking (Craft, 2010), … to imagine how they can move from the way things currently are to how they might be and then go on and take ownership of causing this to happen'.[10]

Education to understand the world and change it for the better

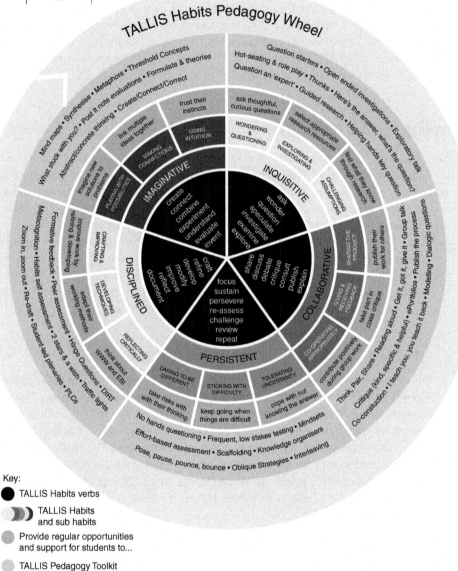

Key:

● TALLIS Habits verbs

◗ TALLIS Habits and sub habits

● Provide regular opportunities and support for students to...

○ TALLIS Pedagogy Toolkit

The **TALLIS** Habits are based on Lucas, Spencer, and Claxton (2013) Progression in Student Creativity in School OECD Publishing.

**FIGURE 11.1** The 'Habits' adopted cross-curriculum; Thomas Tallis School

**FIGURE 11.2** Thomas Tallis 'Character' illustrates the five core traits

**FIGURE 11.3** Thomas Tallis 'Character' illustrates the five core traits

The following factors created by Craft are judged important for a creative school culture. These provide a useful checklist that can be used by senior and middle leaders to test the thermometer of the school's ethos and culture.[11]

- focusing on pupils' motivation to be creative;
- encouraging purposeful outcomes across the curriculum;
- fostering in-depth knowledge of disciplines;
- using language to stimulate *and* assess imaginativeness;
- offering clear curriculum structures; involving pupils in creating new routines;
- encouraging pupils to go beyond what is expected;
- helping pupils find personal relevance in their learning;
- modelling the existence of alternatives in the way information is imparted; helping pupils understand existing conventions;
- encouraging pupils to explore alternative ways of celebrating their courage to be different;
- giving pupils time to incubate ideas;
- encouraging the adoption of different perspectives.

The Durham Commission's report on Creativity and Education[12] makes recommendations for promoting creativity, so all schools resource and teach creativity as part of the curriculum. One proposal is for a network of teacher-led 'creativity hubs', that supports teaching for creativity.

The report identifies the positive impact of creative thinking skills across all disciplines; Arts, Science and Social Sciences. Creative thinking is seen as important for young people's rounded development and as an issue of fairness, 'for young people from disadvantaged backgrounds'. The report criticises the 'knowledge-based education system' for not 'equipping young people with skills … confidence and resilience to shape their lives'.

With increasing emphasis on the EBacc subjects, since 2014, there has been nearly a one-third decline in the uptake of creative subjects,[13] although in 2019 a welcome 10 per cent increase in Art and Design. These are subjects that would normally, but not exclusively, lend themselves to students enhancing creativity skills. As we noted, with the ever-evolving landscape of employment – a move towards entrepreneurial skills and automation in the workplace, creativity thinking skills are now key.

## Creative thinking from our global competitors

Countries such as Australia and Singapore are reviewing curricula with a view to implementing creativity. There is a strong belief that their respective education systems need to prepare young people for the Fourth Industrial Revolution.

Singapore's educational attainment and standards in Science, Reading and Mathematics peaked in the PISA (OCED) assessment in 2015.[14] The major curriculum reform comes at a time when Singapore is transforming itself into a 'smart' nation by investing in emerging digital technologies across industrial sectors. Students 'need to be resilient, adaptable and global in their outlook and feel curious and eager to learn for the rest of their lives'.[15] Its education system has facilitated those students who are more academically inclined, to learn at a faster pace, but those that are disadvantaged do not achieve as well. This is not dissimilar to the disadvantage gap in attainment pattern in England. The Singaporean three-path levels system from 2024 is replaced with teachers facilitating critical thinking skills through projects. The importance of reducing examination pressure and giving opportunities for students to be creative and to acquire passion for new skills for life-long learning, essentially, underpins the curriculum shift.

In Australia, a recent report[16] acknowledges students require a blend of knowledge, skills, creativity and understanding: 'creative, connected, and engaged learners with a growth mindset' with a focus on 'problem-solving, interactive and social skills, critical and creative thinking' and references this to 'shifts in technology and jobs'.[17] In the Australian state of Victoria critical and creative thinking has been measured in 15 year olds for the past three years.

## Summary

In conclusion, transforming our curriculum so that it provides *an appreciation of human creativity and achievement,* can only be successful through structured opportunities across the subjects and extracurricular activities that broaden students' horizons and develop creativity. Each subject provides a vehicle for the teacher and student to explore and to collaborate together, so that the creative skills that result enhance their knowledge. Creative learning environments can stimulate students' attainment through critical and creative thinking approaches. Creativity is founded on deep understanding; finding new ways to see, act or behave. This is a sought-after skill by employers. Young people, more than ever require the ability to think 'outside the box'.

The creative industries such as film, radio, TV music, theatre, museums and digital creative industries are all part of a thriving sector that contribute significantly to the UK's GDP. If the sector is to continue expanding, the decision to exclude the arts from the EBacc needs to be reviewed.

Potentially, through fostering creativity skills across the curriculum, and by ensuring students can access creative and arts subjects, more students would gain a qualification in a subject they enjoy doing at GCSE, and importantly, continue with that subject post-16. All students should be given the opportunity to experience a curriculum that does not uniquely favour knowledge at the expense of creativity and the arts.

## Notes

1   Bernstein, B. (1970). Education cannot compensate for society (pp. 344–347). London: New Society, 38.

2   E. Kashefpakdel et al. (2018) Joint dialogue: How are schools developing real employability skills. Available at: www.educationandemployers.org/research/joint-dialogue/ (Accessed: 14 October 2019).

3   J. Guilford (1950) Creativity. *American Psychologist*, 5: 444–54.

4   S. Horton, H. Kim and E. Care (2017) *New Data on the Breadth of Skills Movement: Consolidation*. Brookings Institution.

5   OECD (2015) *Intervention and Research Protocol for OECD Project on Assessing Progression in Creative and Critical Thinking Skills in Education*. Paris: Centre for Educational Research and Innovation (CERI) Governing Board.

6   OECD Directorate for Education and Skills (2018) *Framework for the Assessment of Creative Thinking in PISA 2021* (second draft). Paris: OECD.

7   Thomas Tallis School (2019) Thomas Tallis School. Available at: www.thomastallisschool. com/creative-manifesto.html (Accessed: 29 November 2019).

8   Ibid.

9   B. Lucas and E. Spencer (2017) *Teaching Creative Thinking: Developing Learners Who Generate Ideas and Think Critically*. Bancyfelin: Crown House Publishing Ltd.

10   A. Craft (2010) Possibility thinking and wise creativity: Educational future in England? In: R. Beghetto and J. Kaufman (eds), *Nurturing Creativity in the Classroom*. Cambridge: Cambridge University Press, pp. 289–312.

11   Ibid.

12   N. Serota et al. (2019) Durham Commission on Creativity and Education. Available at: www. dur.ac.uk/creativitycommission/ (Accessed: 20 November 2019).

13   Bacc for the Future (2019) GCSE results day: Further decline in creative subjects. Available at: https://baccforthefuture.com/news/2019/gcse-results-day-2019 (Accessed: 12 November 2019).

14   PISA 2015 Results (Volume I) (2016) *Excellence and Equity in Education, PISA*. Paris: OECD Publishing, p. 208.

15    J. Lee (2019) Singapore eases up on school testing to foster creativity. Available at: https://asia. nikkei.com/Politics/Singapore-eases-up-on-school-testing-to-foster-creativity (Accessed: 8 November 2019).

16    A. Harris and L. de Bruin (2018) Yes we can greatly improve the teaching of creativity in Australian schools and yes we can measure it. Available at: www.aare.edu.au/blog/?p=2993 (Accessed: 8 November 2019).

17    H. Durrant-Whyte et al. (2015) The impact of computerisation and automation on future employment. In *Australia's Future Workforce*, Melbourne: CEDA, pp. 56–64, p. 61.

# 12

# Cultural capital and citizenship

## Introduction

In this chapter we define cultural capital within the curriculum. We argue that broadening students' horizons through a curriculum that fully embeds 'diverse cultural capital' helps ensure that our young people become informed global citizens. To this end, we explore how citizenship within the curriculum can actively develop both knowledge and skills and incorporate cultural capital.

Our students live in a multicultural pluralistic society and deserve to experience a thought-provoking and relevant curriculum. By this, we mean a curriculum that contextualises rich cultures and stimulates students' curiosity for learning; whilst ensuring that students have critical literacy and thinking skills. This gives them the tools to challenge the familiar world and prepare for the unknown. They will learn not to accept unquestioningly what is taught.

We contend that the 'mosaic of knowledge' students learn must have sufficient breadth, depth and diversity. This cannot be divorced from structured opportunities for learning about global citizenship, through students appreciating their own heritage cultures and those of others. This is especially important at a point where the UK has reached a historic watershed, post departure from the European Union. Forging new relations and understanding with countries worldwide is now an economic imperative. The students of today will potentially seek employment in these countries, or work for foreign employers investing in the UK.

## Cultural appropriateness: Whose culture is it?

OFSTED's understanding of 'knowledge and cultural capital'[1] echoes the National Curriculum's aspiration (Department for Education, 2018[2]) as we saw in Chapter 11 '… the best that has been thought and said … to *engender an appreciation of human creativity and achievement*' [our emphasis].

What this 'essential knowledge' is; how it is selected and by whom, is key. The appreciation of 'cultural knowledge' presents schools with a challenge. This philosophical concept, is largely dependent on all students having the motivation and skills to be receptive to learning about a culture, that some, possibly cannot relate to.

As we know, students are an amalgam of human and cultural capital. They arrive from a variety of different cultures and socio-economic backgrounds shaped by experiences outside of school, their families, peers and local communities and, of course, by an increasingly influential interconnected media.

We operate in an unequal society. John Yandell[3] asserted that schools might not be able 'to facilitate social change within an unequal society'. Michael Savage's social class model[4] refers to the most deprived of all as 'precariat' with low levels of economic, cultural and social capital. Arriving at the 'elite' class, depends on exposure to highbrow cultural pursuits. Therefore, he contends that if schools can expose all students to this cultural capital, they increase their chances of moving beyond the precariat class.

The prime question is – who is defining what constitutes 'highbrow culture'? In aspiring to upward mobility by accessing *only* highbrow culture, and not including what may be perceived by students as relevant to them, do we risk alienating some students for whom this is not the natural cultural environment? The notion of what constitutes cultural appropriateness requires genuine consultation with the staff, students, governors and parents. Otherwise, the result may well be the imposition of a monocultural curriculum on a multicultural and diverse societal culture; 'the effects of this alienation are sometimes permanent, it is precisely "one's own" culture which sometimes fails to survive the culture of the school'[5].

## Cultural literacy and tolerance of other cultures

The ideology of cultural literacy was drawn up by E. D. Hirsch, the American educationalist,[6] who argued that reading comprehension requires not just formal decoding skills but in addition wide-ranging background knowledge. His 'Core Knowledge Foundation' and theories influenced the National Curriculum design and the EBacc suite of subjects in 2012. Rather than critical thinking skills, he proposed that a 'well-rounded, knowledge-specific curriculum can impart needed knowledge to all children and overcome inequality of opportunity'. To this end, he stated that through learning set ideas /concepts and lists of knowledge, students become culturally literate and therefore, upwardly mobile in society. This in turn, would redress the barriers of cultural shortcomings that create under-achievement. Hirsch asserted that broadly studying arts, the 'cognitive wastelands' (Hirsch, 2009) was not valuable. The cultural status quo he defined as 'the classics', 'commonality of language requires commonality of knowledge ... the next logical step'.[7]

British values are about 'tolerance of other cultures'.[8] Cultural capital, based on Hirsch's ideology however, may imply a white middle-class cultural model. 'Lists of "key course content" seem to have returned us back to a time when the classroom prioritised classical, canonical texts and theories', is the view of Greg Sloan, head of Media Studies at Haggerston School in London. He teaches his students the Media Studies set scheme of learning and expects them to 'co-curate texts and ideas from their own cultures and new topics that are relevant to their lives'.[9] This 'cooperative student-focused' practice through blogs and websites is arguably richer and more diverse than any form of top-down approach to cultural capital, asserts Sloan.

## Diversity of cultural capital

Certain forms of cultural capital are more highly regarded than others in particular sectors of society. For example, classical music or opera may be viewed more favourably than listening to rap music. Similarly, reading Shakespeare is judged to hold more cultural capital than reading celebrity gossip magazines. If we are engendering an 'appreciation of human creativity and achievement', should we promote Stormzy alongside Schubert, or Handel with Hendrix?[10] Outside of, and within, the creative arts curriculum, we must question whether Western, classical and traditional music and art are given equal status with popular, contemporary, classical forms of expression enjoyed by a larger proportion of the world's population?

If we turn to GCSE Media/ Film Studies, some exam boards provide wide-ranging film examples for study, including Hollywood, British, European, Middle Eastern and Japanese. In another exam board, however, the examples for study are Western, and largely British. In Year 10, for instance, students may only study *Dr Strangelove* and *I, Daniel Blake*. Whilst these are all perfectly good film choices, we could go one step further.

The Bollywood film industry has the greatest reach worldwide, and, in some cases, this is greater than Hollywood, with massive fans in countries as diverse as China, Nigeria, Poland, Germany, Egypt, Taiwan and others. In none of the exam boards do students ever encounter even a glimpse of films from the largest film industry in the world. However, selected excerpts from a Bollywood film with a social theme based on a real-life biography would extend horizons. One such film, *Dangal CPS* (the biggest non-Hollywood film in China in 2017), recounts how a father overcame patriarchal norms and cultural taboos in a rural village, and trained his daughters as successful professional wrestlers –one of whom went on to win Gold at the Commonwealth Games (2010). It resonated with the Chinese audience, as the producer Shetty pointed out because of 'sacrifices you make to achieve excellence … a common theme in both Indian and Chinese culture … an emphasis on hard work and the correct support or guidance of your parents'.[11]

Aside from the widening of cultural perspectives, a comment on *human achievement* against the odds, and an *appreciation of human creativity,* would be inspirational for young girls aspiring to be successful in a male-dominated sport, breaking stereotypes and the common glass ceiling challenge faced by young girls and women worldwide.

Other than during Black History Month, students would benefit from being exposed to other cultures or other heritages, interwoven through the curriculum. This cannot be just through PSHE/SMSC sessions, if we are to avoid stereotypes and influence young people. Students need to acquire a genuine appreciation of world wide human creativity and achievement through subjects. A celebration and recognition in History, then not only of the achievements of Martin Luther King, Mandela, Ghandi, Harriet Tubman (as civil rights, political and peace activists), but importantly, in Science, of the first Black African American female astronaut Jemison in space (1992). In Mathematics, Mohammed ibn-Musa al-Khowarizmi (773 AD) demonstrated the zero in algebraic equations, and by the ninth century, the zero had entered the Arabic numeral system, as we know it today. This example can sit alongside the German mathematician Gottfried Leibniz's invention of the Step Reckoner (1671); a calculus based on the binary system, the genesis of the computer. Also, Katherine Johnson, a Black American mathematician, referred to as a 'computer', whose calculations of orbital mechanics (armed with pencil, paper and slide rule) as a NASA employee was critical to the success of the first US crewed space flight.

In GCSE History, cultural capital will depend on the vagaries of examinations board and the choices made by subject leaders.[12,13] Students might be taught of the impact of the British Empire and concepts such as imperialism, social Darwinism and civilisation. They may gain an understanding of how the identity of the people of Britain has been shaped by their interaction with the wider world through the legacy of the Empire resulting in migration patterns to the UK, such as Windrush, Asian exodus from East Africa, Jewish migration post war, and so on. Conversely, teaching to a different examinations board will mean that students might be taught about the Weimar Republic and Nazi Germany, 1918–39; British America, 1713–83; Empire and revolution; and The American West, c.1835–c.1895.

Two key points emerge from this; firstly, the World History taught should not be viewed uniquely through the selective lens of the British. For a balanced perspective, resources and historians should include Black, Asian and Jewish writers and others and students need to be taught to be critical of information they access. Secondly, Black Caribbean, African, South Asian students sitting in the History lessons must be given opportunities to learn the history of their own heritage or culture. White British students need to know the contributions made by other nations to the UK economy and society. For instance, if students learn of the two world wars, are all students aware of the military importance of the African, Asian and ANZAC troops? If they learn of the British Empire, are students aware of the lasting legacy of the East India Company's employees in 'acquiring' riches, and investing these in Britain's finest eighteenth-century buildings, even 'buying' a seat in Parliament? Thomas Pitt, famously founded the dynasty of two prime ministers (William Pitt and his son) through the purchase of a diamond whilst he was Governor in India![14]

The alienation of some Black Caribbean and Black African students may in part be attributed to a curriculum, where the contributions and histories of Black people in Britain are not incorporated or openly acknowledged in schools. For instance, it is usually more common for students to become familiar with Britain's involvement in the abolition of slavery in the nineteenth-century, than with the financial benefit Britain gained from the slave trade in the two centuries beforehand.[15] The Black Lives Matter movement in 2020 gathered momentum in the UK[16] owing to deep-rooted unrest and a sense of alienation experienced by young Black people. Teaching about positive Black role models across the curriculum, would contribute to young people feeling more valued and feeling pride in their heritage.

A geographical divide exists in the UK where students attend school with a predominantly White British pupil population and elsewhere, where a high proportion of students are from ethnic backgrounds. It is undeniable that all students equally benefit from a broader, balanced and culturally diverse curriculum.

## Extracurricular 'cultural capital'

If we are staying with the notion that cultural capital has the potential to create a level playing field for our students, then we must move away from paying lip service to 'add-on' extracurricular activities. A review must pose the question: 'Is every opportunity for learning outside of the classroom an activity that students opt into?' In some schools, the package of shows and trips risk becoming experiences for a select few. These then become the 'cultural capital' aspect of the school; but do not feature as integral to curriculum planning. The curriculum should be about what all students get to do, learn, see and experience in lessons, additionally around school, through the broad reach and wide participation in extracurricular activities by all. Examples are available through the Busy Bodies, Busy Minds Program.[17]

Undertaking an audit of the impact of extracurricular student participation reveals interesting conclusions about those students who do not sign up and why as below.

## CASE STUDY: 11–19 ACADEMY

This academy demonstrated a strong commitment to extracurricular activities, including competitions in sport and music but with 80 per cent of the students identified as the same students participating in sporting and musical activities. Subject leaders were not hooking-in those who were not attending. Some students, questioned about why they did not attend, reported the activities were 'too cliquey' or that they did not perceive themselves to 'be good enough'. Others identified a diverse range of activities they would choose to attend, if offered; performance arts, chess, languages, creative writing, debating skills. Other ideas included environmental and film production societies; coding/digital skills; APP design; yoga; mindfulness; Philosophy for Children (P4C); book clubs; young enterprise groups; and robotics.

The academy scheduled activities based on staff expertise on a half-termly carousel basis from a drop-down menu of activities. The model integral to the school curriculum's intent, meant *participation by all students*, thus deepening and widening their exposure to 'cultural capital'.

Students developed knowledge and transferable skills, relating to curriculum subjects and outcomes evaluated for impact against the Duke of Edinburgh Award skills.[18]

The Enterprise group following *The Apprentice* model,[19] produced a product, alongside a business plan, marketing and brand promotion. These included an online game and a T-shirt with a personalised logo! The spirit of collaboration and competitiveness provided a real-world context for students. They acquired these valuable wide-ranging co-curricular skills:

Organisational skills, teamwork, problem-solving, communication and leadership, negotiating income and expenditure (*mathematical skills*); business planning (*the Four Ps – Product, Price, Place, Promotion – Marketing Unit Business Studies*), creativity skills; logo, promotional material (*Design and Art*); oracy, written and persuasive skills; product promotion (*English Language skills*); digital skills (*Computing Studies*).

## Teaching citizenship

A symbiotic link exists between *cultural capital, values* and *citizenship*. Teaching 11–16 students about citizenship requires learning about civic responsibilities through relevance and collaboration in the classroom. The Citizenship curriculum comprises key concepts (democracy, justice, rights and responsibilities, identities and diversity) that students need to understand, along with the key processes and skills (critical thinking and enquiry, advocacy and representation, taking informed and responsible action).

Through a knowledge model, citizenship education is defined as the education of young learners for growth as informed citizens who participate in decisions about society.[20] The programme intent is to deepen students' understanding of democracy, government and the rights and responsibilities of citizens. Students must hone their research skills, weigh up evidence, make persuasive arguments and substantiate their conclusions.

## Understanding 'fake news' through critical literacy

Knowing about democracy means that students must have the *skills to engage with democracy* as active, informed and responsible citizens. The critical literacy skills together with the ability to distinguish between what is authentic and what is 'false news' are now essential, but largely absent from the Citizenship curriculum. Without this skill, the online proliferation of fake news can make children trust the news less, thereby making them less aware of the world around them, or their democratic rights. This is a definition that could fit the notion of helping students to distinguish fake news:

> to discern truth from rhetorical manipulation … as well as knowledge and techniques to help them to make informed and ethical judgements. These opportunities to listen, critique, analyse and compose will improve their skills of critical literacy, political literacy and self-expression.
>
> (Holmes–Henderson, 2014)

Only 2 per cent of British children have the skills to spot whether a story is fake or real,[21] an All-Party Parliamentary Group report identified. Children with the poorest literacy skills, such as boys, as well as those from disadvantaged backgrounds, were found to be the least likely to be able to spot fake news. 'Sometimes you can't actually tell when it's real and you never really find out, so you kind of believe it and then … you … have a hint that it might not be but you never fully know' (Year 9 pupil). In the surveys conducted, whilst half of older children accessed news from websites and social media, only a quarter of these actually trusted online news sources. Half of teachers believed that the National Curriculum did not equip children with the critical literacy skills they needed to identify fake news, and a third voiced that these taught skills were not transferable to the real world.

We must give students every opportunity to practise these skills through placing them in the core of the curriculum, alongside oracy and literacy skills. Facilitating a critical approach to different texts becomes 'an important aspect of critical literacies perspectives' (Olin-Scheller and Tengberg, 2017).[22] Oracy skills, leading to critical debate and discussion, together with reading skills (comprehension and inference), enable students to 'look behind' the text and consider how an author's use of language might position them as readers. An excellent resource is 'The Day', a daily online newspaper for schools, which links news stories to the National Curriculum and encourages students to debate and engage with local and global issues.[23]

Encouraging critical questioning of all texts *across all subjects* is an effective way of embedding critical literacy practices, promoting deeper engagement and metacognition in students through critical reflection. It is important that students develop their critical questioning skills by extending these to beyond the traditional GCSE subjects of English, History, Citizenship, PSHE. At 'A' Level, students apply interrogation and higher order thinking skills to, for instance, Philosophy, Economics, Law, Politics, Psychology and Sociology. The skills of asking perceptive questions, weighing evidence, sifting arguments, and reasoned arguments should extend also to Science, Geography and Mathematics.

OECD Director, Andreas Schleicher (as cited in Siddique, 2017[24]) argues, teaching critical literacy is:

> building skills to help discern the truth into all lessons, from Science to History.

A system change is required linking critical literacy to the real world and making it relevant for children and young people outside the classroom. Students evaluating news articles independently can only happen once critical literacy is integrated into lessons alongside current affairs and real-life links to online/social media.

Owing to the prime importance of this skill, a whole school strategy would better ensure the consistency and interrelated approaches to embedding digital, oracy and critical literacy skills.

> We teach our pupils … to search out for bias, to be analytical and to question and aggregate information because that's how the modern economy works. We are preparing them for third level education … the world of work, but we also want them to access the … interactivity that comes with using technology.
>
> (Fergal Moane, Deputy Headteacher and IT Strategy
> Lead at Sandringham School, St Albans, Hertfordshire)[25]

## International citizenship models

Both France and Finland re-evaluated their thinking on the citizenship element of their respective National Curricula, when confronted with external 'threats' of fake news and, or terrorism. Following the terror attacks in Paris in 2015, Moral and Civic Education (l'Enseignement moral et civique) curriculum is now mandatory across primary and secondary education, focusing on knowledge and skills. The intent was to reinforce the Republic's values and promote community values. The implementation includes training for teachers, a yearly charter signed by student and parent, community service assignments for student misbehaviour, and an annual day of 'laïcité', or secularism. It is more prescriptive than the English model and comprises four main themes: Sensitivity (understanding your feelings and those of others), Rules and Rights (understanding your legal rights and the rules of society), Critical Thinking (making rational decisions) and Social Responsibility (learning to become a responsible member of society).

In a similar vein, when Finland became the target of fake news from Russia, the Finnish[26] government in 2016 developed an educational plan with a multi-platform, cross-subject component of the National Curriculum. This means that students are taught, for instance in Maths, how statistics can lie; how images in Art can be manipulated; in History, propaganda analyses and through language to discern words that can confuse or mislead. The emphasis is on critical thinking, fact checking and evaluating information in each subject. A Finnish head of school is quoted as saying that children 'don't look for news, they stumble across it on social media … or an algorithm selects it for them – they must approach it critically'. One of his students is quoted as saying she had learnt that, 'you must always fact check … no Wikipedia and three/four different reliable sources across every subject'.

## Summary

In conclusion, we endorse cultural capital across the curriculum through subjects rather than a stand-alone approach in PSHE or SMSC, for the reasons explored. Opening *all* students' horizons through global cultural influences is best threaded through a school curriculum. There is an imperative to better prepare our young people in becoming world-informed citizens, with a deep understanding and respect of other cultures.

We propose strengthening the National Curriculum Citizenship model so that it places critical literacy skills at its core. This enables students to become more questioning of the knowledge they learn and to forensically distinguish between fake news and authentic information. For a whole-school approach to teaching critical literacy, as in the Finnish model above, teachers must be provided with the necessary CPD and resources so they can teach critical literacy actively and explicitly, within every subject.

In addition, national assessment frameworks should reflect the need for students to acquire critical literacy skills more explicitly, thus capturing the changing digital landscape and the threats posed by fake news.

These approaches together facilitate a proactive understanding of citizenship, and result in students, regardless of their background, knowing how to engage intelligently and enthusiastically with public life; having the skills to articulate sustained, well balanced arguments and importantly, knowing when and how to influence change.

## Notes

1    OFSTED (2019) *The Education Inspection Framework*, 1st edn, www.gov.uk/government/publications/education-inspection-framework: OFSTED.

2    Department for Education (2018) *The National Curriculum*. Available at: www.gov.uk/national-curriculum/key-stage-3-and-4 (Accessed: 5 November 2019).

3    J. Yandell (2019) Editorial, *Changing English*, 26(4), 337–8.

4    M. Savage (2015) *Social Class in the 21st Century*, 1st edn. London: Penguin Books Ltd.

5    J. Guillory (1995) *Cultural Capital: The Problem of Literary Canon Formation*, 2nd edn. Chicago: University of Chicago Press.

6    E. D. Hirsch (2017) *The Making of Americans: Democracy and Our Schools*, 1st edn. New Haven, CO: Yale University Press.

7    E. D. Hirsch (1988) *Cultural Literacy: What Every American Needs to Know*, 1st edn. New York: Random House.

8    DfE: 'We want every school to promote the basic *British values* of democracy, the rule of law, individual liberty, and mutual respect and tolerance for those of different faiths and beliefs. This ensures young people understand the importance of respect and leave school fully prepared for life in modern *Britain'* [our emphasis].

9    G. Sloan (2017) Curriculum: The influence of ED Hirsch. Available at: www.sec-ed.co.uk/best-practice/curriculum-the-influence-of-ed-hirsch (Accessed: 19 September 2019).

10   Handel & Hendrix London (2019) Handel & Hendrix London. Available at: https://handelhendrix.org/learn/ (Accessed: 29 October 2019).

11   L. Shakleton (2017) What the West can learn from the surprise success of 'Dangal' in China. Available at: www.screendaily.com/features/what-the-west-can-learn-from-the-surprise-success-of-dangal-in-china/5120116.article (Accessed: 21 November 2019).

12   AQA (2020) AQA GCSE History specification. Available at: www.aqa.org.uk/subjects/history/gcse/history-8145 (Accessed: 21 February 2020).

13   Edexcel (2020) Edexcel GCSE History specification. Available at: https://qualifications.pearson.com/en/qualifications/edexcel-gcses/history-2016.html (Accessed: 21 February 2020).

14   S. Tharoor (2017) *Inglorious Empire: What the British Did to India*, 1st edn. C. Hurst & Co Publishers.

15   www.thersa.org/discover/publications-and-articles/rsa-comment/2020/07/myth-busting-our-curriculum

16   Black Lives Matter (2020) Protests related to the death of George Floyd by a police officer in the USA. 25 May. https://blacklivesmatter.com

17   Quebec (2019) Examples of extracurricular activities that schools can organize as part of the Busy Bodies, Busy Minds program. Available at: www.education.gouv.qc.ca/en/school-boards/financial-support/busy-bodies-active-minds/a-few-examples/ (Accessed: 20 November 2019).

18   Duke of Edinburgh Award (2020) Skills examples. Available at: www.dukeofed.org/skill-examples-and-ideas (Accessed: 3 January 2020).

19   A US and UK series following a group of hopefuls completing a series of 'business challenges' who are whittled down to leave one victor who wins an investment.

20   C. Thaxton (2017) Citizenship education: Goals & importance. Available at: https://study.com/academy/lesson/citizenship-education-goals-importance.html (Accessed: 19 October 2019).

21   National Literacy Trust (2018) *Fake News and Critical Literacy*. London: National Literacy Trust (APPG).

22   C. Olin-Scheller and M. Tengberg (2017) Teaching and learning critical literacy at secondary school. The importance of metacognition. *Language and Education*, 0(0), 1–14. Doi: http://dx.doi.org/10.1080/09500782.2017.1305394

23   The Day (2020) The Day. Available at: https://theday.co.uk/ (Accessed: 14 January 2020).

24   H. Siddique (2017) Teach schoolchildren how to spot fake news, says OECD. *Guardian*. Retrieved from www.theguardian.com/media/2017/mar/18/teach-schoolchildren-spot-fake-news-says-oecd

25   D. Hinds et al. (2019) Realising the potential of technology in education. https://assets.publishing.service.gov.uk/government/uploads/system/uploads/attachment_data/file/791931/DfE-Education_Technology_Strategy.pdf: London: Department for Education (DfE).

26   J. Henley (2020) The upside. *Guardian*, 29 January.

PART

# V

# Curriculum intent, implementation and impact

# 13

# Curriculum intent and vision

## Introduction

Curriculum design is steered by the mission and values of the school leadership; academy and/or multi-academy Trust and shaped by a spectrum of contextual factors; most importantly, finance. Leadership of teaching and staffing, including the proportion of temporary/supply staff and of course students' motivations, their aspirations, attitudes and behaviours for learning, are major influencers. OFSTED has focused rightly on the impact of the whole school and how effectively it shapes each student's experience. Senior school leaders are heavily focused on outcomes, especially where students may not achieve predictable positive outcomes. The reasons may relate to staffing issues, funding or a 'challenging' student profile, including students who require additional support, alternative pedagogy, do not have the correct attitudes to learning, have SEND needs, are frequently absent and so on. Whilst these points may all be valid in themselves, it is incumbent on each school to review and adapt the curriculum, so that students' life chances are not affected adversely, at a crucial point in their education, by an inappropriate curriculum. Schools need to consider all these factors when planning the curriculum and to review intent and implementation in line with students' outcomes and the local context.

The OFSTED EIF 2019 is a potential catalyst for transforming the curriculum through providing a 'single conversation at the heart of inspection'. This represents a major shift from the previous inspection framework which focused heavily on student outcomes. An analysis comparing progress 8 scores to OFSTED grades in 2017/18 (Figure 13.1),[1] appears to support this argument. In this chapter, we explore the shaping of the curriculum intent and implementation, so students 'can know more, remember more and do more'. The curriculum is 'rooted in the leaders' solid consensus' of the knowledge and skills needed by their students. This will largely depend on how well the school leadership, genuinely gets 'under the skin of its students' and creates a relevant curriculum.

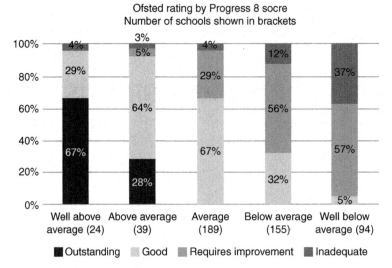

**FIGURE 13.1** Demonstrating the link between OFSTED grading and progress 8 score in 2018 under the old EIF
Source: FFT Datalab

## Establishing a 'Vision' and intent

Websites of different schools and Trusts indicate much variance in the quality and coherence of their Visions. The best examples of 'Vision Statements' are focused on the output for all students. Cabot Learning Federation have a clear and concise Vision of what is important for their students.[2]

This Vision (Figure 13.2)[3] works because the HEART values focus on the whole child, translate to every aspect of school life and are easy for all stakeholders to remember.

A Vision does not 'belong to', or reside uniquely with the senior leadership team; the Vision must be owned by every stakeholder, including staff, governors, Trustees, parents, students, the local community, employers, Third Sector organisations, local authority and former students (alumni). It is more meaningful when a broad range of stakeholders are genuinely consulted on the school's Vision and curriculum plans (Table 13.2).

| | |
|---|---|
| Establish | **H**igh expectations<br>for all that we seek to achieve |
| Create | **E**quity of opportunity,<br>removing disadvantage |
| Champion the success and life chances of | **A**ll children |
| Furnish pupils and staff with the | **R**esilience to succeed<br>as lifelong learners |
| Promote | **T**olerance and respect for ourselves,<br>our communities and our environment |

**FIGURE 13.2** Cabot Learning Federation's shared vision based on five key words
Courtesy of CLF; for more information on CLF see https://clf.uk/

**Table 13.1** Shaping the curriculum: Questions for leaders to consider

### 'Intent'

How does the Curriculum fit in with the school vision?

How does the school ensure an inclusive and equitable curriculum for all students?

How appropriate is the Curriculum given:

- The nature of student profile and intake

- The local context

Is the National Curriculum fully covered across Key Stages?

- Is there anything taught, not on the National Curriculum? Are there elements of the National Curriculum not given appropriate time?

- Is a three-year KS4 model appropriate? Can students access a broad range of subjects in KS3? Is there a rationale for a two-year KS3 relating to impact on learning?

### 'Implementation'

- Do subjects use a 'spiral curriculum/ interleaving' to revisit concepts; end of term, year, key stage?

- How are consolidation and challenge built into learning?

- Can Curriculum leads rationalise the sequence of knowledge and skills, in students' interests?

- How do leaders evaluate the quality of curriculum so it informs future planning?

- Do middle-leaders/teachers evaluate teaching and assessment processes for impact with all students; especially those with learning difficulties and/or literacy needs/more able?

- How effectively do teachers and teaching assistants work together to teach students?

- How effective is induction and transition for Year 7 students/mid-term arrivals, and those for whom English is a second language?

### 'Impact'

- Do the previous years' outcomes; the quality of education for student cohorts; students' progress across subjects and the standards they reach, inform curriculum planning?

- Are student patterns of absence or frequent exclusions (internally or FTEs), or 'managed moves', evaluated for the relevance of curriculum/learning in meeting their needs?

- How effective is the monitoring of addressing knowledge and skills gaps for students who miss chunks of education? What are the checks and balances so that those who miss lessons do not miss out on the sequencing of knowledge and skills?

- Do students act on teacher feedback and 'next steps'? Is there evidence of students understanding, retaining and applying knowledge and skills over time; 'recall, transfer and apply' (metacognition skills)?

- Is a 'love of reading' instilled across all age groups?

- Are students regularly accessing Tier 2 and 3 vocabulary? Do students understand and deploy domain specific words where appropriate?

- Are students leaving to go to appropriate destinations, in line with their aspirations? Are subjects linked into CEIAG and career pathways?

**Table 13.2** 'What' questions that focus on students' experience of the school and the curriculum

- What do we want students' educational experience to feel like across the curriculum?
- What are the values and aspects of ethos which will set students apart from students of other schools?
- What are students' destinations patterns and qualification patterns, particularly by student cohort (SEND, vulnerable, more able, disadvantaged, gender, ethnicity)?
  - What are take-aways for students once they leave the school? What do they remember the school for?
  - What is degree of variability and relevance that they experience of the quality of education across the subjects?
  - What is extent of enjoyment and 'hook-in' into learning?
  - What are strands of *core knowledge, skills, including, employability skills?*

## Gathering accurate information

Patterns of study, student destinations and their staying on rates post–16/post–18 usefully inform curriculum intent and implementation.

We need to critically examine the information we gather. For instance, if a disproportionate number of students gain Level 4 English and Maths and do not reach their potential, or a significant number fail to gain a GCSE in English or Maths; does this mean they received a poor quality of learning. Or is this indicative of an unsuitable examination syllabus, or students who perceive they can retake the exams post–16 in a FE college or sixth form, or a blend of all reasons?

If the majority end up in local employment, what is the primary local industry? If students are entering service-based industry; a focus on customer focused skills such as communication, social skills and empathy is necessary; are these taught explicitly? If the local industry is primarily finance, or engineering-based, higher credence might be given to analytical and problem-solving skills.

The role of CEIAG is intrinsic in collating the patterns of outcomes and destinations to usefully inform curriculum planning and intent. Reviewing post-16 destinations data for Year 11, followed by targeting potential NEETS (not in Education Employment or Training) in Years 10/11 can be facilitated through RONI (Risk of NEET Indicator Tool).[4] This is commonly used in local authorities for tracking purposes and is a useful source of data.

## Synergy between Vision and students' needs and aspirations

The Vision statement reflects significant differences that exist in terms of local context and intake, and between faith schools, non-faith schools, free schools, UTCs and academy trusts. It is clear that all schools intend aspiration and ambition for their students. What is key is reviewing the Vision with reference to the local context and a changing student profile so that this is translated into reality.

For instance, if a school's intake over a three-year trajectory indicates an increasingly high number of students with special educational needs; the school's Vision must be sufficiently flexible to reflect this reality within the curriculum intent. In other words, the priority of meeting these students' needs must be clearly stated.

If a school is experiencing a disproportionate rise in its fixed term exclusions or absence, it is incumbent on the school to focus on this aspect. One way is through restating its Vision's commitment to engaging with parents and carers of 'hard to reach' students.

A school with a large intake of disadvantaged students with low outcomes would inform the Vision through its strategies. A school's population may comprise a diverse range of cultures; its Vision might focus on a celebration of its heritage cultures and/or languages. Schools might emphasise a specialism such as a STEM curriculum, or an arts, creative or business curriculum. A faith school will express spirituality and the values of the faith within its curriculum. This is seen as holistically shaping students' education as in the case study below.

## CASE STUDY: ALL SAINTS CATHOLIC COLLEGE, LONDON

The mission *Orare, laborare, servire* influences the curriculum intent of *Educatio, Formatio and Iustitia Socialis* and the skills that students will acquire.

- Develop lively, enquiring minds, particularly the ability to question and argue rationally.
- Approach tasks logically with planning and perseverance and to carry them through successfully.
- Develop understanding, knowledge, mental and physical skills which will help them in adult life.
- Use language effectively in listening and speaking, reading and writing.
- Use numbers effectively to cope with different situations and to develop and appreciate mathematical skills.
- Develop creative and artistic skills and appreciation.
- Acquire scientific knowledge and skills.
- Acquire IT knowledge and skills.
- Develop personal moral values, respect for religious values and tolerance of other races, religions and ways of life.
- Understand the world in which we live, appreciate cultural differences, realise the independence of individuals, nations and our environment.

The agreed Vision *must* become integral in the school's day to day practice; all stakeholders should be familiar with the content that is translated into the curriculum plans. The *curriculum 'intent'* is better considered as a summary of what should be covered with an end goal constantly in mind–at end of year /key stage/ Year 11.

The case study below illustrates a Vision of a curriculum design built on concepts of *head, heart and hand* linked to subjects and a curriculum aim that develops 'students who make beautiful work which makes a difference to the world'. The school asserts that its subject domains are 'coherent and sequenced from reception to Year 13'.

## CASE STUDY: SCHOOL21

An elective project for students researches moral and ethical issues.[5] The curriculum map on the school website, whilst not explicitly stating the skills that underpin the topic- based knowledge taught, provide a structured opportunity for Year 8 students to combine an academic subject and a creative subject into a project.

Examples include interdisciplinary History/Drama and Science/Design and Technology projects, potentially practising students' creative, critical and problem-solving skills. Students have cross-curriculum opportunities, 'making linkages and consolidating fundamental concepts'. Additionally Year 10 students receive 'a twelve week Real World Placement with a partner organisation; thus developing students' employability skills … for the world of work'.

The powerful synergy between curriculum intent and implementation in turning around a failing school is best illustrated in the case study of Kingsley Academy. In addressing the challenges he faced, Elroy Cahill, the Headteacher, had a vision of a relevant curriculum that ensured challenge and support for students and included all the stakeholders in its implementation. He wanted students to acquire the knowledge, ambition and skills for success in higher education, further training and employment. Knowledge Organisers were not seen as an 'add-on', but integrated into teaching and learning and shared purposefully with the academy's learning community of staff, students and parents. Over the period of eight months, the impact of the redesigned curriculum at Kingsley Academy has been significant, with the academy judged as 'Good' by OFSTED, the first time in the school's history. The impact on its students is far reaching, with outcomes showing radical improvement with 20 per cent increase in the number of students achieving top grades in a wide range of subjects, including English and Maths in 2019. In 2020, the academy retained over half of its Year 11 students, the highest number ever; a testament to the curriculum's success in preparing students for post-16 study.

## CASE STUDY OF IMPACT FROM A RAPID 'TURN-AROUND' CURRICULUM

### Kingsley Academy (11–18) – Hounslow, West London

Kingsley Academy was marred by years of low exam results, a revolving door of staff, weak leadership and two successive OFSTED reports of 'Requires Improvement'. The curriculum followed by students was not preparing them for the next stages of their lives. This included a large number of students who had not had a primary education in the UK, with EAL needs, as well as a high proportion of disadvantaged students.

'We looked at our end points', says Elroy, 'and then thought what knowledge, experience and skills does a student need to be successful at A Level in each subject and then "reverse" planned what was required. Middle leaders started revisiting their passion for their subject and considering how their subject would allow students to achieve the curriculum intent.'

Assistant Headteacher, Prab Govender maintained that, 'The power behind the use of Knowledge Organisers to scaffold students' learning was immense to combat huge gaps in knowledge"' Students had an easy to access store of key concepts and subject specific vocabulary. Students use Knowledge Organisers for knowledge recall, homework tasks, 'Do Now' low stake quizzes, and to prepare for assessments and homework. Deputy Headteacher, Bhavin Tailor explained, 'We devised our "Great 8 for teaching" with opportunities for knowledge recall, and the explicit practising of skills evident in lesson visits. Teachers could immediately see gaps in learning and this supported them with moving students forward.' Training parents and students was integral so that all were clear on how to use Knowledge Organisers and why learning core knowledge and concepts was so vital. The implementation of the curriculum has been a labour of love; staff, students and parents have all bought into it.

## Curriculum implementation/sequencing of knowledge and skills

Although generic schemes of learning form a good starting point, they will not be linked to the school's curriculum intent. They are unlikely to include specific references to quality assessments, for evaluating how well students are acquiring knowledge and skills. In simple terms, they may tick some of the 'implementation' boxes but cannot meet the individual 'intent' requirement and will possibly not fit in with the Vision of what constitutes 'impact'.

This Science department has developed the memorable concept of CPR for delivery of its curriculum.

### CASE STUDY: ALL SAINTS CATHOLIC COLLEGE, LONDON

The curriculum intent is to make directed synoptic links across the Sciences, with the use of Kerboodle scheme of learning in KS3. The concept of CPR (Consolidation, Preparation and Retrieval) is used in planning homework with 'Consolidation' based on the most recent lessons that have been taught; 'Preparation'– homework designed to prepare pupils for the next lesson, or a future lesson; 'Retrieval'–homework based on previous lessons.

## Spiral curriculum and interleaving

Deploying a spiral curriculum, with linear subjects, such as Maths, Science and Languages is a structured way of developing progression and enquiry-based learning. Bruner's theory on cognitive growth[6] means that teaching and revisiting a wide variety of concepts and/or topics; allows students to deepen their understanding, within contexts of ever-increasing levels of complexity. Therefore, in the teaching of Science, this could mean a linear progression to a web of linked ideas, with recall through regular low stakes quizzes. Elaborative Questioning skills requires students to make connections between topics.[7]

An example might be the introduction of 'molecules' in Year 9, taught through 'early atmosphere'; followed in Year 10 by studying molecules relating to the forces within and between them, in the context of the separation of crude oil. This leads to modifying the properties of polymers in Year 11. Students apply their conceptual knowledge in unfamiliar contexts and at various points within KS4. They are encouraged to actively recall, transfer and apply what they learn through real-life tasks/activities.

The connections and continuity in learning are made through start and end of lessons with the prompts on 'What are we learning today?' or 'What are we learning next?' This allows for logical progressions from simplistic to complicated ideas, and encourages students to make links between old learning and new learning, whilst also encouraging critical thinking skills and self-reflective learning. For those who progress to Chemistry or Physics 'A' level this approach provides a firm foundation.

Interleaving as opposed to block teaching, is a technique mixing together different topics or forms of practice, helping students retain new information, acquiring new skills, and knowledge in a wide range of domains, including in English, History, Maths, Music and Sports. 'Spacing' refers to revision throughout the course of study, while 'interleaving' means switching between ideas while learning. Despite memorable teaching of a unit or topic or literature book in September, students will forget key skills and concepts later on, when revisiting the information. Both techniques can help boost students' long-term memories and retrieval of key information.

Herman Ebbinghaus' theory of the 'forgetting curve'[8] identified the increased likelihood of not remembering information over time, unless we regularly revisit. The issue with memory is clearly a key consideration when planning curricula, especially as the current GCSE model requires students to retain information over a two- (or sometimes three-) year period and for core and EBacc subjects a five-year period.[9]

A classroom-based study[10] presenting learners with images of butterfly, in two different patterns (representing interleaving practice), found that while spacing had a short-term negative impact on learner performance, interleaving counteracted this problem. Combining interleaving and spacing may help learners make meaningful connections when learning new concepts.

## Curriculum additionality

A school should evaluate the overall curriculum intent based on its curriculum map with respect to gaps. Balancing the imperative to complete the scheme of learning against curriculum elements identified as missing or important is key. The latter can be delivered through bespoke lessons, or through the use of 'enhanced' curriculum days. An example of this might be if a school required an opportunity to programme simple robots as part of a STEM activity, an enhanced curriculum day provides the time and space for this concept to be explored properly.

In another example, the National Curriculum for History insists upon students covering 'The development of Church, State and Society in Britain (1509–1745)'.[11] This means that most students will not necessarily cover the complex political, religious aspects of 'The Glorious Revolution (1688)'. Politically, this major event, seen as the 'bloodless invasion' for England, was the beginnings of democracy and greater power for the English Parliament. It acted as a catalyst for much of the political and cultural unrest, which reverberates across the British nations today, post-Brexit; and therefore, has relevance for the British constitution.

Curriculum leaders identifying gaps or additionality, need to take into consideration, students' prior learning, their experiences, and their human and cultural capital. Acknowledging that students are not 'tabla rasa', or vessels to be filled with isolated bits of knowledge is fundamental.

The additional knowledge and skills we choose, because they lie genuinely in the students' best interests, are at the core of how we define our curriculum intent. As leaders, we must consider valuable 'additionality' in knowledge, because of its intrinsic value and relevance to students' lives. Education is not confined to slavishly teaching to bullet points on the National Curriculum, or rote learning of common questions on an examination paper. Broadening students' horizons will help to foster cultural capital and increase motivation in learning. As we have seen, if students are motivated, they are more likely to retain information in their long-term memory, through the process of metacognition.

## Interconnectedness of skills – cross curriculum

Setting learning objectives through revising knowledge and skills from other subjects; ensures that students are aware of how their lessons fit into the 'bigger picture' of the curriculum.

One recommendation is to use a visual clue for students so they identify the key strands of knowledge, across the whole school learning 'map'. For example, all subject resources relating to 'solving equations' in Mathematics could use the same graphic on schemes of learning and displays, thereby increasing the chances that students retain the information.

For example, if the icon (Figure 13.3)[12] is attached to every aspect of school work, or a display where algebra skills are required, students would better understand the skill's use across subjects and in real life. Examples include students balancing chemical equations in Science or when calculating profit in Business Studies.

**FIGURE 13.3** Graphic icon denoting algebraic skills within a task in any subject

## Post-16

Linking aspects of different courses becomes more complex, as students may study three qualifications with little relevance to each other. An identifiable list of core skills can be extrapolated and linked to the core skills embedded in each subject. We might expect students to analyse quantitative data in a number of formats; an integral skill for a significant number of post-16 courses.

However, where there is no easily identifiable core skill across the three subjects studied by the student, practice in the skills can be tailored outside of the classroom during guided study. This ensures that as a minimum expectation all students acquire core skills necessary for their next steps.

Figure 13.4 shows how two skills can be linked to different subjects, building the core 'missing skills' into the post-16 curriculum.

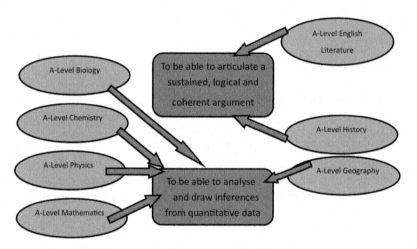

**FIGURE 13.4** Post-16 education: Identifying subjects incorporating 'core skills'
Copyright Nick Haddon

## Summary

A school with a genuine Vision can optimise the intended 'output' in terms of the knowledge and skills that students should develop; this, in addition to their National Curriculum entitlement. The Vision informs the school's ethos and values, as well as the curriculum intent and design. It truly sums up what it is to be a student at that school.

The relevance of curriculum intent should be reviewed through a constant feedback loop using real-time assessment data and information, on a school's changing student profile, as well as student destinations. This will help to continuously improve educational outcomes for subsequent intakes.

By extending their knowledge through co-curricular strands of learning, students have increasing opportunities for connections between different aspects of knowledge and skills and conceptual thinking. As we see, appropriate implementation of spiral, interleaving and spacing techniques allow for recall, transfer and application across a subject, cross-subjects and key stages; thereby accelerating students' progress.

## Notes

1    P. Nye and S. Rollett (2018) How did Ofsted ratings relate to Progress 8 scores in 2017/18?. Available at: https://ffteducationdatalab.org.uk/2018/10/how-did-ofsted-ratings-relate-to-progress-8-scores-in-2017–18/ (Accessed: 17 November 2019).

2    Cabot Learning Federation (2019) Our vision – Cabot Learning Federation. Available at: www.clf.uk/ceo-welcome/our-vision/ (Accessed: 24 November 2019).

3    Used courtesy of Cabot Learning Federation. For more information about the Cabot Learning Federation go to www.clf.uk/

4    CEDEFOP (2020) Risk of NEET Indicator Tool (RONI). Available at: www.cedefop.europa.eu/en/toolkits/vet-toolkit-tackling-early-leaving/resources/risk-neet-indicator-tool-roni

5    School21 (2019) Real world learning. Available at: www.school21.org.uk/rwlp (Accessed: 15 December 2019).

6    J. Bruner (1976) *The Process of Education*, 2nd edn. Cambridge, MA: Harvard University Press.

7    J. Dunlosky (2013) Strengthening the student toolbox: Study strategies to boost learning. *American Educator*, 37(3): 12–21.

8    H. Ebbinghaus (1908) *Psychology: An Elementary Textbook*. New York: Arno Press.

9    L. Tsabet (2019) Why an 'interleaving' curriculum could improve knowledge retention. Available at: www.tes.com/news/why-interleaving-curriculum-could-improve-knowledge-retention (Accessed: 20 January 2020).

10   M. Birnbaum, N. Kornelland, E. Bjork et al. (2013) Why interleaving enhances inductive learning: The roles of discrimination and retrieval. *Memory & Cognition*, 41(3): 392–402.

11   Department for Education (2013) National Curriculum in England: History programmes of study. Available at: www.gov.uk/government/publications/national-curriculum-in-england-history-programmes-of-study/national-curriculum-in-england-history-programmes-of-study (Accessed: 1 November 2019).

12   https://thenounproject.com/search/?q=maths&i=2385659

# 14

# Implementation: Curriculum pathways

## Introduction

Having explored the skills that are essential for successful learning, we now focus on optimising the school's resources, through locating the best fit models for a broad and balanced curriculum, integrating both knowledge and skills. We explore the OFSTED focus on a three year KS3 curriculum, with the intent of ensuring students' choices are not narrowed. We propose practical solutions to curriculum planning, staffing and what is relevant for the local context. Four models in KS3 are presented as follows:

1.  *Model 1*: reconciling the length of KS3 and 4 through a *'halfway house'* model of option choice

2.  *Model 2: a work-related learning model* for a three year KS4, with quality time for employer engagement. Using one day per fortnight for the delivery of cultural capital, the new RSE commitment and CEIAG ensures an engaging and responsive curriculum, and also transforms students' perception of school, thereby improving behaviour and attendance.

3.  *Model 3: Curriculum pathways – Adaptive models* has three strands:

    (i)  *Academic support for students* during KS3 and 4 through an *'Engage and Achieve Unit'*. Re-engaging students who are internally excluded and those at risk of exclusion. These students typically have gaps in their learning and need an 'academic curriculum space' for ensuring continuity in the sequencing of their knowledge and skills. We also propose how this may be funded.

    (ii)  *Transition curriculum* for those students who are *Not Secondary Ready* (NSR); needing further consolidation of their literacy and numeracy skills.

    (iii)  *Secondary ready* – preparing KS3 students for EBacc with a greater focus on History, Geography and MFL.

4.  *Vocational routes through KS3 with a skills entitlement.* A blend of vocational and academic knowledge and skills is central so that there is greater relevance to students' aspirations, and to their future destinations.

5.  *Model 4: KS4 'Pathways' model* focuses on individual students' abilities and aspirations

6.  *Lecture style delivery*

7.  Consideration of models for course selection and curriculum pathways, *post-16*, maximising potential outcomes for students.

## Exploring the KS3 curriculum models

The models are designed on an average 8 form entry school with a two week, 50 period timetable as this seems to be the norm amongst most schools. The models are mutually exclusive and the advantages, disadvantages and solutions for each are proposed.

'MES' is included in all of the models and refers to a weekly two-hour *'Mandatory Entitlement to Skills' module*. This is aimed at future-proofing the curriculum and preparing students for the world of work they will enter. The assessment of the following students' skills will inform the scheme of learning for this module:

■   oracy skills;

■   critical literacy;

■   computing/digital literacy skills;

■   financial literacy and enterprise skills.

A 'National Curriculum' app[1] is now available which is an excellent starting point for subject areas when it comes to reviewing how closely a KS3 intent covers the National Curriculum.

For students with low starting points in terms of English, a project such as CLIL[2], 'Content and Language Integrated Learning', is primarily concerned with students learning in a non-native language. This approach is suitable for students with low reading ages, facilitating elements of History, Geography and even Science to be taught in line with the National Curriculum, whilst improving students' literacy skills and knowledge.

## How long should KS3 be?

OFSTED's priority, namely a *'broad and balanced KS3 curriculum'*, has resulted in many schools reviewing the two year KS3, which allocates more study time for three-year KS4, through implementing option choices at the end of year 8 from the compulsory subjects listed.

Evidencing that this decision is not detrimental for students' 'broad and balanced education' will be key.

■   English

■   Maths

■   Science

- History
- Geography
- Modern Foreign Languages
- Design and Technology
- Art and Design
- Music
- Physical Education
- Citizenship
- Computing[3]

> If a school has shortened key stage 3, inspectors will look to see that the school has made provision to ensure that pupils still have the opportunity to study a broad range of subjects, commensurate with the National Curriculum, in Years 7 to 9.
>
> (EIF OFSTED, 2019)

Following the OFSTED survey (2011), 'KS3: The Wasted Years'[4] the National Curriculum review recommended a *condensed KS3 curriculum*. The panel suggested that a three-year KS4 allowed students to study a broader curriculum, covering courses in greater depth, whilst benefiting from more interaction with subject specialists. If this is the case, then it seems sensible for schools to gain clarity about which model they follow, based on the best interests of the students.

We have to consider whether the impact of a two-year KS3 truly detracts from a school's broad and balanced curriculum. It is worth considering how much of the current Year 7 curriculum might be a repetition of KS2 knowledge and skills. The purpose of early assessment at the beginning of secondary school is to guide schools in finding appropriate levels of challenge for all students within the first term and also identifying the gaps in their knowledge and skills.

Let us consider the varying levels of wealth of knowledge and skills that Year 6 students bring to a typical secondary school. This is reduced to two standardised SATs numbers for Maths and English that informs all teachers how to judge their students' understanding and ability in every subject. It is not surprising, therefore, that schools may tend towards a 'one-size fits all' approach to the KS3 curriculum. Reframing the transition curriculum KS2/3 must ensure that prior learning is taken into account. The intent of KS3 is a stepping stone that consolidates and extends the knowledge and skills, taught in KS2. Assessments, such as GLS tests and others will reveal gaps in learning to be addressed, for all students. On the other hand, by not identifying the more able students and those who are non-secondary ready, means potentially dumbing down the KS3 curriculum for all. This results in disengaging the more able students and lowering their potential for academic progress.

> Many of the senior leaders ... accepted that some pupils would repeat some of what they had done in Key Stage 2 ... repeating work is more of an issue in Mathematics and English than in the foundation subjects.[5]

The same is true for students who either have learnt a MFL language in primary school or who through their heritage are fluent in a MFL language. Despite the primary curriculum's intent to dovetail more effectively into the higher GCSE standards of knowledge and skills; it is still the case that the KS3 curriculum is largely dependent on each secondary school's willingness to plot its curriculum outlines, taking into account the prior knowledge and skills of its students.

## A case for a 'condensed KS3'

Where options are chosen at the end of Year 8 and not Year 9, the rationale proposed by the National Curriculum review of 2011 was true then as it is now, and has greater relevance with the higher standards and demands made through the EBacc curriculum. The advantages of a two-year KS3 are:

- Students may find the work in KS3 more challenging owing to the increased pace.
- Students with gaps in their knowledge and skills; especially disadvantaged students and SEND require three years to fully cover a GCSE scheme of learning and acquire depth of learning.
- Students will not potentially be disengaged over three years of a five-year secondary education, by covering work they have already covered in primary school.
- Schools could use time gained by reducing the number of subjects being covered in Year 9 to increase the scope for enrichment activities and work-related learning.
- Students could benefit from a greater choice when deciding options. By allowing three years to deliver options subjects, it is possible to allow students to study one subject at greater depth or pick additional supplementary GCSEs like GCSE Statistics which can support other subjects.

Figure 14.1 illustrates Westminster Academy's five-year GCSE curriculum outline. This expresses aspirational, well-envisioned intent so all students experience a broad range of KS3 subjects, including digital and enterprise skills. Students are given good structured opportunities for a sound foundation by the time they decide their three-year KS4 curriculum options at the end of Year 8.

### CASE STUDY: WESTMINSTER ACADEMY, LONDON

The ethos of this International Business and Enterprise Academy is built around Global Citizenship through both the International Baccalaureate Diploma Programme (IBDP) and the International Baccalaureate Career-Related Programme (IBCP). Rather than focus on two-year or three-year KS3, the Academy's intent is that its students are on a Year 7–13 curriculum journey. Students at Westminster Academy follow a KS3 curriculum that includes digital and enterprise skills and a combined humanities subject (Geography, History and RE) that provides a broad and balanced foundation in Years 7 and 8, enabling all students to experience all NC subjects. Subsequently, senior leaders believe students are best placed to excel in the three-year GCSE programme of their choice.

Westminster Academy's KS3 curriculum booklets outline term by term what students will learn and usefully identify the necessary skills they need as a starting point, as well as the technology they will use; for instance; 'chrome book to do research on key texts and present your ideas to the class'. The curriculum booklet also provides an intended outcome 'by the time you finish you will be a creative, keen and critical writer'.[6]

The academy's Curriculum Vision states that 'internationally minded, relevant, concept-driven and challenging curricular demands of IB courses inform curriculum planning in Key Stages 3 and 4'.[7]

## MODEL 1: 'THE HALFWAY HOUSE'

A hybrid model in Table 14.1 allows KS3 students to select options early while also maintaining the breadth of curriculum they need for Year 9. Table 14.2 projects the pathway for Years 10/11.

**Table 14.1**  Hybrid pathway: Years 10/11

| Year 7 | Hours per fortnight | Year 8 | Hours per fortnight | Year 9 | Hours per fortnight |
|---|---|---|---|---|---|
| English | 8 | English | 8 | English | 7 |
| Maths | 8 | Maths | 8 | Maths | 8 |
| Science | 8 | Science | 8 | Science | 8 |
| History | 4 | History | 4 | History | 4 |
| Geography | 4 | Geography | 4 | Geography | 4 |
| Citizenship | 2 | Citizenship | 2 | Core PE | 3 |
| Core PE | 4 | Core PE | 4 | Option A | 4 |
| Computing | 1 | Computing | 1 | Option B | 4 |
| MES | 1 | MES | 1 | MES | 1 |
| MFL | 4 | MFL | 4 | MFL | 4 |
| DT | 3 | DT | 3 | Arts* | 3 |
| Arts* | 3 | Arts* | 3 | | 50 |
| | 50 | | 50 | | |

Year 9 Citizenship delivered through 'alternative curriculum days', includes opportunities for students to meet the Gatsby Benchmarks[8] and engage with employers as part of the Work-Related Learning element.

Adjustments can be made to the model, dependent on the context of the school, GCSE outcomes and the agreed Vision for the curriculum.

**Table 14.2** Work-related learning/citizenship pathway

| Year 10 | Hours per fortnight | Year 11 | Hours per fortnight |
|---|---|---|---|
| English | 8 | English | 8 |
| Maths | 8 | Maths | 8 |
| Science | 8 | Science | 8 |
| History/Geography | 5 | History/Geography | 5 |
| Option A | 5 | Option A | 5 |
| Option B | 5 | Option B | 5 |
| Option C | 7 | Option C | 7 |
| Citizenship | 1 | Citizenship | 1 |
| Core PE | 3 | Core PE | 3 |
| | 50 | | 50 |

Copyright Nick Haddon

| **Advantages** |
|---|
| • EBacc qualifications and the EBacc element of the progress 8 |
| • Broad range of subjects (academic and creative) through a language and an arts subject |
| • Continue with History and Geography in Year 9 |
| • Students choose one humanity subject at the end of Year 9, and another open subject Y10-11 |
| • Broad and balanced KS3 curriculum; increased curriculum time for two options subjects |
| • Third option with significantly more time: in Year 10 and 11 |
| • Splitting the options process across 2 years allows students and staff to address inappropriate decisions, resulting from Year 8 choices |
| **Disadvantages** |
| • No design technology option |
| • Citizenship not taught; delivery during 'alternative curriculum days' or within the MES slot |
| • Complicated CEIAG and options process; students select in Year 8 and 9 |
| **Solutions** |
| • Year 9 choose from two option blocks: technology and computing subjects; dependent on the school's track record in these GCSEs. |

# MODEL 2: WORK RELATED LEARNING

The concept of a 'work related learning lesson' is for students to have meaningful encounters with employers. Depending on the location of the school, work experience could be scheduled to weekly afternoons.

In Table 14.3 students select all options at the end of Year 8, with a reduced number of hours for each subject to allow the 'breadth of curriculum' to continue.

**Table 14.3** Broad/flexible three year GCSE pathway

| Year 7 | Hours per fortnight | Year 8 | Hours per fortnight | Year 9 | Hours per fortnight |
|---|---|---|---|---|---|
| English | 8 | English | 8 | English | 8 |
| Maths | 8 | Maths | 8 | Maths | 8 |
| Science | 8 | Science | 8 | Science | 8 |
| History | 4 | History | 4 | Option A | 4 |
| Geography | 4 | Geography | 4 | Option B | 4 |
| Citizenship | 2 | Citizenship | 2 | Option C | 4 |
| Core PE | 4 | Core PE | 4 | Option D | 4 |
| MES | 2 | MES | 2 | Core PE | 4 |
| MFL | 4 | MFL | 4 | Arts | 4 |
| DT | 3 | DT | 3 | WRL | 2 |
| Arts* | 3 | Arts* | 3 | | 50 |
| | 50 | | 50 | | |

Copyright Nick Haddon

A more flexible model that allows for decisions in Year 9 that genuinely set the student on an individual KS4 pathway towards his/her future destination – academic, creative, technical or vocational training through a blend of subjects.

| |
|---|
| **Advantages** |
| • Core PE time is protected at 4 hours per fortnight |
| • Work related learning period devotes real time to employer engagement |
| • Students access a significantly more guided learning hours curriculum for level 2 courses. This leads to in-depth study with more scope to explore concepts |
| • Impartial CEIAG advises Year 8 students on best subject combinations for future destinations |
| **Disadvantages** |
| • Not all Year 9 students choose *History, Geography, or Citizenship* options |
| • Some students study an 'arts' subject, alongside the compulsory 'arts' subjects |
| **Solutions** |
| • All students select from one humanities subject and a technology subject to ensure that these aspects of the National Curriculum are met; otherwise the school progress 8 outcomes maybe affected by students not fulfilling their EBacc elements |
| • Creative arts subjects in Year 9, such as Drama are used to teach a number of PSHE related topics by involving students in exploring real life scenarios. As Drama is a non-compulsory subject,[9] PSHE schemes and concepts can be woven into the teaching. It is desirable for all subjects to include aspects of cultural capital. |

## MODEL 3: ADAPTIVE CURRICULUM PATHWAYS: ENGAGE AND ACHIEVE

### Creating relevant and appropriate curriculum pathways

The school curriculum's intent moving towards 'Adaptive Pathways' considers the differing student cohorts and responds to their needs within the curriculum (Figure 14.4). KS3 students are prepared for appropriate KS4 pathways by taking into account their starting points and potential, highlighted through their KS2 attainment. The *NSR Pathway* addresses KS3 students who require a different curriculum model with 'catch up' in English and Maths skills. The *Engage and Achieve Unit* (EAU) sits outside the pathways and constitutes KS3-4 supplementary provision. The EAU intent is targeted learning for students with sequential gaps in their knowledge and skills. In both cases, Academic Intervention is the only way to ensure these students are able to fulfil their potential, so that they access the mainstream curriculum successfully. The case study linked to the EAU model is located in Part III, Chapter 5.

The *Secondary Ready Pathways*, as outlined in the first and second models above (*Half Way House and Work Related Learning Models*) are anticipated for the majority of Year 7 students who do not fall significantly below the KS2 national standard in English and Mathematics.

### Non Secondary Ready

For schools, that serve a significant proportion of students with significantly below national averages, in relation to KS2 attainment/standards; an accredited 'pathways' model (see case study below) can be structured around Ark Mastery English and Mathematics/Passport to Maths,[10] Computing Skills, Art, Prince's Trust (*Employability and life skills*). The inclusion of financial literacy, oracy skills (ESB) and digital skills means that students gain the Mandatory Key Skills. Through 'Pathways', students are able to spend additional time in a primary style learning environment. Clearly, the number of groups for each Pathway is dependent on the nature of the school student profile and its resources. Schools with a lower ability intake could create more than one group of this nature; some schools may not require one at all.

This case study illustrates the Pathway implementation, where the main focus is on English and maths given the students' low starting points.

---

**CASE STUDY: ACADEMY IN NORTHAMPTONSHIRE**

The 'Not Secondary Ready (NSR)' group typically presented with standardised SATs scores below 95.

The students in the English 'catch-up' group follow the Mastery foundation route and study the same text as their peers, but on a more accessible level. Most of the students study the abridged version of *Oliver Twist* combined with extracts from the original text.

The NSR group follow the Foundation Pathway, spending three lessons weekly on the literature text with two further English lessons per week, on a fortnightly rota. Three of the four lessons focus on English Mastery Writing.[11] Students improve their writing skills through the booklet's three levels. In these sessions, the NSR group work through Mastery writing using booklet 1.

During the library lesson students read with the Accelerated Reader, completing quizzes, and 'reading for pleasure'. In the reading for pleasure sessions, the students read through a class reader and learn new vocabulary.

Students follow Numeracy (four x one-hour lessons per week); two out of the four lessons constitute Passport Maths.[12]

The academy is prioritising the importance of reading, and consequently, writing skills. A significant number of students arrive in Year 7 with reading ages below ten years of age. Students who identify as 'red flag profiles' are classified as emergency intervention with a specific needs profile; these students are re-engaged with 'Read, Write Inc. Fresh Start'.[13]

The '*Vocational*' band is appropriate for students who aspire to a vocational or technical career rather than an academic one. CEIAG would advise on the right subject combinations where the curriculum pathway/subject combinations permit. Curriculum guided learning hours in EBacc subjects are reduced in favour of increased hours in a technology subject, such as Food or Design Technology, with a view to this leading onto a vocational route at GCSE. Along with Science, Maths, Computing, and Technology, students start to prepare for KS4 courses, such as Engineering.

Creating space, time and funds for an '*Engage and Achieve' unit* enables students who have missed large portions of schooling, or who have been excluded from lessons, not to fall behind academically and become disengaged from learning.

For these students, and the NSR group, their learning should follow a bespoke curriculum model. Both groups have different needs, either because they are removed from lessons resulting from internal exclusion, or because they need 'NSR catch-up'. A model that allows for small group work and one-to-one is key. It also makes best use of the pupil premium funding and 'catch-up' funding to contribute towards staffing subject specialists within this unit.

## Engaging the most aspirational

In addition to a broad and balanced curriculum, we consider the needs of aspirational and the most able students. Creating a targeted and super-curricular programme which takes place outside of lessons can be used as a vehicle to not only inspire these students in lessons, but also to prepare them for further and higher education. The programme activities students could include:

- specialist trips to areas of historical, cultural or scientific interest;
- mentoring from older students;
- visits to universities and local employers;
- a suggested reading list;
- lectures delivered at lunchtimes by staff volunteers with lunch provided.

Programmes of this nature foster aspiration and encourage students to develop a love of learning.[14] In the interests of equity, all students would greatly benefit from inspirational learning and re-engaging with a creative and stimulating curriculum. Each

| | 1 | 2 | 3 | 4 | 5 | 6 | 7 | 8 | 9 | 10 | 11 | 12 | 13 | 14 | 15 | 16 | 17 | 18 | 19 | 20 | 21 | 22 | 23 | 24 | 25 | 26 | 27 | 28 | 29 | 30 | 31 | 32 | 33 | 34 | 35 | 36 | 37 | 38 | 39 | 40 | 41 | 42 | 43 | 44 | 45 | 46 | 47 | 48 | 49 | 50 |
|---|---|---|---|---|---|---|---|---|---|---|---|---|---|---|---|---|---|---|---|---|---|---|---|---|---|---|---|---|---|---|---|---|---|---|---|---|---|---|---|---|---|---|---|---|---|---|---|---|---|---|
| **Sec Ready** | Maths | | | | | | | | English | | | | | | | | | Science | | | | | | | | History | | | | Geography | | | | Core PE | | Cit. | | MFL | | | MES | | DT | | Arts | | | | Co | |
| **Vocational** | Maths | | | | | | | | English | | | | | | | | | Science | | | | | | | | History | | | | Geog | | | Core PE | | | Cit. | | DT | | | MES | | MFL | | Arts | | | | Co | |
| **NSR** | Maths | | | | | | | | English | | | | | | | | | Core PE | | | | | | | | Primary topic style lessons in one bespoke classroom | | | | | | | | | | | | | | | | | | | | | | | | |

**FIGURE 14.1** Adaptive Curriculum Pathways

*co = Computing

Copyright Nick Haddon

would come away with a 'take-away', in line with their own starting point, fostering academic knowledge, creative skills and cultural capital.

## Lecture style delivery

A fortnightly subject 'lecture', led by one experienced member of staff and supported by other teachers (who could benefit as a CPD exercise) and/or teaching assistants has great benefits. Giving students timetabled 'lecture style' lessons can be an extremely powerful tool for the following reasons:

- Staffing costs are reduced as support staff are used to help supervise/guide students.
- Students perceive these sessions as 'different'; the unique aspect supports retention of key information.
- Teaching techniques/formative assessment are easily modelled for professional development.
- Students are exposed to a style of teaching, they will encounter in further and higher education.
- Students make Cornell style notes during the session or use a graphic organiser.
- Teacher uses a visualiser to profile examples of students' work; students share their work developing confidence in oracy/presentation skills.
- The session can be used to deliver a whole school aspect; such as distinguishing 'fake news' for citizenship.

## Ensuring value for money

With schools in only 18/553 constituencies being better off in real world terms in 2019 than in 2015,[15] schools are increasingly rationalising staffing expenditure in relation to curriculum. Staffing costs generally represent 70 per cent of total school expenditure.[16] These are a direct consequence of the number of students on roll, but importantly, reflect the intent, implementation and impact of the curriculum planning. The financial decisions taken, whether these are imposed through constraints, or for other reasons, will reflect a school's priorities.

OFSTED are researching new methods that examine schools' financial decision making as part of the leadership and management and quality of education judgements. Professor Muijs is quoted as saying:

> We will be looking at financial decision making on inspection, to see whether this gives us more insight into the quality of leadership and management.[17]

In the light of this, leaders, should be prepared to explain why staffing decisions have been made, and how ringfenced funds have been deployed towards an equitable and inclusive curriculum for all students. By comparing outcomes with the average cost of a lesson,[18] leaders can generate a clear picture of which teams are delivering 'value for money'.

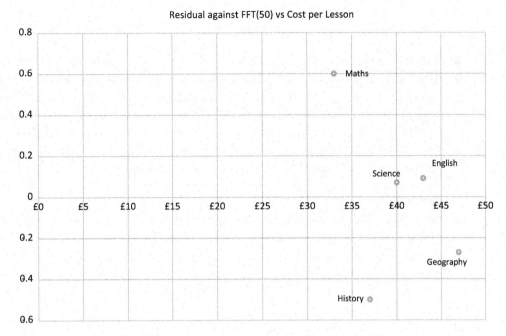

**FIGURE 14.2** An example of how subject performance can be quickly compared to lesson cost to assess 'value for money'
Copyright Nick Haddon

Figure 14.2 shows a simple version of how this could look. FFT(50) is used below but could easily be replaced with whichever target setting method the school uses. It is clear to see which subjects are delivering the best 'value for money' in terms of outcomes for students. In this example, History and Geography are clearly a concern evidencing a high cost per lesson with negative outcomes. The reasons can be investigated along with evidence from work scrutiny, Pupil Progress Reviews and so on. There may of course be other factors such as staff absence, or insufficient professional support for staff, that influence student outcomes.

All these calculations provide another strand of valuable hard data that form part of the professional dialogue, exploring how best a school can deliver a curriculum in line with its intent. Forward planning in this manner allows schools to migrate into the staffing structure they want in the best interests of the students. This potentially avoids restructuring which is costly and most importantly, unsettles and demotivates staff and students. The instability can disrupt the sequence of learning and have a detrimental impact on the outcomes and experiences of students.

## Funding an Engage and Achieve Unit

This dedicated space supports students who are removed from lessons, or facilitate reintegrating students back into school. If we assume a typical scenario where ten students might have fairly regular access to this space, we can consider how this space could be funded. This unit is staffed with subject specialists so that students get the best learning. These hours should be planned in at the curriculum planning stage, and not as an afterthought, deploying residual 'unspent hours of leftover' staffing.

- Firstly for pupil premium students, this would be a viable use of the £935 per year.
- If we assume 27.7 per cent of the students accessing this space would be pupil premium (as this was the national figure for 2018), this would potentially be 14 x £935 = £13,090. Coupled with the £4386 age weighted pupil unit funding (national average) this would generate an additional £61,404.
- For any students with behavioural SEN needs, this hub is likely to be a core part of the day-to-day strategy for managing these students. The amount that would be factored in would depend on the SEND and Additional Educational Needs funding, but in some schools, this could be significant.
- Student support hours required on EHCPs outside of lessons can be covered in this space, particularly if 'small group work' is a recommendation.
- It is also worth factoring in the significant cost that many schools spend per year on alternative provision to manage those students who are not permanently excluded but may be accessing another provider for a proportion of the week. The cost of these placements can be around £17,000 for a full-time placement in an AP (Figure 14.3).
- Three students accessing full-time schooling as opposed to being directed towards alternative provision would save £51,000 per annum. This could cover the cost of potentially two specialist members of staff. The students would also be far more likely to be accessing quality curriculum and completing a higher number of approved qualifications.

Figure 14.3 illustrates the potential high expenditure associated with a FTE placement in every key stage. Consideration of disruptions to students' life chances needs to be taken into account with the real possibility of unsuccessful GCSE outcomes. Schools need

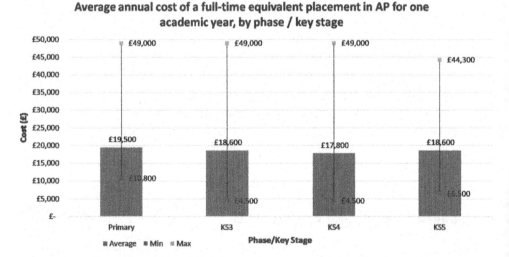

**FIGURE 14.3** The true cost of alternative provision by key stage

Source: Department for Education (2018a) *Alternative Provision Market Analysis.* London: Department for Education.

to reflect *long term* on the potential cost of losing students and the associated expenditure, and balance this against the short- to medium-term costs of establishing the Unit. A multi-academy trust typically may top slice up to 10 per cent of an academy's budget to resource its centralised staffing infrastructure, whilst possibly off rolling students or placing them in an AP. Retaining students in their learning will pay greater dividends in the long run.

## MODEL 4: CHOOSING PATHWAYS

Figure 14.4 is intended to provide a bespoke set of teaching hours dependent on the individual students' needs. For schools with a lower ability intake there would most likely be more 'pathway 3' type groups. In a school where students are skewed towards high prior attaining, more 'pathway 1' type groups would predominate.

For students with scaled scores below 95, accessing EBacc subjects may not be the best option, as these students should focus on improving their English and Maths. It is essential to remember that career choices should be the determining factor above all else (Part VII, Chapter 19). As an example, if a student with a SATs scaled score of 120 wants to train to be an engineer, pharmaceutical lab technician, or construction designer, a pathway leading to a vocational/technical course would be the most appropriate. Therefore, a T-level leading to HE or an eventual Higher Apprenticeship, might be the best Level 3 pathway. Students with lower scaled scores need the best opportunity to progress onto suitable Level 3 courses. These may well include T-levels. The transformative effect of engaging students in practical activity that fits in with their ambitions motivates them to remain focused and to enjoy learning.

Pathway 3 allows for increased employer engagement during the vocational option time; this is intended to replicate the proposed style of the T-level qualifications. At this point, it is equally feasible for students to follow qualifications such as Prince's Trust or ASDAN.

Graveney Academy illustrates a pathways approach to curriculum with a focus on work related activities, providing a real scope for 'closing the gap.' Attitudes to learning beyond the classroom are seen as key to developing students, including an overnight residential. The curriculum is implemented through an accredited bespoke programme of physical and creative skills, and volunteering experiences.

'A Next Steps' booklet demonstrates how the KS3 outcomes inform the pathways into KS4 options. In KS4, the curriculum for English and Maths is informed by the needs of three distinct student cohorts.

### CASE STUDY: GRAVENEY ACADEMY, LONDON

*Accredited KS3 Diplomas rewards*: Excellent Academic Progress, Exceptional Attitude to Learning, Commitment to Learning Beyond the Classroom through a Graduation process.[19]

KS4 Careers/Work Related/Enterprise Curriculum: to learn through work, for work and about work, to become aware of possible career pathways, transferable employment skills and personal finance issues.

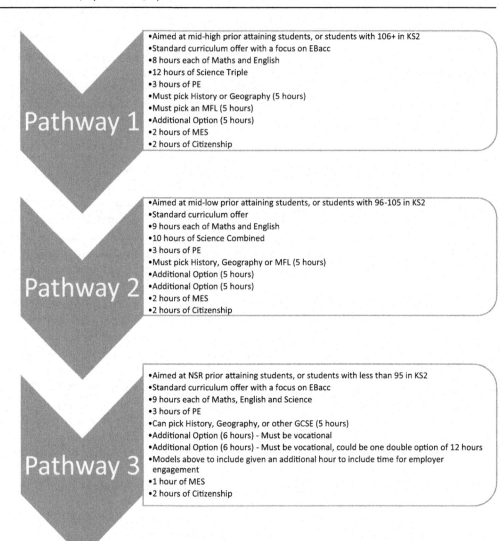

**FIGURE 14.4** A KS4 pathways approach for students based on their KS2 starting points or CATS scores
Copyright Nick Haddon

## Post-16 curriculum modelling

In much the same way, we consider students' individual needs and create a bespoke programme of study in KS5. A number of schools adopt this approach. One such, Ormiston Bushfield Academy's model, separates[20] students into pathways based on their GCSE results. For example, a student achieving five 9–4 GCSE is directed towards the 'blended pathway' which encourages a mix of BTEC and A-level qualifications.

King Edward VI in Nuneaton[21] has a well thought out website which arranges courses into clusters such as 'People, Law and Government', including vocational options alongside traditional A-levels. Within each potential career pathway, all students are catered for. Bespoke entry requirements are also included, so the school is able to cater for a diverse intake of students.

It is also important to include ample opportunity for timetabled independent study lessons for completion of assignments. This means the school can ensure all students are meeting their guided learning hours, and for students this develops the independence skills and work ethic required for their next step.

## Summary

By adopting a pathway approach in both KS3 and KS4 curricula, individual students' needs can be catered for. Schools who manage to successfully implement a model of this nature are demonstrating a clear 'intent' that strives for all students to achieve their potential.

A 'one-size-fits-all' approach to curriculum planning will always leave some students behind. Having a well-staffed and well managed Engage and Achieve Unit which students regularly access to ensure they cover key educational concepts and skills will ensure the curriculum does not leave behind the most vulnerable. Making good use of 'catch-up 'funding and disadvantaged funding to employ subject specialists is integral to an inclusive and equitable curriculum. A bespoke model for differing abilities ensures that all students focus on the most important aspects of their curriculum, allowing students with lower standardised scores in English and Maths, the time and expertise to improve, whilst those students who excel in these subjects can deepen and broaden their experience.

It is possible that a broad and balanced National Curriculum is delivered during a two-year KS3 alongside offering a reduced set of GCSE options in KS4. This will suit those students who need the additional curriculum time to adequately prepare for GCSE examinations and achieve successful outcomes. The key here is to ensure that the specific *elements* of the National Curriculum are being met in KS3 through the selection and sequencing of the knowledge and skills taught to students. This means that for those who choose this as a GCSE subject, they gain a solid foundation that is extended and consolidated in KS4.

In relation to finances, schools need to prioritise which elements of their staffing and curriculum they wish to protect. Schools and multi-academy Trusts are always faced with a financial balancing act; leaders, governors and Trustees have a choice about what to fund. This refers back to the Vision and intent of curriculum. These priorities might include investing in a Mandatory Key Skills programme, quality alternative provision for NSR students, a drop-down day for WRL or cultural capital, or ensuring continuity in sequencing of learning for excluded students and others.

## Notes

1    The National Curriculum.com (2020) The National Curriculum.com. Available at: https://thenationalcurriculum.com/the-app/ (Accessed: 3 January 2020).

2    University of Cambridge (2019) www.cambridgeenglish.org/images/168750-teaching-history-through-english-a-clil-approach.pdf. Available at: www.cambridgeenglish.org/images/168750-teaching-history-through-english-a-clil-approach.pdf (Accessed: 5 January 2020).

3  Department for Education (2018) The National Curriculum. Available at: www.gov.uk/national-curriculum/key-stage-3-and-4 (Accessed: 5 November 2019).

4  Department for Education (2011) The Framework for the National Curriculum: A report by the Expert Panel for the National Curriculum review, https://assets.publishing.service.gov.uk: Department for Education.

5  OFSTED (2015) Key Stage 3: The wasted years?, https://assets.publishing.service.gov.uk: OFSTED, Crown Copyright.

6  Westminster Academy (2019) Curriculum. Available at: www.westminsteracademy.org.uk/ (Accessed: 11 December 2019).

7  Westminster Academy (2019) Curriculum – Key Stage 3. Available at: www.westminsteracademy.org.uk/224/curriculum-key-stage-3 (Accessed: 11 December 2019).

8  Complete Careers (2019) The Gatsby benchmarks – a summary by Complete Careers. Available at: https://complete-careers.com/gatsby-benchmarks/ (Accessed: 9 November 2019).

9  Department for Education (2013) National Curriculum in England. Available at: www.gov.uk/government/publications/ (Accessed: 1 November 2019).

10  Mastery Programme (2019) Mastery Programmes. Available at: https://arkonline.org/ (Accessed: 23 December 2019).

11  English Mastery Programme (2019) English Mastery Programme. Available at: www.englishmastery.org/programme/ (Accessed: 23 December 2019).

12  Maths Mastery Programme (2019) Maths Mastery Programme. Available at: https://arkonline.org/news/mathematics-mastery-needs-new-recruits (Accessed: 23 December 2019).

13  Ruth Miskin Training (2019) Read Write Inc Fresh Start. Available at: www.ruthmiskin.com/en/programmes/fresh-start/ (Accessed: 26 December 2019).

14  The Brilliant Club (2020) The Brilliant Club. Available at: https://thebrilliantclub.org/strategies-for-stretching-your-most-able-students/ (Accessed: 1 March 2020).

15  S. Weale (2019) Most schools in England worse off next year than in 2015, study says. Available at: www.theguardian.com/education/2019/nov/09/most-schools-england-worse-off-next-year-than-2015-study-says (Accessed: 17 November 2019).

16  Department for Education (2018) School resource management: top 10 planning checks for governors. Available at: www.gov.uk/guidance/school-resource-management-top-10-planning-checks-for-governors (Accessed: 27 November 2019).

17  J. Roberts (2020) School finances could face even more Ofsted scrutiny. Available at: www.tes.com/news/school-finances-could-face-even-more-ofsted-scrutiny (Accessed: 18 January 2020).

18  Total staffing costs for this department divided by the number of lessons delivered per annum by these staff.

19  Graveney Academy (2019) Curriculum Intent Statement. Available at: www.graveney.org/Curriculum/ (Accessed: 22 December 2019).

20  Ormiston Bushfield Academy (2019) Ormiston Bushfield Academy. Available at: www.bushfield.co.uk/sixthform/curriculum-pathways/ (Accessed: 9 December 2020).

21  King Edward VI College (2019) King Edward VI College. Available at: https://kecnuneaton.ac.uk/ (Accessed: 9 December 2020).

# 15

# Impact: Quality assuring education

## Introduction

> If leaders have an *accurate evaluative understanding of current curriculum practice and have identified appropriate steps to improve curriculum quality and develop curriculum expertise across the school,* inspectors will evaluate 'intent' favourably when reaching the holistic quality of education judgement.
>
> (EIF 2019 OFSTED; our emphasis)[1]

To all intents and purposes this is broadly how OFSTED might define a whole school quality assurance system. We propose a simple process that forensically evaluates these factors:

- impact of the curriculum against its intent;
- implementation of the sequencing of the knowledge and skills towards agreed end points;
- how the intended curriculum addresses social disadvantage through closing gaps in students' knowledge and skills and develops cultural capital;
- the typical quality of all students' educational experience in and out of the lessons (barriers and facilitators);
- the progress that students make against their potential and the standards they attain across the curriculum, across subjects and key stages, including their attitudes to learning.

The versatility of the quality assurance process described here means that it can be used within subjects, departments and across key stages from primary through to sixth form as we are focusing on students' acquisition of knowledge and skills, and not the 'teacher' or teaching. In addition, at a time when students are learning through a blend of online learning and classroom learning, it give insights into the usefulness and impact of both.

The system is called a *Pupil Progress Review* because it does precisely what it says on the tin! The intent, implementation and impact of the curriculum is viewed through the lens of the students. We would all agree that curriculum intent should be equitable and inclusive. Therefore, the system of evaluating this is both equitable and inclusive for staff and students, moving away from judgements set in stone to professionally evaluative and developmental next steps for staff.

At the same time as the process seeks to identify barriers and facilitators in learning within student cohorts, or for individual students, it also offers a genuine model of professional development and capacity building for teaching staff. There are key differences between a 'learning walk' and a Pupil Progress Review (PPR). The PPR is specific in focus and impact and is captured through what students acquire in sequenced knowledge and skills over time, as opposed to the curriculum intent. A 'learning walk' dips in and out of lessons and risks not gathering tangible information that can usefully inform middle and senior leaders on the quality of curriculum. The PPR, on the other hand, is a powerful tool that leads to continuous improvements in learning. This enables leaders to improve curriculum quality and develop curriculum expertise across the school.

Throughout the book we focus on developing students as 'leaders of own learning'. The entire thrust of cognitive science/metacognition; the research that lies behind the EIF is to develop self-reflective learners. Therefore, what better way to demonstrate the impact of the curriculum, the patterns of students' learning over time, the quality of teaching and effectiveness of assessment on driving students' progress, than through speaking with students about the knowledge and skills they have acquired and can apply.

We have included examples in the appendices from schools that have embedded PPR quality assurance systems.

## Overview: PPR–single joined-up educational conversation

OFSTED's inspection methodology underpins Figure 15.1 through identifying the sources of evidence specific to curriculum implementation. These include schemes of work and discussions with middle leaders and teachers, but most importantly, 'assessing observations of and interviews with pupils or classes in lessons, including scrutinising the pupils' work'.

In evaluating the implementation of the curriculum, these are the points of accepted wisdom that inspectors (EIF) look for in relation to the impact of teaching and assessment on students' learning. The expectations are teachers,[2]

1.  with expert knowledge of the subjects; are supported to address the gaps in their knowledge, so they do not disadvantage their students, through ineffective teaching;

2.  enable students to understand key concepts, encouraging appropriate discussion, checking students' understanding and correcting misunderstandings;

3.  ensure that students embed key concepts and knowledge in their long-term memory, apply them fluently;

4.  use assessment to check students' understanding in order to inform teaching, and to help students use knowledge fluently, develop their understanding, and not simply memorise disconnected facts.

**Single joined-up educational conversation**

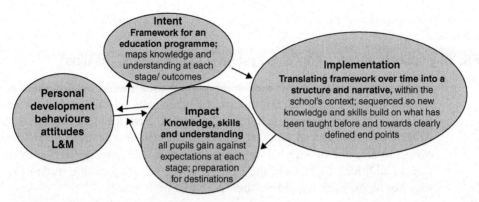

**FIGURE 15.1** How the new Education Inspection Framework judges sources of evidence specific to curriculum implementation
Copyright Meena Kumari Wood

**Pupil Progress Review: Evaluating impact of curriculum**

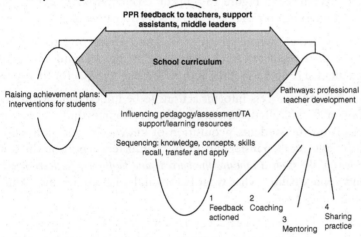

**FIGURE 15.2** How the process of Pupil Progress Review effectively evaluates the curriculum
Copyright Meena Kumari Wood

In the above PPR diagrammatic process (Figure 15.2), the focus is shifted away from the *teacher* and moves to the *impact of the teaching of the curriculum* in its broadest sense, upon students' learning in the here and now and over time. This means that the actual processes of learning, however these are arrived at, are evaluated for their effectiveness. This becomes a powerful tool within the school's quality assurance process. The *Pupil Progress Review Quality Assurance* system does precisely all of the above.

There are two key outcomes from the process. At the heart of the process is the actual PPR that can lead to identifying interventions and/or support for individual students which is captured in a *Raising Achievement Plan*. At the same time, rather than senior and middle leaders observing teachers and creating 'grades on their quality of teaching', we use the findings from this process to inform continuous *professional development pathways* for individual teachers and learning support staff.

## PPR: Why schools should adopt this system – 13 compelling reasons!

1. Students, who may not be *making the progress* they should against their potential and based on their starting points, are principally selected to be reviewed in the lessons. Other criteria include: students who have low reading age, dyslexia, ADHD or other special educational needs, and those who have missed lessons, owing to absence or internal/external exclusion, ethnicity, gender or disadvantage. In addition, the focus of the PPR may well be on more able students as they may not be on track to achieve their potential high grades.

2. The PPR process can effectively evaluate the experiences of students across Year/Key Stage/subject. Concerns about specific students can be evaluated across the subjects. This will help identify the reasons behind the *spikey profile of their learning* with peaks of understanding in some subjects and troughs of 'blind spots' in others. In the case of significant underachievement and/or other barriers to learning, middle leaders put in place a Raising Achievement Plan (RAP) which you can see in Figure 15.8 in this chapter. A RAP revisits students to assess their progress against the plan and this forms part of the process.

3. For the sake of balance, when selecting students, identifying those who are achieving above their predicted levels gives insights into learning processes that work best for them and might usefully inform *learning strategies* for their peers.

4. The feedback from the process informs actions to be undertaken by the teacher, and/or support staff; typically informing teaching, resources and assessment. The primary focus is on the students' acquisition of knowledge and skills and their metacognition skills (recall, transfer and apply). Ultimately, capturing the teaching through the *lens of the student captures the barriers and facilitators for learning*, during the lesson and contextualises what went before and what comes after. This then, exemplifies the *learning sequence*.

5. At *individual teacher level*, the process identifies strengths and any gaps in a teacher's subject expertise that might lead to *'ineffective teaching'*(EIF).[3] Leaders provide the necessary professional support through guidance on teaching/assessment strategies, creating opportunities for the teacher to visit other teachers' lessons, shadow and, or team teach, provide a mentor or coach. The outcomes from the PPR process are logged as evidence towards *continuing performance management* for the teacher; assisting with continuous staff development, along with other evidence, such as appraisal and formal lesson observation. This is a *three-dimensional* approach to developing staff.

6. In *evaluating curriculum*, PPRs are conducted on lessons or year groups and assess the *quality of learning across Key Stages*. It is possible to test out the sequencing of knowledge and skills over time. EIF: Curriculum is sequenced so that new knowledge and skills build on what has been taught before and pupils can work towards clearly defined end points.

7. PPRs across a Key Stage determines whether the learning in KS4 is more effective than KS3, or vice versa, as the school may be more reliant on academic interventions in KS4. The focus could include evaluating whether out of class interventions are proportionate or compensating for ineffective teaching in either Key Stage.

8. Conducting a PPR across a suite of subjects in a faculty or department gives insights into the variability, enabling middle leaders to identify good and weaker practice and why students achieve better with certain teachers or subjects, than others.

9. Conducting a PPR into online learning ascertains the impact and usefulness to students and identifies those students with variable digital and metacognition skills in navigating online learning. Factors such as focus, concentration are key to learning online. What do students do when they come across obstacles to learning independently?

10. A departmental in-depth focus is conducted by SLT and the curriculum leader of the department. The focus can also include a *peer review*, by including a curriculum leader of another department. Subjects pairings can be identified as Maths and Science, Maths and DT, English and History, MFL and English, Geography and RE, Citizenship and RE, Media Studies and Music, Media Studies and Drama, Art and DT, Food Technology and Textiles. This gives good insights into how *core subjects are threaded* across the curriculum such as English, Maths and Science.

11. A PPR conducted on a *cross curriculum theme* can include implementation of teacher assessment/feedback/dialogic marking; literacy, numeracy, oracy, digital skills, or good practice in developing students' metacognition skills and attitudes to learning. In this way, it is possible to evaluate the quality of cross school practice and impact on students; *identify strengths for sharing and weaker areas* that need addressing.

12. A PPR *identifies good practice* within all subjects; *recall, transfer and apply techniques;* formative feedback (teacher/peer/self); formative assessment against success criteria; questioning; impact of the subject curriculum (sequencing of knowledge and skills through spiral curriculum/interleaving and other outlines); impact of teaching/ learning assistants in and out of lesson.

13. When communicating with parents it is possible to provide specific feedback on students' *observed performance* in lessons, drawing from PPRs conducted over the course of the academic year. For instance, if a student does not complete a response to teacher feedback or lacks concentration/focus in lessons.

## PPR: Getting started on the process

The Pupil Progress Review (PPR) process commences with selecting three students, identified from the school's data tracker in particular subjects/Key Stage/Year group. This is determined by the progress they currently make. The actual PPR should take around 20 minutes in the lesson, with ten minutes' preparation time to collect information relating to the students beforehand. Using the questioning prompts in

Figure 15.7 (p. 183) and by reviewing their books, the reviewer can evidence the sequencing of knowledge and skills, students' experiences of learning in the subjects or subjects, the progress they make over time. This is gathered through evaluating predicted targets against the actual standards.

It is an excellent opportunity for reviewers to evaluate first hand the impact of graphic/knowledge organisers, if these or other methods are being used by the school to assess whether students are able to recall, transfer and apply knowledge (their meta-cognition skills) as well as their attitudes to learning and behaviours.

The PPR observer is able to evaluate the aspects of effective teaching and barriers to learning, not only for the three selected students, but by extension for their peers. During the PPR, it is proposed that the reviewer observes and samples a couple of other students' work to compare. This approach as we can see sits perfectly with the OFSTED inspection methodology. It allows a more in-depth look at the impact of curriculum on student cohorts, rather than viewing a teaching group as a collective.

The impact of teaching and the appropriateness of the curriculum are importantly interpreted through the student's lens. Prime in this are:

- standards and sequencing of knowledge/skills;
- gaps in learning;
- impact of teacher feedback/student follow-up;
- metacognition skills;
- questioning techniques; extending and consolidating understanding;
- addressing subject misconceptions;
- relevance of tasks and activities/pace of learning for students' abilities/ educational needs;
- barriers stalling learning;
- factors facilitating or accelerating the acquisition of knowledge, skills, concepts over time.

A combination of work scrutiny and questioning of students on their knowledge and skills take place during the lesson. This helps gather reflections on the students' educational experiences and the progress they are making. The questions in Figure 15.7 (p. 183) can also be used outside the lessons with a focus group of students and their work. This helps corroborate the evidence from the PPR review gained from the lessons.

More specifically, the PPR reviewer can observe the impact of teaching on learning as reflected in the following:

- assessment, verbal and written/peer/self-feedback and next steps (follow up of Next Actions);
- teachers' expectations of students;
- the use of information on students' ability levels/progress/prior knowledge to inform and plan apposite tasks, activities, questioning, pace of learning and outcomes;

- whether greater challenge exists for all students, especially More Able, to reach the higher levels and fulfil their academic potential.
- disadvantaged, lower ability students; those with special educational needs and learning difficulties access learning successfully;
- reframing of activities/tasks during lessons, takes place, if necessary, *after* checking students' understanding of knowledge and skills;
- structured learning opportunities exist for extended writing skills and presentation skills;
- using sophisticated subject specific extended responses whether literacy, oracy and numeracy skills are practised (including Tier 2/3 vocabulary; referencing skills, computational and digital skills);
- higher order thinking, critical reasoning and analytical skills: using students' prior learning as a resource; students become '*leaders of own learning*';
- collaborative approaches between teacher and TA facilitates 1:1 and small group learning;
- students assisted in consolidating metacognition skills – 'recall, transfer and apply'
- deployment of digital resources (including for homework) to consolidate, extend and deepen learning.

## Evaluating and not judging

Figures 15.3–15.6 illustrate a Pupil Progress Review in a History lesson as part of a KS3-4 departmental humanities review. More able students were selected as GCSE outcomes did not evidence the high grades that most students were predicted and did not reflect their academic potential. During this PPR, the learning of more able students was stymied by all students working on the same task and at the same pace (recall of facts). Students were not given sufficient opportunities to transfer and apply the knowledge or to address the source evidence in depth, and importantly, to develop their extended writing skills.

All students evidenced sound verbal recall of the facts halfway through the lesson as this was a revision lesson. Therefore, most would have been sufficiently confident to start practising more sophisticated writing, using their source retrieval and analysis skills. Books evidenced good factual recall, but not the higher order critical thinking skills. The final evaluation at the end of the PPR is a comment on the quality of students' educational experiences in the lesson and over time and therefore, the facilitators and barriers in learning. The action points for the teacher target practical professional strategies (template and example of whole school subject analysis are available in Appendix 15.1, at www.routledge.com/9780367900878).

The action points following the PPR are agreed with the teacher, after reviewing the evidence that is gathered. For the PPR to be effective, it is important that the discussion that takes place has engages the teacher and is used constructively as professional development. Actions in this case include shadow opportunities for the teacher to observe good practice and a follow-up PPR.

## PUPIL PROGRESS REVIEWS

## XXXX SCHOOL – Pupil Learning and Progress Review (PPR)

Teacher: T1     Year Group: 9 Set 2     Subject: History     Student Observer: Ob 1     Date: 13 /07/16

Learning Objectives: WW1: Battle of the Sommerole of General Haig using source evidence to develop extended writing

| Student Name: | Student Name: Pupil 1 | Student Name: Pupil 2 |
|---|---|---|
| **Working towards:** | Working towards: 5+ (secure) | Working towards: 5-(developing) |
| **FFT 20 Target:** | FFT20 Target: 6 | FFT 20 Target: 6 |
| **Attendance Pattern:** | Attendance Pattern: | Attendance Pattern: |
| **Student Group**: | Student Group: | Student Group: |
| **(PP, SEND, EAL, G&T, other)** | (PP, SEND, EAL, G&T, other) | (*PP*, SEND, EAL, G&T, other) |

## Challenge/support in tasks/activities

*Challenge in task is insufficiently challenging for those @ 6+ to acquire mastery.*

Pupils 1+2 working at 5+ and 5-; both pupils are aiming for Target 6 but written work – *standard of extended writing does not reflect this high level, although pupils have good grasp of information and knowledge.*

Pupil 1's work is well marked against LO: describe 2 different interpretations (the Learning Objective); he can articulate his reasoning effectively to the reviewer.

Pupil 1 reports lesson is a revision but today focuses on why interpretations have changed over time.

Too much time spent revising 2 interpretations (first half of term) so that pupils have only completed 2 questions – would have had greater gains in progress and learning by focussing on extended writing / skills of *retrieving source evidence*. Pupils working below 5 show limited superficial understanding. Those working at 5 + and 5- lack challenge in the current task as they are reasonably confident with the subject matter. Pupil 2 reported that the task is a repeat and did not know 'why they were going over it again'.

Challenge for pupils could come from manipulating *specialist vocabulary*, encouraging pupils to transfer to different historical context i.e. compare and contrast WWI Butcher of Somme with any situation that they may know in current day war and this would help develop SMSC.

FIGURE 15.3 Pupil progress review example – History lesson

## Assessment for learning and literacy/numeracy

> Monitoring and checking of learning (peer reviews, self-assessment, mini plenaries, modelling of answers/use of Directed Activities Related to Texts (DARTs) / scaffold materials / writing frames / teacher checking learning and reframing activity before students start task (if necessary)

> Differentiated questioning techniques: deeper questioning for more able/ support for less able

> Assessment of books: teacher feedback and impact of Next Steps (challenge and consolidation of gaps)

> Literacy, Language and Numeracy skills / presentation of work (is their work neat, well labelled, presented well?)

*Questioning techniques*: targeted and extended questioning also used – 'helping hand' is a good technique. This helps pupils model answers and ensures that less able and less confident pupils contribute to Q+A and are learning.

*Assessment/Spelling/Presentation* in Pupil 2's book shows no sign of feedback or evidence of marking. Work on 23/01/16 not marked evidences serious errors in spelling. Teacher's detailed narrative in WWW/EBI would benefit pupils through precise feedback and Next Steps; focus on extended writing skills would help move pupil to next level.

Pupils respond well to the excellent prompts on board on the pros/cons of General Haig as the 'Butcher General'.

*No dictionaries* available to students and self-checking not in evidence hence poor SPG in the books scrutinised. Literacy errors not picked up by teacher through assessment and marking. Pupils given glossary of specialist vocabulary and could use this well within context but this could have been extended to other contexts.

Depth of knowledge and skills

*Retrieving and analysing* source evidence requires *higher order skills* (critical, persuasive and high-level literacy skills) – pupils are not given sufficient practice in effective answers using these skills.

Too little time is spent on this task (10 mins before the end of lesson). Therefore extension/challenge especially for higher level pupils missed opportunity to move to *mastery*.

FIGURE 15.4  Pupil progress review example – History lesson

## Behaviour for learning

➢ Are students off task? Is there off task chatter (low level disruptive behaviour)
➢ Can students work independently/collaboratively – attitudes to learning?
➢ Attendance and punctuality to lesson

Good attitudes: pupils enthusiastic and keen and enjoying their learning. No off task chatter. Responsible learners but not evidencing leadership of learning/reflective learning as not given opportunities through deeper questioning and requiring students to develop extended writing skills.

## Summary evaluation

Describe what students have learnt:

- The knowledge/concepts or skills acquired in the subject
- The barriers or factors that have had an impact on their learning
- Refer to emerging/ developing/secure/ mastered age related expectations observed in lesson and over time for individual students you are observing
- Refer to learning and progress of their peers
- Refer to Go4Schools data on working towards and FFT 20 Target.

Students' progress is outstanding/good/requires improvement/inadequate because . . . . . . . . . . . .

- Good references to 'horrors' of WW1 on battlefield. Pupils can select suitable quotes to illustrate their subject knowledge. Extension to modern day wars would have challenged more able students using historical and current newspapers sources (also 'Dulce et Decorum est' – poem by Wilfred Owen on horrors of battlefield, studied in English anthology)
- Spoken skills and subject knowledge are good and most pupils can articulate effectively and make expected levels of progress with over time a small minority below 5 making secure progress (Go4Schools)
- More able pupils (6 and 5+) are plateauing and not making the progress they should
- There is too little challenge in written task and insufficient time spent in preparing all students for using the source evidence 'higher level' task; skills of thinking wider and drawing on other historical sources including contemporary issues and structuring writing skills; this means that attainment (secure and mastered) not evidenced for all pupils
- SPaG (errors in literacy – extended writing skills); precision in writing /including the use of specialist vocabulary is inconsistent across pupils' work – this is preventing pupils from making good progress in their writing skills as they work towards GCSE and will cap their development of these important skills.

**FIGURE 15.5** Pupil progress review example – History lesson

Action points for teacher:

- A differentiated task approach on one task with different activities linked to appropriate success criteria from below 5 to 6 so that more able pupils may fulfil potential and acquire mastery; PP pupils.
- Prioritise 'higher level' skills of analysis/critical thinking so that source evidence may be easily accessed by pupils and extended writing using English Literature techniques is practised.
- Present students with scaffolded writing and exemplars of good writing using source evidence
- Develop extended writing skills – SPG (greater accuracy and precision in writing) – homework task
- Precise Next Step for students in feedback/marking and identify SPG
- Develop SMSC through extension to using wider range of source evidence (practise compare and contrast: WWI/modern day and use of poem (building on recent anniversary of WW1: 1914–2014)

Feedback given and accepted /Teacher comments:
Next Steps agreed:
Date of next review:

FIGURE 15.6    Pupil progress review example – History lesson

## Pupil Progress Reviewer dialogue with student

✓ Can the student explain what they are learning?

✓ Is this a concept/skill/knowledge that they are familiar with or revision?

✓ Can he/she transfer this to another context – does he/she have a wider understanding of what he/she is learning?

✓ Can he/she demonstrate deeper understanding or a superficial understanding of what is being taught?

✓ What did he/she learn previously?

✓ What is he/she going to learn?

✓ How is the teacher's feedback and assessment helping the student to improve? Can the student give an example? Are Next Steps sfollowed through?

✓ Can the student give an example of a piece of work that they are proud of? How did the teacher help with his/her understanding of the concept/skills/knowledge?

✓ Is there a piece of work/unit/concept/skill that the student is struggling with? Has the teacher acknowledged this and given the student feedback / extension /consolidation that has helped?

FIGURE 15.7  Pupil Progress Reviewer dialogue with student

## Importance of PPR reviewer dialogue with students: 'Leaders of own learning'

### Gathering evidence

The *dialogue* that happens in lessons during class activities, or out of lesson has a clear focus on speaking with students about what they know or can do, what they remember in the sequence of learning and the effectiveness of feedback in helping them improve. Specific examples from their books/folders of work are referenced by the reviewer. The evidence gathered through the review is valid as the learning reflects the progress that students make from their starting points and their attainment at a given point in time. The following extracts in A and B are from actual PPR reviews conducted in schools by the subject leaders.

## (A) PPR focus on embedding concepts and addressing misconceptions

In these lessons visited, students' understanding of the knowledge would have been greatly enhanced by the teacher periodically checking concept acquisition, through higher order, targeted questioning in lessons, or reframing activities where students had not fully understood. In addition, allowing students to work on tasks at own pace and with different learning objectives would help those with specific educational needs.

1. In a French lesson, all Year 7 students displayed positive, enthusiastic attitudes to learning, yet, two-thirds had not fully grasped the *conceptual difference* between definite/indefinite articles, despite this being a key learning objective and a revision session. Questioning two 'more able' students, and reviewing their previous two months' work with them indicated that they were unable to give appropriate examples that distinguished between *le/la/les* and *du/de/des*.

2. *Pace of learning*; in History Year 10, short bursts of activity on a worksheet, did not give slower or less able students sufficient time to complete the task. Students had to outline *conceptual* reasons for Hitler's rise to power between 1929 – the Wall Street Crash up to 1934 and his appointment as Fuhrer. Most had accurately memorised details and facts regarding the rise of Hitler in the early 1930s during the Weimar Republic, evidenced through question and answer session and reflected in the written work. Questioning three students on the importance of the events leading to Hitler's rise to power and how this related to the start of the Second World War required conceptual thinking. Students needed to make connections; using skills of prediction and hypothesis. Only a handful of the most confident students were able to articulate a deeper understanding, when questioned. Most presented a superficial or partial grasp of the facts.

3. In the Science lesson, following questioning of three students, one student arrived at a very good understanding of *concept*: 'density–correlation of mass and volume' after the investigative practical. He articulated a clear explanation. Two others demonstrated insecure knowledge of the learning objective and one reported that she would not be able to complete the homework (write up) 'without googling the information'.

4. In some cases, *misconceptions* were not being addressed; in Spanish in Spanish (spellings, tenses), and Maths (algebraic equations in geometry and volume and area of cylinder). Over time, these misconceptions and partial understanding, were showing gaps in the written knowledge and skills. The gaps were reinforced through questioning of students with their work, outside of lessons, by the reviewer.

## (B) PPR: Impact of written/verbal feedback on progress over time

In the first example below if the teacher had checked that students had *completed the actions* detailed in her feedback, they would have benefited by extending and consolidating their knowledge in subsequent activities. In the second example, *referencing assessments against the subject success criteria* and identifying students' strengths and areas for development are helping students to make the progress they should. They become reflective and independent learners.

1.  In Geography, the facts of coastal processes and sea erosion were well understood by the three Year 10 students questioned during the lesson. However, clear feedback actions identified by the teacher in their books were not actioned by them all. This resulted in missed opportunities for students to broaden and deepen their understanding of the unit being taught over time and understanding the interconnectedness of coastal processes and coastal management.

2.  In an English Year 9 lesson, constructive feedback to students in their written work on the Christmas Carol meant that a student could easily articulate what he needed to do in the 'Do Now Action' to help him progress. He and other students were developing as leaders of their own learning and acquiring independent learning skills. Assessed work mapped against the success criteria for literature and language identified students' strengths and areas for development, in relation to conceptual knowledge and skills. The standards of work seen in the books of four students of low and middle ability were carefully presented, evidencing their enjoyment of the subject.

## Addressing underachievement through the RAP and PPR

A Raising Achievement Plan (RAP) arises out of a review of achievement data, absence from lessons, attitudes to learning and other pastoral/academic reasons, including literacy, numeracy or learning difficulties. Typically, it would be the Head of Year who receives the feedback from the subject leader, regarding the student's underachievement. This information is collated by subject into a grid (Figures 15.8 and 15.9).

The Head of Year has overall responsibility for presenting this RAP at review meetings, attended by curriculum middle leaders and senior leaders responsible for curriculum and behaviours. Each student is considered and the effectiveness of the strategies evaluated for impact. Barriers to learning are identified, along with strategies for improvement. These may be academic interventions, mentoring, pastoral support, deploying a teaching assistant, consulting the SENDCo and so on.

The student who is in the spotlight agrees to these. These are logged in an Individual Learning Plan or L2L Diary and the parent/s are informed. Dependent on the staffing context and size of the school, the monitoring of the strategies will typically be by the subject teacher through to Head of Year, or may involve the form tutor. If the student is significantly underachieving in only one or two subjects, then the most likely route is monitoring by the subject teacher and subject lead. If the student is underachieving in more than two subjects than the best route would be through the Head of Year and Form Tutor. Reviewing the students' progress can also form part of a PPR review within a subject. There are a number of additional benefits to this approach that serve schools well as a part of the overall quality assurance system.

## Recording Outcomes from PPRs

Through a *centralised spreadsheet, PPR outcomes are recorded alongside the students' names,* creating a detailed profile of student performance. Collating average grades for individual cohorts, by including residuals from data tracking makes it possible to ensure that this information is constantly triangulated against predicted levels/ grades.

These allow further *inferences to be drawn*. For example, the sheet could be filtered to review disadvantaged SEND and EAL students and their lesson experiences, the learning grades they have been apportioned and in which subjects. This allows weaknesses to be identified, alongside areas of best practice.

Inputting the data as in Table 15.1 below (for ease we have used grades 1–4) and giving each *PPR review a score against each of the National Teaching Standards* presents valuable information. This can be modified each time reviews take place, following professional dialogues between reviewer and teacher, on the best way forward. We deploy the Teaching Standards rather than the OFSTED EIF as the former are universally set, whilst the latter are modified through each successive framework. Importantly, the PPR outcomes are not 'definitive judgements' about a teacher. They comprise successive evaluations of the impact of teaching and assessment practice on students' learning and can be triangulated through other evidence. Tables 15.1, 15.2 and 15.3 evidence the different ways the data can be collated.

Where schools use the process of entering a target grade and forecast grade, gathering this information prior to the lesson and then checking this alongside the students' book work and lesson experience is a *detailed form of moderation*. This facilitates a professional dialogue between the reviewer and the teacher on the synergy or disconnect between the grades and what is actually in the work books.

**Table 15.1**  PPR outcomes by class

| Teacher | Year Group | Teaching Group | Key Stage | Subject | Lesson Topic | PPR Observer | Date | Latest Residual | Average Learning Grade |
|---------|-----------|---------------|-----------|---------|--------------|--------------|------|----------------|-----------------------|
| AGT | 11 | 11D | 4 | DT Food | Food Science | JGN | 11/2/20 | –0.2 | 2 |

**Table 15.2**  PPR outcomes by student cohort

| Cohort | 1.85 |
|--------|------|
| PP | 1.98 |
| PP Boys | 2.00 |
| PP Girls | 1.96 |
| SEND | 1.75 |
| EAL | 2.40 |
| LAC | 2.10 |
| MPA | 1.79 |
| LPA | 1.92 |

**Table 15.3**    PPR outcomes by subject

| | 1. Set high expectations which inspire, motive and challenge pupils | 2. Promote good progress and outcomes by pupils | 3. Demonstrate good subject and curriculum knowledge | 4. Plan and teach well-structured lessons | 5. Adapt teaching to respond to the strengths and needs of all pupils | 6. Make accurate and productive use of assessment | 7. Manage behaviour effectively to ensure a good and safe learning environment |
|---|---|---|---|---|---|---|---|
| Art | 3.00 | 4.00 | 2.00 | 4.00 | 3.00 | 4.00 | 2.00 |
| Biology | 2.00 | 2.00 | 1.00 | 1.00 | 2.00 | 2.00 | 1.00 |
| Business Studies | 1.00 | 1.50 | 1.50 | 1.50 | 2.00 | 1.50 | 1.50 |
| Chemistry | 2.00 | 2.00 | 1.00 | 2.00 | 2.00 | 2.00 | 1.00 |
| Criminology | 1.60 | 2.00 | 2.00 | 1.60 | 1.60 | 1.60 | 1.60 |
| Design Technology | 1.00 | 1.00 | 2.00 | 2.00 | 1.00 | 2.00 | 1.00 |
| DT Food | 1.00 | 2.00 | 2.00 | 2.00 | 2.00 | 2.00 | 2.00 |

Raising Achievement Plan (RAP) 3 – **Head of Year**

*For discussion at the Learning Evaluation and Academic Progress (LEAP) meetings*

Year Group: _____    Head of Year: _____

| Pupil Premium: | EHCP / Statement: | | High Attainers: | |
|---|---|---|---|---|
| Looked After: | SEND Support: | | Middle Attainers: | |
| | | | Lower Attainers: | |

**Progress**

Term: _____

| | English | Maths | Science | Languages | Humanities | Technology / ICT | Expressive Arts |
|---|---|---|---|---|---|---|---|
| **Group 1** - Students whose last assessment grade was 1 fine grade below, equal to or exceeding their end of year target | | | | | | | |
| **Group 2** - Students whose last assessment grade was 2 fine grades below their end of year target grade | | | | | | | |
| **Group 3** - Students whose last assessment grade was more than 2 fine grades away from their end of year target | | | | | | | |
| **Group 4** – Other / Pastoral Issues | | | | | | | |

| Student | Student cohort focus PP/SEND/more able | Reason for Intervention e.g. poor attitudes to learning /low literacy/sporadic attendance SEND/at risk /vulnerable /repeat disruptive behaviours | Strategies to raise attainment by subject | Intended Outcome e.g. specify progress/fine levels to be achieved and by when. Indicators and monitoring by whom and how? |
|---|---|---|---|---|
| | | • See attached list for examples | • See attached list for examples | |
| | | • | • | |

**FIGURE 15.8** An example of a Raising Achievement Plan (RAP) a Head of Year or Pastoral Leader could undertake with a student

The PPR reviewer is more likely to notice *learning difficulties*, such as a lack of focus for students with ADHD or dyslexia that may not have been detected by the SENCO or be apparent to the teacher. This can lead to more effective support and teaching strategies for the students. This information can also be used to track students' progress for informing EHCP applications and reviews. Pupil Progress Reviews log a profile of student progress and engagement over time and can be used in class and online. Online

PPRs can conduct the dialogue with students in a tutorial online or observe learning as an additional participant.

| | Identifying the barriers to achievement and potential strategies |
|---|---|
| **Potential barriers to underachievement. Provide details on what strategies have been put in place so far.** | ☐ Low literacy levels are affecting progress<br>☐ Low numeracy levels are affecting progress<br>☐ Lack of homework completion affects progress<br>☐ Students(s) is/are frequently off task in lessons<br>☐ Poor attendance has affected progress<br>☐ Significant behaviour issues affect progress<br>☐ Lack of specific skills, knowledge or understanding is affecting progress. Please specify<br>☐ Teaching and assessment strategies are not entirely appropriate to accelerating the learning (please explain)<br>☐ Feedback and Next Steps are not helping the students to progress in their learning<br>☐ Other factor is affecting progress. Please specify<br>. . . . . . . . . . . . . . . . . . . . . . . . . . . . . . . . . . . . . . . . . . . . . . . . . . . . . . . . |
| **What practical strategies could be used to remove these barriers?** *Please consider if pupil premium funding can help remove/break down these barriers?* *Catch Up Year 7* *Reading and literacy strategies* | ☐ Regular updates on progress to parents<br>☐ Differentiated tasks in lesson<br>☐ Feedback and Next Stoppes Extended and differentiated questioning<br>☐ 1:1 intervention Small group intervention<br>☐ After school/lunch time catch-up<br>☐ Personalised homework tasks<br>☐ Behaviour Management Plan – PSP?<br>☐ Use of specific rewards/incentive<br>☐ Specific support for SEN – IEP/EHCP?<br>☐ Other specific strategies |

**FIGURE 15.9**   Potential barriers to learning and strategies

**FIGURE 15.10**  How we build a picture of student progress and engagement

For any students who are identified as underachieving, the monitoring of progress and outcomes is then contained within a *Raising Achievement Plan (RAP)*. Figures 15.8 and 15.9 provide examples of RAPs.

## SCHOOL A: CASE STUDY
## WHAT DID THE PPRS TELL US NEEDED TO IMPROVE?

### Example 1: Marking and feedback across school

- Written and verbal feedback in a subject and across a department was variable and not consistently helping students to move to the next level.
- Teacher's next steps/actions were missing in some books; students were not given the necessary practice to address the gaps in their learning.
- In some cases, teacher feedback was insufficiently differentiated for students; not taking into account the challenge necessary for students to attain the higher levels and not helpful for students with a lower reading age or other learning difficulties. One student could not read the teacher's feedback owing to the quality of the handwriting and so was not able to act on it.
- Students who had missed lessons or incomplete classwork had missed the 'sequence in learning', demonstrated superficial knowledge when questioned by the reviewer; the gaps had not been followed up by the student or teacher.
- Where a number of students had not understood a concept or skill, this had not been planned into subsequent teaching activities to help students consolidate.

As a result: the school relaunched its assessment policy with particular emphasis on differentiated feedback. Activities addressed misconceptions such as 'plugging the gaps' in the sequence of knowledge and skills and sharing good practice activities that reinforced metacognition skills.

## CASE STUDY
## WHAT DID THE PPRS TELL US NEED TO IMPROVE?

### Example 2: Low ability disadvantaged boys (D&T)

- Students' writing of product design was of a poorer quality then their product design specifications. This was because they were not encouraged to apply the techniques they had learnt in English on how to write effective evaluative text.
- Students had not developed the necessary basic skills (SPAG) they needed to move onto the next level.
- Students struggled to apply/ transfer their knowledge of mathematical skills to the practical everyday contexts being used.

As a result

- Construction and Engineering 'Literacy Mats' were produced to support students.
- Whiteboards were added to each table to help calculate mathematical problems.

## The Big Five accelerators that impact on learning

From the teaching perspective, the PPR process is practical with specific actions, genuinely providing insights into improving teaching. By changing teachers' mind sets, they can focus on the *impact of the teaching* rather than the teaching in itself, means that *each* teaching/assessment activity can reflect the *Big Five* below.

- structured teaching opportunities to all students (SEND, more able, disadvantaged) develop in-depth subject knowledge, skills, language and literacy skills (oracy and written);
- challenge for all and consolidation of learning gaps through feedback and next steps task;
- checking understanding before setting on or during the task or activity;
- raising expectations through extended and differentiated questioning (student/student and student/teacher);
- tasks that develop metacognition skills (recall, transfer, apply).

## PPR: Hands-on professional development

### Mentoring and coaching of teachers: follow on from PPR process

The mentoring and coaching of teachers is part of: *continuous professional development, performance management, appraisal and review.* It develops the quality of teaching and learning practice, leadership development and succession planning. Through developing trust, a coach will offer targeted support identified through the PPR process. In addition, coaching through Pupil Progress Reviews can identify good practice in pedagogy, assessment, marking and feedback. This is then shared more widely.

### How is coaching used?

Coaching targets high performance and improvement, focusing on specific skills and goals that need addressing, identified through PPR process. The process typically lasts for a relatively short defined period of time, and forms the basis of continuous professional development.

### How is mentoring used?

Mentoring involves the use of the same models and skills of questioning, listening, clarifying and reframing, associated with coaching. Mentors will be allocated to teachers who are less experienced or who will benefit from developing new pedagogies and assessment for learning techniques. In addition, in PPRs, it would be helpful where particular student cohorts are consistently not making the progress they should in a subject.

### The international context of school systems

High-performing countries like Canada, Estonia and Singapore demonstrate the value of respected and well-supported teachers. The success of these countries has been researched by the National Centre on Education and the Economy and demonstrate two points.[4] Firstly, the countries have invested in '*building effective systems*, opting not to chase silver bullets or short-term, narrow-focused solutions'. Secondly, they hold 'at the core of their work *a commitment to professionalising teaching* as an occupation'.

If we look at the Finnish education system, there is no Finnish word for 'account-ability', explains the Director of the Finnish Ministry of Education. He elaborates that '*accountability is left when responsibility has been subtracted* ...'[5] There are no league tables of top performing schools or teachers, an environment of co-operation, not competition is the norm.

Estonian students perform at a consistently high level, within a context of an aging teaching population and have difficulty attracting new teachers. The propor-tion of low-performing students is the smallest in Europe and the world. Estonians describe their curriculum as one in which schools, school leaders, and teachers have a considerable amount of autonomy. Other than providing a minimum number of course hours in core subjects, and mandatory citizenship across all age groups, schools can emphasise particular subjects, like the Arts, Technology or the Natural Sciences. Consequently, some students may choose more hours of Maths and Science, others more in Art and Languages. On average, Estonian students still demonstrate consist-ently high and equitable performance.[6]

As we explored in earlier chapters, autonomy for a school to decide the shape of that curriculum, according to the local context, enables choice for students and can led to greater equity.

In conclusion, reviewing national and international evidence, we would argue that migrating towards an inclusive and equitable curriculum requires two essentials. Firstly, school leaders develop greater autonomy in designing the curriculum. Secondly, a QA system that generates greater responsibility and respect for teachers as professionals. Investing in proportionate development of staff through a school's QA system means that teachers and middle leaders no longer jump through judgmentally numbered hoops, located within ever-changing inspectorial goal posts.

Inspired by countries that attain higher standards than ours, we propose a system that is genuinely fair; a process that supports educational professionals at the chalk face to carry responsibility for their students' learning. The focus on professional development through coaching and mentoring, ensures that cooperation across a school, or across a multi-academy trust is embedded through the sharing of best professional practice. We expect students to become responsible leaders of their learning; similarly, we should expect teachers to be responsible for ensuring that all students fulfil their potential.

## Summary

Looking forward to the 2019 EIF, HMCI Amanda Spielman reported in 2017[7] that inspection was about exploring what lay behind the data and asking how results had been achieved. She referred to

> *looking underneath the bonnet to be sure that a good quality education − one that genu-inely meets pupils' needs − is not being compromised.*

The PPR creates a forensic lens on the progress of pupil groups (disadvantaged, SEND, more able, boys and so on), across departments and across key stages and gets 'underneath the bonnet of education'. Figures 15.2−15.7 demonstrate the PPR process and provide an example of how this would be completed. Arising from this process is the Raising Achievement Plan, put in place for students who are significantly underachieving. They gain additional mentoring and this scrutiny leads to incremental improvements and changes in attitudes to learning. Example templates are available in Figures 15.8–15.10.

Moving away from 'judgemental observations' of teachers creates a more meaningful professional and open dialogue with teachers and TAs based on a wider evidence base. The interconnectedness of outcomes from the PPR provide genuine professional development opportunities, including mentoring and coaching. This leads to less defensiveness when teachers are being appraised.

The QA system used effectively promotes systemic professional development within an individual school/ academy or across a suite of academies, within a MAT or LA. The added advantage of broadening the QA system to a wider range of schools is the development of peer subject reviewers who provide useful expert insights for the subjects they manage or teach in their own school.

Therefore, a systemic whole school quality assurance process that captures the student's learning experience and the progress that he or she is making across all subjects is key to raising aspirations and addressing failings. Only through the PPR will schools position their students at the heart of the curriculum, creating a genuinely joined-up educational conversation. Leaders are then able to assess the relevance and breadth of curriculum intent, along with the quality of the implementation and the true impact this has on each of their students.

## Notes

1   OFSTED (2019) *The Education Inspection Framework*, 1st edn. www.gov.uk/government/publications/education-inspection-framework. London: OFSTED.
2   Ibid.
3   Ibid.
4   NCEE (2019) Empowered educators. Available at: http://ncee.org/empowered-educators/ (Accessed: 20 November 2019).
5   M. Colagrossi (2018) 10 reasons why Finland's education system is the best. Available at: https://bigthink.com/mike-colagrossi/no-standardized-tests-no-private-schools-no-stress-10-reasons-why-finlands-education-system-in-the-best-in-the-world (Accessed: 3 December 2019).
6   International Education News (2017) 10 surprises in the high-performing Estonian education system. Available at: https://internationalednews.com/2017/08/02/10-surprises-in-the-high-performing-estonian-education-system/ (Accessed: 18 November 2019).
7   Spielman, A. (2017) Amanda Spielman's speech at the Festival of Education. Available at: https://gov.uk/government/speeches/amanda-spielmans-speech-at-the-festival-of-education (Accessed: 11 November 2020)

PART

# VI

# Redefining social disadvantage and cultural capital: The extended learning community

# 16

# Human and social capital

## Introduction

As we transform the curriculum towards a more equitable and inclusive education for all, one of the prime influencers is the congruence between school, home and the broader society; drawing together school, social, familial values and aspirations. In previous chapters, we explored a values rich curriculum underpinned with a reformative behaviour strategy that focuses on motivation and attitudes to academic learning.

Through research-based evidence we now explore the importance of factors that contribute to the variable rates of achievement for disadvantaged ethnic groups, including White British. We need to fully understand the implications before designing a curriculum that addresses 'social disadvantage'(OFSTED EIF). Parental aspirations and the values they transmit to their children regarding education are key in motivating them to succeed. Conversely, where parents are not positive influencers this results in a negative impact on their children's attitudes towards learning. Considering the background data on the reasons why gives insights into how we can turn the negatives into positives.

Human capital can be summed up as what the student largely internalises; knowledge, skills, behaviours and attitudes. Social capital, culture and background are the context that influence this.[1] Cultural capital was first defined by the French sociologist Pierre Bourdieu 1973, as 'the *accumulation of knowledge, behaviours and skills* that a person can tap into, to demonstrate one's cultural competence and social status'.[1]

We examine in turn the 'home' factors that influence children on their educational journey; these include: aspirant cultures and the 'immigrant paradigm'; the 'absent father' factor; role models and family/student aspirations that may not be in line with the school's educational intent. OECD maintains that 'high performance and greater equity in educational opportunities and outcomes are not mutually exclusive'.[2] Can English schools balance out home factors and create high achievement for all through a more equitable curriculum? We review the evidence in our current society and educational landscape.

## Human capital

As we know educational outcomes by ethnicity are significantly variable. Rothon (2007),[3] measured 'Human capital' in relation to students' attainment from different ethnic groups, demonstrating that the actual attainment of British Indian and Chinese against their predicted outcomes was proportionately much higher than that of their ethnic peers. Even at the point at which this research was undertaken, the myriad influences on human capital, although not quantifiable, were recognised. These factors constituted parental expectations, parental ability to help with learning and resources; students' aspirations and role models, students' work ethic and natural ability, peer attitudes to learning, teacher expectations of student, and extra-curricular opportunities.

Some educationalists acknowledge performance differentiation between sub-groups, but attribute this to teaching strategy 'failure'[4]. Whilst this may be a valid assertion, the importance of human capital factors in learning must be acknowledged. These contribute to the differential rates of achievement for some groups, over others, especially when the groups may in fact, all experience the same effectiveness of teaching. This is a complex area for educationalists and indeed, within the wider societal policy arena. However, by not developing the debate, we risk applying the premise that *all* students have equally receptive minds and skills, to appreciate both the learning of academic knowledge and the 'cultural knowledge' in lessons. The reality, as every teacher knows, is far from the truth.

Reinforcing the earlier research, a recent 2018 study identified that immigrant students' positive attitudes towards education might be *'contagious'*,[5] in improving their peers' attitudes. The students from an immigrant background were two-thirds more positive about education and its benefits than their peers. No sign of differences in *outlook* between first- and second-generation immigrants, were identified: 'people who emigrate are ... more aspirational and risk-taking ... grit and determination passed from parents to children ... manifests in the school environment'. If indeed, students with higher aspiration, motivation and resilience can positively influence their peers in classroom learning, this potentially raises implications for curriculum design. For instance, a school wide model can identify students as 'leaders of own learning'; including, for instance, peer mentors, leading debates, micro-teaching slots and modelling of questioning and answers by students for peers. The case study below illustrates a pro-active use of bilingualism in the classroom.

### CASE STUDY: ACADEMY IN SOUTH WEST LONDON

In one school, students with heritage languages such as Spanish, Portuguese and French were deployed in modern language lessons by the teacher as 'monitor traducteurs' (translators)'. The teacher operated a 'target language only policy' and relied on her monitors to translate into English, on those occasions where the majority of students had not necessarily understood her instructions. She also extended classroom questioning to a higher level through the students with the heritage languages. She successfully modelled communicative everyday life situations.

The knock-on impact was positive, as all students increasingly developed confidence in speaking in the target language. A number of previously less confident students who were subsequently volunteered to become 'monitors'.

## The 'student disadvantage' factor in achieving successful outcomes

If Bernstein[6] were commenting today, he might well feel vindicated that his theory on speech codes, and how they prevent educational progression within the working classes, could go some way to explaining the increasing attainment gap between disadvantaged and non-disadvantaged students. In general, the attainment gap between disadvantaged and non-disadvantaged students is attributable to socio-economic factors. Disadvantaged students consistently attain much lower grades than their non-disadvantaged peers across all ethnic groups.[7] However, Bernstein's theory would not explain the relatively higher attainment trajectory, over the years, for disadvantaged students from specific ethnic groups. Their attainment, taking into account social class and poverty, is not as disproportionately affected as for others.[8]

Chinese, Indian, Bangladeshi, White Other and Black African students achieve much higher outcomes in comparison to their White British and Black Caribbean disadvantaged peers. The 2019 GCSEs outcomes evidence this trend[9] whilst longitudinal trends from 2011 onwards,[10] indicate the gap between the different disadvantaged ethnic groups is continuing and, widening. What is more surprising is the extent of the attainment gap at 16 points between the second largest ethnic group Indian (disadvantaged) and the White British (disadvantaged) populations, with Chinese students achieving well above all the disadvantaged ethnic groups.

In designing our curriculum intent, we must surely be cognisant of this factor; allowing it to influence our thinking on aspirational and motivational strategies for certain student cohorts. We cannot blindly follow the clunky governmental and OFSTED model of uniquely scrutinising achievement of *disadvantaged versus non-disadvantaged students.*

## Aspirant cultures and the 'immigrant paradigm'

As we can see from the differing student outcomes for disadvantaged ethnic groups, research conducted over a decade ago (Sutton Trust, 2005;[11] Strand, 2007[12] concluded a link between students' academic outcomes,[13] and parental attitudes.

Strand[14] identified parental educational aspirations as a key factor that mediated the pernicious effects of social class and poverty. Where positive, this resulted in influencing students' educational motivations, academic self-concept and resulted in a positive impact on attainment. The greater progress of Indian students was partly explained by 'advantaging factors' in their family and home lives; high parental and student aspirations, and hard work that, 'offset the relatively negative disadvantaging effects of social and economic circumstances'.

Explanations provided by Winder (2004)[15] referred to the 'immigrant paradigm' that valued education as a way out of poverty as these parents viewed their children's academic achievement as a route towards upward social mobility and security; 'the children of immigrants … devote themselves to the acquisition of knowledge'(Caplan et al., 1991;[16] Modood, 2003).[17]

Strong motivation and aspiration provide the bedrock for positive attitudes to learning and both are integral to successful outcomes. This is illustrated by the research[18] conducted on British Chinese parents regarding the consistently high value they place on education 'regardless of social class, gender or ability'. This was valued by the Chinese students interviewed during the research. They perceived the less strict English parents as more liberal, 'as long as their daughter tries her hardest'. Another Chinese student refers to the pressure to achieve the highest standards and to get a professional job as what differentiated Chinese parents from White British parents.[19]

Can the explanations surrounding the 'immigrant paradigm' explain the cross gen-erational impact with third and fourth generation British African, British Chinese and British Indian students? It would appear so. Little research has been carried out on the GCSE outcomes for more recent European immigrant arrivals, for instance, Polish, Portuguese and Eastern European. If we assume that these students describe themselves as 'White Other', the data would suggest that they may attain higher than their disadvantaged White British peers; therefore, sharing characteristics of the 'immigrant paradigm' / diaspora.[20]

Apart from the research on the immigrant paradigm, we can consider the explan-ation offered by Ball (2005)[21] and Bourdieu (1990)[22] who cite 'cultural *capital*' as a product of parental high expectations, values and close tracking of children's per-formance, as typically associated with middle-class white families. Both maintain that this constitutes a prime factor in the educational success of middle-class children, as opposed to disadvantaged families, where parents may not be as interested in their children's schooling. It could well follow that ethnic families from certain disadvantaged backgrounds, *unconsciously mimic* the high aspirational behaviours of non-disadvantaged white and ethnic parents. This would infer that cultural heritage norms have indeed potential, in some instances, to transcend socio-economic factors and disadvantage.

## Key 'home' factors that may affect lower achievement

### Black Caribbean disadvantaged students

The 'absent father' factor has arguably been cited as a contributor in the lower achievement of disadvantaged and non-disadvantaged Black Caribbean children. Whilst this factor is certainly not unique to this ethnic group, the Runnymede Trust (2014)[23] identified over half of Black Caribbean children were growing up in single parent families, a rate nearly three times as high as the overall average of about one-fifth in the UK. Black Caribbean children were more likely to have an absentee father, or live in a single parent household than many other ethnic groups. This compared with a quarter of White children and less than one tenth of Indian or Bangladeshi children[24] (Connelly et al., 2014)

The author of 'Father absence, Father deficit, Father hunger' (E. Kruk, PhD (2012)[25] reported that:

'Children's diminished self-concept (children consistently report feeling abandoned when their fathers are not involved in their lives). Behavioural problems (fatherless children have more difficulties with social adjustment ... manifest behav-iour problems; in an attempt to disguise their underlying fears and anxieties).'

More recent insights from within the Black Caribbean community appear to support this. A Jamaican Church leader who grew up in Brixton South London commented:[26]

Many males do not grow up with a father. The African home is more of a family with a father. Among the Asian community there is a family with a father. The Black Caribbean community are without fathers and that is the difference.

Although these snapshots present a bleak picture, they create awareness and understanding for schools of possible causes of poor behaviours and patterns of under-achievement. Given that Black Caribbean students are three times more likely to be excluded than white students,[27] in particular boys, the school imperative is to shift the focus from 'the disadvantaged' to targeting students that are *vulnerable*. They are statistic-ally more disposed towards underachievement, or exclusion. Motivational and academic strategies that have been outlined in previous chapters, can help prevent the downward spiral, along with positive role models for the students, as in the example below.

A Black Caribbean male behaviour mentor from a Lambeth school gave his observations:

> 49% of families are led by women. This has a massive effect on our boys. The average pupil goes home, he doesn't eat with his family, and he eats alone. They are latch-key kids. This has been brought about by Black Caribbean culture. If the family foundation is not solid you have lots of problems.... The boys and girls have a particular bond with you as a man.

## White British disadvantaged students

The 'anti-school' culture for white working-class boys is well researched.[28,29] This cul-ture helps shape post-16 choices but also has a negative effect on attainment while at school. Research evidenced through Evans (2006)[30] and Demie and Lewis (2010)[31] confirmed that a gap existed between the culture and values of white working-class families and that of the inner London schools attended by their children. OFSTED, (2008)[32] identified good leadership practice in schools with White boys from low income backgrounds, where school leaders prioritised strong partnerships with a wide range of agencies for social, educational and practical support. This benefited the boys and their families, raising low aspirations.

> ... they don't necessarily have high educational aspirations, because they don't see education as instrumental in leading to the kind of outcomes that they want.
>
> (Strand, 2014, Oxford)[33]

Where school leaders ensure that the cultural values and school ethos drive the quality of teaching, this can overcome teacher stereotyping of achievement levels for particular groups, who then successfully enable underachieving students to catch up with their peers.[34]

> ... students who don't have that parental support, don't have that aspiration, don't have that follow-up at home ... they are already miles behind everyone else. So, we have to put more in to catch them up.
>
> (Tom Knott, Assistant Principal,
> The Totteridge Academy)[35]

Existing research suggests that role models are most effective when students can see similarities between themselves and the role model.[36] On this basis, it seems likely that white working-class male university role models or higher apprentices as academic/vocational/technical mentors, can have a positive impact on white working-class students.

Cultural and curricular norms have been cited as reasons for the underperformance of both disadvantaged white and ethnic minority groups. In focus groups undertaken by Lambeth Council, White British working-class parents highlighted a perceived lack of white culture in the National Curriculum and a sense of marginalisation in their own communities.[37] Interestingly, this sense of non-representation in mainstream schools was partly why Black supplementary schools, were founded. This constituted a response to how the National Curriculum portrayed (or did not portray) black history.

Through recognising the human and cultural capital of all students' backgrounds, much more can be done to ensure that the disparate communities believe they are represented in the curriculum and this is relevant to their lives. For both student groups, for different reasons, we cannot underestimate the importance of all staff consistently articulating higher expectations of what students can achieve, providing positive role models and of course, active partnerships with parents from different ethnic and socio-economic groups, in motivating their children during their schooling.

## Summary

Our evidence strongly suggests there is a correlation between human capital and/or a diaspora culture and its values, as this may confer greater, or lesser motivation and a desire to succeed in education.

There are a complex range of interconnecting factors at play. Students require a mindset; as we have seen that includes motivation, resilience and academic self-esteem. Other factors to consider include attitudes to learning, and counteracting reactive behaviours, especially when faced with challenges presented in lessons and towards authority figures. Patterns of absence, truancy and exclusion will clearly influence the educational prospects for all students. Those students who lack the aspiration to succeed and are not encouraged by their parents are especially at risk of not achieving their potential. We have evidenced that parental factors clearly have a stronger bearing in determining high attainment levels than socio-economic status or disadvantage alone.

These factors must be taken into account when planning curriculum intent and the funding of an extended curriculum involving parents and other community stakeholders.

Once the pattern of underachievement is identified in KS3, schools should ideally adopt a proactive, rather than a reactive firefighting approach. Strategies include the early identification of 'at risk' students through the PPR process described in Part V.

In too many cases, there is often over reliance on KS4 academic interventions, as back up, with parents only invited in, as and when, their children are perceived as 'problems'. In Chapters 17 and 19, case studies illustrate meaningful engagement between the school and its wider community through positive role models, mentors and importantly, parents in their children's learning. All of this must form part of transforming the Extended Curriculum.

A reductionist binary model of reviewing attainment for disadvantaged and non-disadvantaged students is not helpful if we desire curriculum reform. There exists a matrix of complex interactions between ethnicity, gender and factors, relating to dis-advantage and socio-economic status. Presenting accounts of educational achievement framed uniquely in relation to only one of these factors is not helpful if schools wish to adopt strategies that effectively address these inequalities. The national trajectory of GCSE results to date should challenge educational researchers to develop more nuanced and evidenced accounts of educational success, or failure in relation to the curriculum.

Schools receive funding for closing the gap between disadvantaged students and their peers. It appears that Black Caribbean and White British disadvantaged boys, maybe more pre-disposed, on account of 'home' factors, towards slipping into the category of underachiever and into the category of excluded. It would be true to say that many students within these cohorts do overcome these challenges and succeed against the odds.

Nevertheless, schools are urged to deploy this funding more proactively to invest in people resources that effectively prevent those students, from falling off the cliff edge and off the radar of the school.

# Notes

1  P. Bourdieu (1990) *Reproduction in Education, Society and Culture*, 2nd edn. New York: SAGE Publications Ltd.
2  OECD (2016) *PISA 2015 Results (Volume I): Excellence and Equity in Education*, PISA, Paris: OECD Publishing, p. 206.
3  C. Rothon (2007) Can achievement differentials be explained by social class alone? An examination of minority ethnic educational performance in England and Wales at the end of compulsory schooling, *Ethnicities*, 7(3): 306–22.
4  T. Sherrington (2017) *The Learning Rainforest*, 1st edn. London: John Catt Ltd.
5  University of Bristol (2018) Immigrant pupils more likely to think school can help them succeed than UK-born peers. Available at: www.bristol.ac.uk/news/2018/july/immigrants-education.html (Accessed: 18 December 2019).
6  B. Bernstein (1970) Education cannot compensate for society, *New Society*, 38:344–7.
7  Education Policy Institute (2019) EPI Annual Report 2019: The education disadvantage gap in your area. Available at: https://epi.org.uk/publications-and-research/epi-annual-report-2019-the-education-disadvantage-gap-in-your-area/ (Accessed: 5 December 2019).
8  D. Gillborn and H. Mirza (2000) *Educational Inequality, Mapping Race, Class and Gender*. London: Crown Copyright. Office for Standards in Education.
9  Department for Education (2019) GCSE results ('Attainment 8'). Available at: www.ethnicity-facts-figures.service.gov.uk/education-skills-and-training/11-to-16-years-old/gcse-results-attainment-8-for-children-aged-14-to-16-key-stage-4/latest (Accessed: 25 November 2019).
10 Education Policy Institute, J. Hutchinson et al. (2019) *Education in England: Annual Report 2019*, https://epi.org.uk/publications-and-research/annual-report-2019/: EPI.
11 Sutton Trust (2005) Rates of eligibility for free school meals at the top state schools. Available at: www.suttontrust.comreportsratesofeligibilityforfreeschoolmeals

12    S. Strand (2007) *Minority Ethnic Pupils in the Longitudinal Study of Young People in England: Report on Performance in Public Examinations at Age 16.* London: Department for Children, Schools and Families DCSF – RBO29.

13    S. Strand (2010) The limits of social class in explaining ethnic gaps in educational attainment. *British Educational Research Journal*, in press.http://dx.doi.org/10.1080/01411920903540664

14    S. Strand (2010) The limits of social class in explaining ethnic gaps in educational attainment. *British Educational Research Journal*, in press.http://dx.doi.org/10.1080/01411920903540664

15    R. Winder (2004) *Bloody Foreigners, The Story of Immigration to Britain*, 1st edn. New York: Hachette Digital.

16    C. Caplan, M. Choy and J. Whitmore (1991) *Children of the Boat People: A Study of Educational Success.* Ann Arbor: University of Michigan Press.

17    T. Modood (2003) Ethnic differences in educational performance. In D. Mason (ed.), *Explaining Ethnic Differences: Changing Patterns of Disadvantage in Britain*, Cambridge: Policy Press, pp. 53–67.

18    B. Francis and L. Archer (2005) British-Chinese students and parents' constructions of the value of education, *British Educational Research Journal*, 31(1), 89–108.

19    Ibid.

20    The Economist (2017) Why central and eastern European children lag behind in British schools. Available at: www.economist.com/britain/2017/07/13/why-central-and-eastern-european-children-lag-behind-in-british-schools (Accessed: 15 December 2019).

21    S. J. Ball (2005) *Education Policy and Social Class.* Abingdon: Routledge.

22    P. Bourdieu (1990) Structures, habitus, practices. In P. Bourdieu (ed.), *The Logic of Practice*, Redwood City, CA: Stanford University Press, pp. 52–79.

23    The Runnymede Trust Research (2014) Fatherhood Facts Sheet, www.runnymedetrust.org/projects-and-publications/parliament/pastparticipation-and-politics/david-lammy-on-fatherhood/fact-sheet.html. (Accessed: 16 January 2020).

24    R. Connelly, H. Joshi and R. Rosenberg (2014) Family structure. In Platt, L. (ed.), *Millennium Cohort Study Age 11 Survey Initial Findings.* London: Centre for Longitudinal Studies.

25    E. Kruk (2012) Father absence, Father deficit, Father hunger, *Psychology Today.* Available at: www.psychologytoday.com/blog/co-parenting-after-divorce/201205/father-absence-father-deficit-father-hunger (Accessed: 12 August 2020).

26    F. Demie et al. (2018) *Black Caribbean Underachievement in Schools in England.* Berlin: Researchgate.

27    J. Staufenberg (2017) News DfE to review 'disproportionate' exclusions of certain ethnicities. Available at: https://schoolsweek.co.uk/dfe-to-review-disproportionate-exclusions-of-certain-ethnicities/ (Accessed: 26 February 2019).

28    C. Jackson (2002) 'Laddishness' as a self-worth protection strategy. *Gender and Education*, 14(1): 37–50.

29    N. Dasgupta (2011) Ingroup experts and peers as social vaccines who inoculate the self-concept: The stereotype inoculation model. *Psychological Inquiry*, 22(4), 231–46.

30    G. Evans (2006) *Educational Failure and Working Class White Children in Britain.* London: Palgrave Macmillan.

31    F. Demie and K. Lewis (2010) *Raising Achievement: Good Practice in Secondary Schools with Outstanding Leadership.* London: Research and Statistics Unit, London Borough of Lambeth.

32    OFSTED (2008) White working class boys from low income backgrounds: Good practice in schools. www.ofsted.gov.uk

33    S. Strand (2014) Ethnicity, gender, social class and achievement gaps at age 16: Intersectionality and 'getting it' for the white working class. *Research Papers in Education*, 29(2): 131–71.

34    T. Quong and A. Walker (2010) *Seven Principles of Strategic Leadership.* Available at www.researchgate.net/publication/228506732_Seven_principles_of_strategic_leadership (Accessed: 12 August 2020).

35    W. Millard, K. Bowen-Viner et al. (2018) *Boys on Track – Improving Support for Black Caribbean and Free School Meal Eligible White Boys in London*. London: LKMCo.

36    N. Dasgupta (2011) Ingroup experts and peers as social vaccines who inoculate the self-concept: The stereotype inoculation model. *Psychological Inquiry*, 22(4), 231–46.

37    F. Demie et al. (2018) *Black Caribbean Underachievement in Schools in England*. Berlin: Researchgate.

# 17

# Creating a learning community

## Introduction

Engaging parents in children's learning, when successful, undoubtedly raises and sustains students' educational aspirations[1]. Of 6000 waking hours in a year, the typical UK student spends just 1500 at school. Because 75 per cent of a student's potential learning time is spent at home; parents are a significant influencer of young people's education, making a school's implementation of parental engagement critical for student success. 'It is unarguable now after decades of evidence that parental engagement makes a difference' (Sir Kevan Collins).[2]

'Engagement' is taken to include a variety of aspects:

■ learning at home: help with homework/additional home tutoring;
■ attitudes, values, aspirations;
■ school–home communication;
■ in-school activities: volunteering; helping in classrooms, parents' evenings, field trips;
■ decision making: school governorcommittees and advisory groups;
■ collaborating with the wider community: contributions working both ways between schools, families and communities.

Here, we focus on breaking down barriers to get buy-in from parents for students from different ethnic groups, those with special educational needs and disadvantaged backgrounds. Parents who are viewed as 'hard to reach' by schools, often view the school as 'hard to reach'. However, where schools make concerted efforts to engage and sustain engagement of these parents, there is evidence of improved student behaviour and learning. We can add to this the potential role of external partners in further education, employers and those from the Third Sector (voluntary groups, charities and so on) in engaging students. More research would help inform how parents engage with their children in the home, in order to influence school-based interventions that best respond to the students' needs, behaviours and family values. There is clearly no universal concept of 'parenting', with a set of practices and attitudes understood and commonly shared by all. Those schools with a *parental engagement strategy* as part of the curriculum intent evidence a strong commitment to creating a 'learning community' within an extended curriculum.

There are three main ways that parents can actively support their children's learning as below. The toolkit provided by School Home Support[3] (SHS) helpfully summarises these areas and identifies six imaginative ways in which schools can engage with parents, and in particular, recalcitrant ones.

---

1.  *Parental engagement for learning;* the school takes specific steps to connect parents to classroom learning.
2.  *Parental engagement through learning;* parental study groups or parenting classes held by schools.
3.  *Parental engagement about learning;* parents actively engage with teachers and students about the process of learning so that they gain a greater awareness of the meta-cognitive strategies for improving learning outcomes.

**Six elements must be embedded by schools:**

1.  Communication between home and school is regular, two way and meaningful.
2.  Responsible parenting is promoted and supported; school must support positive parenting by respecting and affirming the strengths and skills needed by the parent to fulfil their role.
3.  Parents' integral role in assisting student learning; students' achievement increases when parents are actively involved in the learning process. Parents must be given the tools and effective means to support their children's educational needs, including promoting certain behaviours and attendance.
4.  Parents welcomed as volunteers; and obtain a better understanding of learning processes.
5.  Parents as full partners in the decisions that affect their children. Schools should actively enlist parent participation, representing the diversity of the student group in decision making.
6.  Parents, school and community collaborate to enhance student learning, strengthen families and improve schools.[4]

---

This case study by SHS illustrates the impact of a Third Sector agency working constructively with a school to re-engage a persistently absent student through establishing communication between the school and the family in a a complex case.

**CASE STUDY**

Hope, aged 14, was absent from school for seven months. Relationships between school and mum were strained as the school had referred the family to court for non-attendance. SHS visits to the family home revealed that Hope's mum was single, living in inadequate living conditions and these were contributing to poor mental health. Both Hope and her mum had become very anxious about Hope returning to school.

SHS helped as intermediaries between Hope and her mum to provide medical records, to create a reduced timetable and, helped Hope's mum to increase her understanding of the importance of Hope attending school. SHS encouraged communication between family and school, building up to attendance at parents' evenings. SHS also advocated on the family's behalf for better living conditions, while guiding and empowering mum to obtain better housing and support for management of her finances.

With support from SHS, Hope started attending school, initially on a reduced timetable. Through the support received from SHS, the mother became more confident, changed her attitude to school, and towards her daughter's education. She cooperated with the school and was no longer obstructive.

## Barriers to parental involvement

Parents may perceive schools as presenting obstacles, for instance, through a lack of encouragement, not informing parents of what they can do, and not fitting around busy working and family lives. Parents themselves face challenges, including costs, time and transportation, low levels of literacy, language and numeracy, a lack of ability in understanding and negotiating the school system. A negative experience of parents' own schooling could reflect a lack of confidence in supporting their children's learning. Some might be working in multiple jobs and are pushed for time. Others are not interested in their children's learning as they believe this is up to the school. As parents, they do not perceive themselves as the 'experts'.

Schools face challenges in sustainability: in particular, retaining motivated and inspiring senior leaders, who believe in the importance of parental engagement, creating high levels of commitment across staff teams, and consistent access to the funding streams to resource successful programmes. Other barriers include reaching out to parents who have chosen not to engage either with their children's school or with their children's learning. Recruiting experienced and knowledgeable staff who know which practices will effectively support parents in engaging with their children's learning is paramount.

Consistency in behaviour management routines and support for academic outcomes must be well communicated with parents. A lack of clarity of a mission or vision, poor communication of this, or demonstrating values or routines contrary to the stated ones will mean ineffective implementation of the stated intent. In addition, there will be a break in trust and belief in what the school is trying to achieve, however aspirational.

A case study conducted by Harris and Goodall (2007)[5] in the Engaging Parents in Raising Achievement (EPRA) programme identified schools partnering with parents and helping their children learn. Schools offering bespoke support programmes, including literacy classes and parenting skills, proved most likely to engage parents in their children's learning. There was a positive correlation between increased parental engagement, particularly amongst the 'hard to reach parents' and improved pupil attendance, performance and behaviour.

Subsequently, EPRA schools sustained a two-way relationship based on mutual trust, respect and commitment, consistently reinforcing that 'parents matter,' through demonstrating improving student outcomes.

Hopkin's research[6] on successful 'twenty-first-century schools' demonstrates, through strong values and high expectations, that schools can 'defy the association of poverty with outcomes'; responding to students' need for clear direction and a disciplined environment, establishing respect for education. These schools aimed to provide a better daytime alternative to being at home, or on the streets.

This proactive approach to working with parents is reflected in the joined up 'Team Around the Child' ethos and strategy in the STEP model and relationship charter below.

## CASE STUDY: PASSMORES ACADEMY

All parents sign a 'Relationship Charter' … created by the students, parents/carers and staff.[7] The expectation is that school staff and students model the behaviour expected of students in and out of school … to protect its good name in the community and digital world, in accordance with the Charter's principles.

The Students Towards Excellent Progress STEP team conduct early interventions for students with behavioural, social, emotional and academic difficulties; re-engaging students through positive reinforcement booklets; observing identified students in lessons with in-class support and advice.

## What schools can do to successfully engage parents

Effectively targeted school communications can actively involve parents. Examples include weekly texts, newsletters linked to learning that promote academic success, or success with behaviours and attendance, use of blogs/twitter, social media and online calendar. Further helpful examples are listed in this *Guardian* article.[8]

- 'One nice thing … a stamped postcard home when my son does a good piece of homework. I like that old-fashioned touch, it goes up on the kitchen noticeboard and becomes a talking point.'
- A simple video, modelling an approach (to Maths) created by class teacher or pupil … uploaded on the learning platform (accessed by parents) can secure engagement.
- 'One school … where most parents didn't have computers at home – put a computer in the foyer of the local supermarket, with videos of teaching on a loop. Whole families came in to watch.'

Parent Advisers, within a Parental Engagement Strategy, play a valuable role as the interface between school and home; building the trust and respect of 'hard to reach' parents; especially for those with low literacy and English language needs. They maintain the relationship through on-going communication, supporting and celebrating children's achievements.

## CASE STUDY: 11–18 ACADEMY

*Student Parent Advisers* were key in ensuring that the Home School contract (Appendix 5.4, available at www.routledge.com/9780367900878) was completed by parents; subsequently, monitoring the student's progress against their targets, through the daily reports. The three-way partnership comprised a target for the parent to support their son/daughter at home, the school to ensure that a mentor was in place, and the student carefully guided and monitored to achieve his/her target. Targets for students were typically around behaviour, and attendance, and always referred to learning attitudes and 'small wins' in learning.

## Engaging parents through learning communities

Two-way communication is invaluable; consulting with parents about how they can be involved can usually lead to more effective home–school relationships; especially with parents who are 'hard to reach'. Restricting communication to parents' evenings will mean that for those students who are underachieving, or whose behaviours or attendance patterns are not acceptable; the only contact between school and parents is likely to be negative, frustrating and lead to dissatisfaction. More productive is a sequence of on-going activities that helps build a strong foundation of communication between school and parents.

Schools planning group-based parenting initiatives (such as regular workshops) at a convenient time and location, leads to trusting relationships. Establishing informal, welcoming environments are key in encouraging parents to attend, with topics ranging from understanding the importance of doing homework, knowing how to make the best use of apps that help with homework, and monitoring students' progress. In addition, showcasing aspects of learning across curriculum, especially in Maths, English, Science, helps parents understand the expectations and educational standards in lessons that their children are expected to reach.

Many schools at Open Days, showcase real learning to parents across subjects in imaginative ways – in a 'have a go' spirit; conducting short science investigations, cooking demo in food technology, constructing a model robot in design and technology, solving mathematical puzzles, displays of historical artefacts, and so on. Thereafter, these events mostly cease, owing to the demands on teaching staff. An Outreach co-ordinator, who continues targeting parents, has resource implications but with long-term benefits. This results in a 'learning community'. Regular short sessions are organised and parents invited in to see videos of staged learning. In addition, they are given opportunities to access resources and online materials that their children use in their lessons. This would fit in very well with parents knowing how to access KOs, APPs, or schemes of learning on the website. This is especially important, given parents may not be so up to date with changing digital technologies. The use of 4Matrix provides digital tools for tracking students' educational performance in key stages 3–5. Students' progress in subjects is analysed along with the progress made by pupil groups, the consistency and impact of teaching, and key school performance indicators. The school can share this information in user-friendly language[9] with parents and students for a real time update on students' progress.

Engaging parents who may not understand the value of education is key. Once they appreciate the importance of their role in motivating their children and how to raise their aspirations, their children can stand a better chance of achieving their educational potential. The school has a prime role not only in creating an educationally nurturing environment for their students but importantly to showcase this to the parents and families. Teachers can preserve students' work in digital files or portfolios, instantly shared with parents. Report card grades are only indicative of the transient stages of potential, while the portfolio shows the actual work, which is proof of achievement and hopefully, provides an example of deeper understanding and mastery.

This is especially important for students with SEND, and those that have dyslexia. Sharing these students' work with their parents, at various stages of development during the year, can hopefully evidence the powerful impact of teacher feedback in assisting the student in making progress and demonstrate to the parents, how their child learns. This alongside the Individual Learning Plan or EHCP will also show the impact of the teaching/assessment/support.

It is crucial for schools to invite parents into Years 7 and 8 Careers sessions. This means they can listen to the CEIAG lead discuss Gatsby Benchmarks. They can, for instance, appreciate the role of parental support during work experience placements, for their children's future destinations. This is especially important where parents are themselves workless. Since the last decade, the influence that parents, carers and family members have on how young people think about education, their future and society is certainly noteworthy and well-researched (Harris, Andrew-Power and Goodhall, 2007).[10]

## Parents contributing to the extended curriculum

More recently, the influencers affecting variability in parental engagement have been identified as socio-economic status, parental experience of education and belonging to certain ethnic and social groups.[11] These factors are now well known by insightful school leaders. Many schools, steered by this, get successful buy-in from their parent communities by creating volunteering opportunities with after-school clubs, school trips, reading buddies or speakers in assemblies, on a passion, hobby or job. When we consider the importance of including parents in their children's learning, through an extended curriculum; let us consider the apt saying by the Chinese philosopher Confucius: 'Tell me and I will forget. Show me and I will remember. Involve me and I will understand.'

In this case study, the parent's first experience of the school was a negative one as she had been unhappy with the repeat detentions meted out to her daughter for disruptive behaviours. After the initial discussion on a mutually agreed way forward for dealing with behaviours, the headteacher talked of the importance of parents volunteering in the school. The parent volunteered her expertise and time to set up a successful scheme with staff, extending learning to outside the classroom.

## Case study of an entrepreneur parent–school partnership in the Midlands

A parent with her own business, helped Year 8 and 9 students in developing 'entrepreneurial skills'. She worked with the pastoral staff, business studies and food, design and technology teachers, in establishing fortnightly, regular Friday lunchtime stalls. Some students decorated pre-bought soaps and T shirts; others made cakes; others brought sketches and paintings; others made toys in design and technology. Three Year 11 students did the 'Maths and Book-keeping' for the sessions; the proceeds were donated to an environmental charity. The event was promoted throughout the school and publicised the importance of environmental issues. Students were invited to contribute a recycled-item for sale (clothing, books, toys). At particular times of the year, invites were sent to parents, coinciding usually with parents' open evenings. These events promoted the school in the local community in a positive light and also showcased students' skills and knowledge, in a practical sense.

## Partnerships with FE and Third Sector

In this FE/school collaboration, the approach adopted resulted in a win–win situation for both partners; the FE college increased enrolments in its adult classes and the school increased attendance at parents' evenings.

## Case study: FE opening doors to hard-to-reach school parents

A local London FE college enrolled adults onto its Return to Learning Maths and English classes. As part of the initiative, the college worked in partnership with local voluntary organisations and a secondary school located in an area of high deprivation, with a high proportion of disadvantaged British White students. Attendance at parents' evenings was traditionally very low. The school was keen to target parents of Years 7–9 students, underachieving in Maths and/or English. After consultation, the college, along with a local charity, established Taster sessions in financial literacy, Understanding Your Child's Homework, aromatherapy, and a Zumba dance session.

Activities were promoted through texting; leafleting in shops, hairdressers, nail salons, takeaways and pubs. The event succeeded in attracting a moderate turn-out and thereafter positive feedback through social media and tweeting by parents attracted more parents to subsequent sessions. This resulted in slowly increasing attendance at parent evenings as college representatives at the Taster sessions stressed the importance of parental involvement. A spin-off was the recruitment of three parents as school lunchtime supervisors; one of whom wished to work as a Parent Support Adviser, subsequently enrolling onto the Level 3 Certificate in Work with Parents course at the college.

## Positive role models, raising aspirations

In the absence of high parental aspirations, the role of alumni in schools can be inspirational. Research from the Charity Future First[12] shows that over a third of students from the poorest backgrounds do not know anyone in a job that they would like to do. This affects young people's perception of their own ability, their expectations of future success and the extent to which they value their schoolwork. The result is that only one in eight children from a low-income background is likely to become a high earner as an adult.

The Charity's mission is to see every state school and college in the UK supported by a thriving and engaged alumni community. Future First has supported more than 1200 state secondary schools and colleges in building networks of former students and helps them manage their community of supporters through a digital platform. The charity reports that the vast majority of young people say 'meeting alumni made them realise that 'people like me' can be successful and they work harder; and teachers report that relatable working role models raised students' motivation to learn'.

One of the charity's good practice case studies showcases the Community Liaison Officer organising mock interviews and social events with alumni at Eggar's School – Alton. Events such as the Lecture Club, with visiting alumni and the school's ten-point challenge offer after-school opportunities, so students develop their talents, and skills alongside their academic studies.

Deploying *behaviour/academic mentors* means that students and, by extension, their parents have the wrap around support they need to raise their aspirations, in relation to education. Positive female and male role models are key; especially where students do not have these in their home background. Those that share the backgrounds of the students and have undergone similar negative experiences in their lives, but pull through successfully are motivational models. These can range from reformed ex-offenders or previous 'gang' leaders, excluded students to students who struggled with special educational needs (dyslexia, ADHD), gaining access to higher education and training.

All illustrate that they have overcome adversity to achieve success.

Below is the case study of Jordan, who, following exclusion, attended an Alternative Provision (AP) and overcame all the odds to go onto university. This provided an inspirational role model for the AP students and their parents who believed it could not be done.

---

**CASE STUDY**

Following exclusion from mainstream school for fighting and a long period of non-attendance, I became a student at the Bridge AP Academy, completing my IB exams. I was the first student to apply and am proud to be in the first cohort to graduate from the TBAP[13] 16–19 AP Academy! Since then, I am studying a Multimedia Sports Journalism University Foundation Course (UCF).[14] I am hoping to become a football sports journalist and have started my own blog. I thoroughly enjoy the lectures; some inside Wembley Stadium, a cunning way of ensuring I get to Uni every Monday! So far, I have learnt about the different techniques employed by those who work in media. Some of my lecturers are seasoned professionals in the industry and I am learning a lot. I look forward to when I will show TBAP my first published article.[15]

---

## Summary

'A school without parents at its foundation is just like a bucket with a hole in it' said Reverend Jesse L. Jackson.[16] If we accept that parental ambition and motivation are key to fostering educational aspirations in our students, then we must work pro-actively with our parent community, to overcome barriers, so that they fully appreciate the value of education and their contribution. The inclusion of 'role models' for students and parents is highly motivational.

Education cannot be just as a means to an end towards qualifications for future destinations, but seen as an end in itself for social, mental and physical well-being, as well as academic success. The school curriculum, if genuinely broad and balanced, widens horizons and gives students the knowledge and the range of skills they need to improve their life chances. We must convince all our parents that the curriculum we decide upon will ultimately be in the best interests of their children's futures. The evidence is in the intent, the implementation in practice, and the impact, in relation to our students' outcomes and their wide-ranging skills. Showcasing this to parents is a powerful tool to evidence the work of the school in helping their children progress.

Creating a 'learning community' and an Extended Curriculum, through school partnerships between school, student and parent through a 'contract', fosters mutual respect and a good foundation for successfully engaging recalcitrant students and their parents.

## Notes

1   We will use 'parent' for ease but this refers to parents/carers/guardians/grandparents etc.
2   House of Commons Education Committee (2019) *Tackling Disadvantage in the Early Years*. London: House of Commons.
3   School–Home Support (2019) Parental engagement. Available at: www.schoolhomesupport. org.uk/wp-content/uploads/2015/11/SHS-Parental-engagement-toolkit.pdf (Accessed: 29 November 2019).
4   School–Home Support (2019) Parental engagement. Available at: www.schoolhomesupport. org.uk/wp-content/uploads/2015/11/SHS-Parental-engagement-toolkit.pdf (Accessed: 29 November 2019).
5   A. Harris and J. Goodall (2007) *Engaging Parents in Raising Attainment – Do Parents Know They Matter?* London: Department for Children, Schools and Families.
6   D. Hopkins (2010) *School Leadership Today; Changing Landscape of School Improvement*. London: Institute of Education, University of London.
7   T. Bennett (2017) *Creating a Culture: How School Leaders Can Optimise Behaviour*, London: The Department for Education.
8   H. Wellham (2015) Top tips for teachers on engaging parents in learning, *Guardian*, 28 June.
9   4Matrix (2020) Welcome to 4Matrix. Available at: www.4matrix.com/ (Accessed: 18 January 2020).
10  A. Harris and J. Goodall (2007) *Engaging Parents in Raising Attainment – Do Parents Know They Matter?* London: Department for Children, Schools and Families.
11  L. Ferguson (2019) 5 ways to boost parental involvement at low-income schools. Available at: www.scilearn.com/5-ways-boost-parental-involvement-at-low-income-schools/ (Accessed: 24 November 2019).
12  Future First (2019) Our purpose. Available at: https://futurefirst.org.uk/our-purpose/ (Accessed: 23 November 2019).
13  TBAP – Tri-Borough Alternative Provision.
14  University Campus of Football Business Wembley.
15  J. Brightman-Charles.
16  See https://leadershipnyc.org/parents (Accessed 11 November 2020)

# The curriculum journey:
# Managing key transition points

# 18

# Primary transition: Head start to secondary

## Introduction

Effective academic transition across key stages (primary/secondary) is central to establishing the high standards of education that students need to be successful in GCSE examinations. This may be an area that is not well-structured or sequenced. The vast majority of primary pupils may in theory experience at least a two to three month 'academic fallow period from mid-May to September', post-SATs. The negative impact of this single factor on the starting points of Year 7 students means that they can regress in their knowledge and skills. If frequency of exposure to knowledge and skills, through the process of recall, transfer and apply is important to its consolidation, then it follows that Year 7 students will be significantly variable in what they know and the level of skills they have. This means that the standards they display in English and Maths upon arrival in Year 7 may be out of kilter with their SATs outcomes. This is before we factor in possible variations in the quality of the curricula they will have experienced across the primary schools. We illustrate a good practice approach from a borough-wide transition project, implemented May-July (post-SATs).

## The importance of KS2-3 transition

Ensuring Year 6 students are secondary-ready is paramount for optimising the progress they make over the next five years of their school journey. Leaders in the secondary sector are responsible for planning a learning journey that develops students' knowledge and skills from 10-19. It is more helpful for us to view this cross-sector curriculum phase as the students' pathway to their final destinations of further training, higher education and employment. Collaborative primary/secondary and secondary/secondary partnerships, within a local context can create a sound springboard for students to gain an awareness of the knowledge and skills they need to become secondary ready. As we have seen in Part III, knowledge is not enough for successful outcomes – having the skills and knowing how to manipulate the knowledge and apply it in a relevant context is essential.

Moving from primary to secondary curriculum involves careful planning and proactive actions. The vast majority of secondary schools deploy staff members who liaise with the primary feeder schools, especially in relation to SEND and vulnerable students, as in the case study below, thereby establishing a positive start to learning. Activities commonly include meetings between secondary and primary staff leading on Transition. In Parkside Academy during the Year 6 spring and summer terms, regular primary school visits are made. The Induction Day enables all pupils to experience sample lessons and fun activities, with a view to building self-confidence for a smooth transition to secondary school.

## CASE STUDY: PARKSIDE ACADEMY

Parkside Academy's programme for vulnerable students and those with SEND, focuses on visual timetables.[1] Students benefit from developing Communication and Interaction skills within a Cognition and Learning programme, a Connect nurture group, a Phonic development programme with 1:1 phonics support; a Connect + literacy and numeracy programme and resilience intervention.

The examples below offer some practical strategies that schools have implemented to ensure that known vulnerable primary pupils are given the best possible opportunities for a head start at the secondary school.[2]

A local authority two-week summer programme operates for vulnerable pupils moving to secondary school. Pupils are supported by specialists such as educational psychologists, and subject specialists in Maths and English. Collated information about the pupil is passed to the pupil's secondary school.

- A secondary academy ran a programme for Year 6 pupils to spend a week at the school before Year 7. This helped pupils get used to the environment and understand the secondary school's expectations.
- A PRU offered a support programme for primary pupils identified as 'vulnerable'. The group meets with pupils for four weeks discussing their feelings and concerns, while staff work with them to promote the skills that will help them make the transition to secondary.

## What can schools do?

The secondary curriculum does not lie in a vacuum and we must be mindful of the fact that the sooner we make the connections in learning, prior to Year 7, the quicker and easier it is for all students to adjust and access the secondary curriculum. We can model their expectations and ensure that they remain on track and are motivated.

Secondary schools usually arm themselves with a plethora of data on the primary pupils they welcome to their school. However, what they do with this information is variable across the curriculum and its impact can be diluted. Rather than be uniquely in the domain of the senior lead, (in charge of) 'Transitions', the most sensible way forward is to ensure that information is made available to subject curriculum leaders. Practically speaking, they can then begin the constructive process of ensuring with their teachers and TAs that resources and materials are prepared in readiness for the diversity of the new Year 7 intake, catering for the more able, to those with special needs and learning difficulties and so on.

There exist a range of commercial and teacher made resources that schools can access to facilitate the transition so that primary pupils may continue the process of acquiring knowledge and skills, post the SATs examinations during the 'fallow period' that precedes September entry.[3]

For History, examples of project resources aim to provide continuity and progression that fall in the remit of both primary and secondary school History teachers.[4] Year 6 pupils need to be ready for History in Year 7 and Year 7 threshold schemes of learning need to progress from the primary experience. However, therein lies the challenge as secondary school History teachers have to take into account the diverse range of primary school starting points. Teachers will invariably locate gaps in their students' learning. At the same time, they must cater for those that are more able, motivated and require greater stimulus as they are ready and poised to move onto the next level. There will be students who are not secondary ready and without the necessary literacy skills for extended writing. The example below illustrates a project-based approach that aims to stimulate and to deepen students' learning from their individual starting points.

## CASE STUDIES OF PREPARATION FOR HISTORY AND SCIENCE IN YEAR 7

An imaginative strand of the project identifies an activity, whereby Key Stage 2 pupils write letters to Key Stage 3 pupils in role as WW2 evacuees, and Key Stage 3 pupils write back as parents. There are links that show Year 6 pupils' evidential thinking, using historic sites. Secondary school teachers who tried out these ideas, extended and shared these. Another resource focuses on preparing Year 6 for aspects of disciplinary history.[5]

In Science, much depends on the teachers' confidence, subject knowledge and opportunities for Year 5 and 6 pupils to conduct simple practical investigations that deepen their scientific skills.[6] KS3 Science transition resources for new Year 7 students, or for Year 6 pupils at the end of summer term, used during a well-structured transition course of activities, in the first week of term can refine students' scientific investigation skills, or be used as part of a baseline assessment.[7]

## Local authority secondary/primary transition partnerships

The challenge faced by secondary schools lies precisely in the complex range of their feeder schools. In recognition of these potential barriers and a changing curriculum in 2014, a local authority project was designed to support the transition of Year 6 pupils. The project intent ensured that the pupils would be better equipped to join Year 7. They underwent a two-week structured scheme of work focused on skills, post SATs in June–July. This was in preparation for the new KS3 and KS4 programmes of study, from September 2015.

The project was a partnership enterprise between the schools and the local authority. The project's participants attended two collaborative events: one before the project start to design schemes of work and the second, at the project's conclusion, to showcase and evaluate the project to schools, pupils and their parents. Outcomes included valued networking and positive relationships between primary and secondary colleagues, resulting in the sharing of expertise, experience and resources. Where possible, pupils visited secondary schools and were taught by secondary colleagues. For instance, in Science, pupils were highly motivated and in relation to attitudes to learning. The project was resourced through National STEM funding. This financed the collaboration between two secondary schools on a professional upskilling programme for the KS2 teachers who were teaching the primary Science curriculum.

Overall key principles included opportunities for primary teachers to visit secondary schools, to observe lessons and to learn pedagogy and assessment techniques. Primary and secondary teachers shared examples of work from Years 5/6 and Years 7/8. Year 7 students, as proud ambassadors for their new school, visited their old primary school and gave an account of their secondary school experience, explaining the challenges and successes they had faced in the first term.

What secondary teachers found especially useful were what Year 6 pupils considered to be their 'best' work in Mathematics, Science, English, Humanities. These they had brought with them and stuck into the front of their exercise book. In this way, teachers and students together with their parents had tangible evidence of the progress that students had made from Year 6 onwards towards Year 7. They gained sense of synergy and educational connectivity in the students' cross phase learning journey.

## The project objectives by subject

The practitioners designing the project strongly believed that for Year 6 pupils to become secondary ready; they needed critical thinking, reasoning and analytical skills as these are required cross-curriculum. A project style delivery enabled pupils to gather evidence of these skills and to showcase these in the work they produced over the two-week project. The outcome was a folder of work entitled 'Passport to Success' that the pupils took to the secondary school.

*English Language–intent*: pupils practised extended writing in different contexts and analysed literary text. The greater variety of text they read; the deeper their understanding. Teachers wanted them to learn how to construct an essay and build a line of argument ('To what extent do you agree that …?'). Crucially, all pupils needed to know how best to respond to a reading text; to write an essay-style response, and through analytical skills focus on what the writer intended and the effects of the text on the reader. For pupils to work towards becoming secondary ready, it was deemed helpful for primary teachers to have different and higher expectations of what their pupils could achieve.

For the project, the English resources created through collaboration between the local authority and the teachers, centred on Charles Dickens and the biographical genre. Primary schools adopted varying, imaginative approaches, illustrated in Figures 18.1 and 18.2 such as:

- Victorian history; research skills;
- Bill Sykes' trial; a series of lessons involving drama; practising persuasive writing skills; pupils had an opportunity to understand the notion of justice (British values and SMSC);
- writing biographies on Shakespeare using the Dickens resources as an example.

Figure 18.1 illustrates the importance of primary school children knowing how to note-take effectively as a key secondary skill.

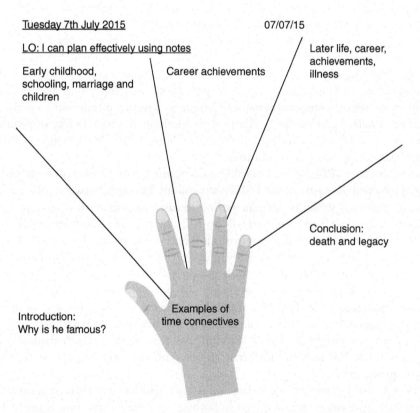

**FIGURE 18.1** The importance of primary school children knowing how to note-take effectively as a key secondary skill

## Language skills

*'Before we wrote a biography of Charles Dickens we had
to research about the Victorian period. We learnt about
how hard it was to survive in their time and, how children
had to work from a early age. We watched a series called
"24hrs in the Past" -it was about modern day people
going "Back in time" to see how life was in the 1800s.
After the series had ended we played a computer game
based on Charles Dickens' life. The aim of the game was
to get on a train that cost 12 shillings to get the money
you had to pickpocket and rob corpses. When you got on
the train you were able to visit Charles Dickens.'*

**FIGURE 18.2** An example of a Year 6 pupil's writing skills analysing what he has learned from studying Charles Dickens

*Mathematics-intent*: building in the cross–curricular elements of the Mathematics and including Functional Mathematics. Primary teachers selected a lower Tier GCSE paper question and through scaffolding, introduced their pupils to the mathematical skills they would be encountering in Year 7 onwards. The emphasis in the transition scheme of learning was on *fluency* in the fundamentals of Mathematics. This included varied and frequent practice with increasingly complex problems over time, so that pupils gained deeper understanding and could recall and apply knowledge rapidly and accurately. Secondly, teachers focused on mathematical *reasoning* by following a line of enquiry, conjecturing relationships and generalisations, presenting an argument, justification or proof using mathematical language. Thirdly, pupils were taught the importance of *solving problems* by applying their Mathematics to a variety of problems with increasing difficulty, including breaking problems down into a series of simpler steps and persevering in finding solutions.

Financial literacy (PFEG) was considered a good starting point that should be continued into Year 7, as part of the PSHE curriculum. Linkages between jobs, pay and progression provided students with an online research opportunity. They also learnt simple facts about the taxation system and how to calculate gross and net income.

*Science-intent*: two practical investigations were conducted (Figure 18.3); one was completed using equipment and resources on site in the secondary school, and the other that the primary school pupils conducted in their classrooms. At GCSE, the investigative skills assessment comprises 40 per cent of the core grade and what was important were *the skills required to complete the investigation, the method and the reasoning behind it.* Much of the new Mathematics curriculum strand of Handling Data was taught at KS1-2 through science investigations. A principle aim was to consolidate this and to familiarise pupils with the safety aspects of scientific enquiry required in KS3.

Teachers listed a range of secondary skills that resulted from the investigations. These included the difference between hypothesis and prediction. Pupils learnt how a hypothesis is made about the behaviour of springs when loaded, and a prediction about what would happen when the force was added. They also learned about variables (dependent, independent and control) and then broadly about the use of values as measurements for the independent variable.

## Year 6 pupils

*'We went to the secondary school and we noted how to spot the hazards in the lab. Next, we labelled the equipment. Afterwards our teacher showed us how to use the Bunsen Burners. Then, we had to fill the boiling tube with water and take the temperature of the water. Next, we had to set a crisp on fire and hold it under the boiling tube. After the crisp was nothing but ashes, we needed to take the temperature again. Finally we did a calculation to help us find how much energy each crisp brand contained- not much!! That surprised us!'*

FIGURE 18.3 A primary student reflection on a practical science lesson conducted in a secondary lab

*'Near the end of Year 6 we started to work on a project for year seven. This project gives our Year 7 teachers an idea of what our strengths and weaknesses are. We had to do a biography of Charles Dickens and also draw a poster of photosynthesis and how it works.'*

$$6\ CO_2 + 6\ H_2O \longrightarrow C_6H_{12}O_6 + 6\ O_2$$

carbon dioxide    water    Light energy from the sun    glucose    oxygen

FIGURE 18.4 A Year 6 students' perspective on the project they are engaged in

Figure 18.4 above summed up a Year 6 pupil's perspective of the project.

The case study below illustrates the experience of Colette Doran-Hannon, the Headteacher of one of the lead participating primary schools and how the good practice within a constructive Transition is sustained year on year.

### CASE STUDY: ST THOMAS MORE ACADEMY

The transition from KS2 to KS3 is a priority and to that end, our intent is to prepare our pupils for life beyond our gates in the best way possible. Once our pupils have completed their KS2 assessments, our focus shifts towards ensuring that our pupils are as prepared for next stages. In previous years, members of our SLT have been part of the local authority Transition Project, where the objective was to find the best possible solution towards a smooth transition for pupils moving between Year 6 and Year 7.

We believe that the work we do across Key Stage 2 should prepare the pupils holistically for secondary school. Core academic subjects are key, but also a Growth Mindset. Emotionally, pupils need to be prepared for the change. Induction days are key, as well as when we talk to pupils about their emotions; 'closing one door and opening another'.

During their final half term at St Thomas More, our pupils are exposed to the standard of work that will be expected of them upon their arrival at secondary school. In English, our pupils move on to study the work of William Shakespeare, *A Midsummer Night's Dream* in particular, where pupils are required to dissect the text and focus on the author's intent and use of figurative language. In Maths, pupils take part in a series of lessons designed to improve their financial literacy skills and that will challenge their problem-solving abilities. In terms of Science, pupils further develop their enquiry skills and their ability to identify dependent and independent variables by undertaking a series of investigations. The expectations are that pupils display their ability to work more independently, direct their own learning and manage their time effectively. The impact of this focus on transition is that our pupils leave St Thomas More as best prepared for secondary school as they can be.

## Non-secondary ready

These are students who gain below 95 in the SATs and are assessed as not having the necessary skills for accessing the curriculum. In Part V we provided a *Transition curriculum pathway* model for these students who are not secondary ready (NSR).

## Literacy skills strategies

Key strategies, such as DEAR (Drop Everything and Read), marking for literacy policy, reading for meaning and for pleasure, teaching extended writing skills are common across schools. Further resources that can be accessed are Reading Wise.[8]

The case study below illustrates the use of software in encouraging reading.

### CASE STUDY: NORTH LONDON ACADEMY: DEVELOPING CONFIDENT YEAR 7/8 READERS

Students enthusiastically embraced the *Accelerated Reader Renaissance*[9]

The AR programme is used weekly in the library alongside Reciprocal Reading practice.

The STAR Reading™ test with computer-adaptive technology continuously adjusts the comprehension questions in line with the student's responses through increasing the difficulty level. The student's 'Zone of Proximal Development' following the (termly) STAR reading test, indicates the range of books that would challenge him/her without causing frustration. This means that students read comfortably and can enjoy the reading. These students gained increasingly high levels of comprehension within their ZPDs and developed self-confidence and motivation.

## Reading skills for access to curriculum through Directed Activities Relating to Texts (DARTs)

Good readers ...

- do not always read continuously;

- choose a style of reading (skim, scan, read closely) depending on the text type and the purpose of the reading;
- read backwards/forwards when they do not understand what they are reading;
- ask themselves questions to make sense of the text;
- connect what they are reading with what they already know.

*Directed Activities Related to Text* (DARTs) is a technique that encourages active reading skills within a subject and increases comprehension through differentiated tasks and activities. This technique uses reading as a way of learning a 'subject' and aims to foster independent reading and actively engage the student with text. The techniques can be practised individually or within a small group, or in pairs, through scaffolding the learning with students who are dyslexic and those who have a low reading age.[10]

The advantages of DARTs activities are many:

1. As problem-solving activities, they promote thinking skills and independence in learning.

2. As students manipulate the text, they can be linked to physical and online activities. This often increases variety and enjoyment in learning.

3. During active learning situations students collaborate and cooperate to solve problems.

4. The activities internalise learning through facilitating recall, transfer and apply.

5. Students are encouraged to be analytical.

6. Students are interacting with text, if they are weak readers.

7. The work is shared and supportive and so can aid the less able.

8. The tasks enable students to go beyond the literal level of understanding and start the process of inferring, deducing, and analysis.

9. The activities challenge the more able as the exercises can be graded in difficulty.

10. They are an excellent way of introducing a new topic or to revise and consolidate a topic at the end of a unit.

As can be seen below, a sequence of four main activities can be deployed to scaffold and access a text meaningfully:

- cloze exercises
- text sequencing
- text marking
- text restructuring

For an example of using these strategies see Appendix 18.1 and Appendix 18.2, available at www.routledge.com/9780367900878.

Figure 18.5 considers the steps to support children in reading. Figure 18.6 outlines the four main reading skills required cross-curriculum. Figure 18.7 links activities to the different stages of reading a text or narrative.

# How do we help pupils to read?

| Pre | • Activating prior knowledge | Create a context – brainstorming, group discussions, displays, diagrams, |
| | • Establishing purpose | Glossaries |
| While | • Adopting an appropriate reading strategy | Highlight organisational devices in text books |
| | • Interacting with the text | Pre-read opportunities for homework |
| | • Making notes to assist memory and help understanding of text | Teacher modelling of reading strategies & discussion about when/why to use |
| Post | • Final outcome | DARTs writing frames, note-taking, diagrams, role play, students writing different genres |

**FIGURE 18.5** The steps to support children in reading

## Types of reading which should be modelled and taught are:

| Type of reading | What is it? |
|---|---|
| Skimming | Looking rapidly through a text for general impression of the main ideas. Getting the gist. |
| Scanning | Looking rapidly through a text to pick out specific information by locating key words. |
| Close reading | Slowed down detailed reading that enables comparisons and connections to be made about the information. |
| Continuous | Reading without stopping, where the reader independently chooses reading strategies to make sense of what they're reading. This may include asking questions of themselves, making links with what they already know, and creating mental images of what they're reading. |

**FIGURE 18.6** The four main reading skills required across all subjects

**Pre-reading activities**

Motivating

Activating or building background knowledge

Providing text-specific knowledge

Relating the reading to students' lives

Preteaching vocabulary

Preteaching concepts

Prequestioning, predicting and direction setting

Using students' native language

Engaging students and community people as resources

Suggesting strategies

**During-reading activities**

Silent reading

Reading to students

Guided reading

Oral reading by students

Modifying the text

**Post-reading activities**

Questioning

Discussion

Building connections

Writing

Drama

Artistic, graphic and nonverbal activities

Application and outreach activities

Re-teaching

A sequence of activities

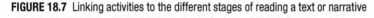

**FIGURE 18.7** Linking activities to the different stages of reading a text or narrative

Using these three stages provides the greatest gains. Reading a text 'blind' without any associated activity, but expecting students to make sense of it, and to simultaneously identify key information is a highly complex skill. Without adequate preparation, moving to questioning, discussion and so on (post-reading activities) can only result in variable levels of understanding of what they read. Therefore ensuring pre-reading activities either in class, or through Flip Learning beforehand, familiarises students with the text structure, vocabulary and gist. This in turn deepens subject knowledge and increases metacognition skills.

## Summary

The Transition project took place at a point in time in the evolution of secondary curriculum. It reflected the concerns of that time around the importance of Transition from primary to secondary. Of note are the principles that underpinned the project for Year 6 pupils. These were key skills within Maths, English and Science that they would need from Year 7, more relevant now than ever.

With the OFSTED emphasis moving from a two-year KS3 to a three-year KS3, together with the need for 'a level playing field', investing in a well thought out Transition programme gives students that extra impetus in their learning. This can positively impact on the pace of progress they make and potentially their GCSE outcomes.

We propose that local authorities play a key role in facilitating Transition, not just for students with SEND, but for all students through working with primary and secondary school leaders in creating a skills mapping exercise. This can ensure all primary school students undergo an induction scheme of learning, post-SATs, that gives all of them a head start.

Even inviting Year 6 primary pupils into secondary school post-SATs and delivering a two-day synoptic scheme of learning based on the above model triggers the process of familiarisation with the standards of skills required in secondary and is reassuring to students. KS3 curriculum intent and design can then be influenced through capturing students' starting points and prior learning through their Year 6 work, along with an initial assessment and the SATs data. It is inevitable that some students are not ready to access the secondary curriculum and need additional input; in particular, for their reading and writing skills.

By not treating the new Year 7 students as tabula rasa, and with an effective Transition programme in place, a curriculum *intent of respect* is voiced equally for all students. This values their past learning and at the same time, raises students' expectations and aspirations.

## Notes

1   Parkside Academy (2019) Parkside Academy. Available at: http://parksideacademy.org.uk/special-educational-needs-disabilities/transition/ (Accessed: 21 December 2019).

2   E. Timpson et al. (2018) *The Timpson Review of School Exclusion*. London: Department for Education, Crown Copyright 2019 [Online]. Available at: https://assets.publishing.service.gov.uk/government/uploads/system/uploads/attachment_data/file/807862/Timpson_review.pdf (Accessed: 1 December 2019).

3   Twinkl (2019) FREE! – Secondary KS2 to KS3 Transition Resource Pack. Available at: www.twinkl.co.uk/resource/t3-p-191-secondary-ks2-to-ks3-transition-resource-pack (Accessed: 20 November 2019).

4   Historical Association (2019) Transition KS2-KS3. Available at: www.history.org.uk/secondary/categories/ks3-transition-ks2-ks3 (Accessed: 21 November 2019).

5   T. Wiltshire (2020) Telling and suggesting in the Conwy Valley. Available at: www.history.org.uk/secondary/resource/1463/telling-and-suggesting-in-the-conwy-valley (Accessed: 19 January 2020).

6   Oxford Secondary (2014) KS2 – KS3 transition: Get ready for science!. Available at: www.tes.com/teaching-resource/ks2-ks3-transition-get-ready-for-science-6438302 (Accessed: 23 December 2019).

7    For articles that examine broader models of progression, from 5 to 18, see the section
     Progression and Assessment (KS3). The report, units and schemes of work from our Key
     Stage 2–3 Transition Project can also be found at www.history.org.uk/secondary/resource/
     1463/telling-and-suggesting-in-the-conwy-valley.
8    Available at www. info@readingwise.com
9    Renaissance (2019) Accelerated Reader. Available at: www.renaissance.com/products/
     accelerated-reader/ (Accessed: 26 December 2019).
10   TeachIt (2019) Directed activities related to texts. Available at: www.teachit.so/index_htm_
     files/DARTS_Information_booklet.pdf (Accessed: 19 January 2020).

# 19

# Next step choices: Careers Education, Information, Advice and Guidance (CEIAG)

## Introduction

Careers guidance must keep pace with the changing national and global employment trends that young people face in relation to their future choices, by not uniquely focusing on an outdated and static idea of a jobs market. We explore the increasing importance of high-quality CEIAG integrated into curriculum, supported by a range of measures, including tasters and mentoring. These act as a springboard in facilitating social mobility 11–19 and beyond. We also review the introduction of technical levels as a vocational pathway to employment and post-16 pathways.

## Post-16

Post-16 education is on the cusp of a revolution. Schools decide how they position themselves between vocational qualifications and traditional academic qualifications as part of their curriculum intent. The pressure on schools to maintain student numbers have resulted in a number of schools offering Level 2 pathways, or 'access years', enabling students to improve on Level 2 outcomes before Level 3 courses. Some schools have used level 2 average point scores to encourage students onto three differentiated pathways of study, a vocational pathway, a 'mixed' pathway and an A-level pathway.

Deciding which courses to pursue in the light of future destinations and careers has been challenging with, in some cases, similar programmes of study leading to BTECs and A-levels courses. For example, a student pursuing a career in Physiotherapy, can choose between a BTEC Sport Diploma or study A-level PE alongside A-level Biology. Schools must invest in impartial advice and guidance that looks at options, not only for those remaining in the school's sixth form, but wider afield, towards apprenticeships and college-based technical and vocational provision. Schools must resist the temptation of advising students, consciously or unconsciously, onto courses that benefit the school's own staying on rates and sixth form academic outcomes.

Guiding students to follow courses *in the best interest of the student* should be the norm, in line with what schools know to be the best route. Stereotyping a student's potential and future academic capacity, based on his/her school track record, is not necessarily an accurate reflection of actual future achievement. This way of thinking is unhelpful, leading to the creation of a glass ceiling. A student risks being perceived as better suited to the 'BTEC way of working', when a fresh start with support on an A-level course of study would be in the best interest of a student's future career prospects. Conversely, the student might be perversely incentivised to study A-levels, despite needing to pursue vocational study.

This poem extract (Figure 19.1) truly encapsulates the frustration felt by many students shoehorned into choosing subjects that they believe are incompatible with their knowledge and skills-set.

---

DEAR MUM, BTEC[1]

I know you don't get it
the pleasure I feel
when I push down the pedal
the turn of the wheel

It's a language that I speak
one that's disappearing
in the forest of the school
my favourite lesson is a clearing

Everything else feels like shoes
that don't fit.
I can't stare at a computer
I can't scribble while I sit

No words. No numbers.
No wasps in my brain
just the weight of the hammer
the bulb of the plane

So don't worry when I tell you
that Uni's not the path I see
I'll build a future for myself, Mum,
and you'll be proud of me.

---

**FIGURE 19.1** 'Dear Mum' – Steven Camden beautifully explains how some students feel on vocational pathways

Source: S. Camden (2019) Dear Mum, BTEC' by Steven Camden, full poem. Available at: www.teachwire.net/teaching-resources/dear-mum-btec-by-steven-camden (Accessed: 2 December 2019).

## Choosing subjects post-16

Globalisation and the effects of technology are reshaping every profession. Increasingly, graduate jobs now require a combination of knowledge from the science and non-science worlds. The idea that at 16, everyone must decide on a narrow range of subjects that they want to study now is starting to seem out of date. Delivering social mobility and access to aspirational employment opportunities relies on schools opening doors for all young people.

The binary choice about whether students are 'arts people' or 'science people' or whether male and female students favour Science or Arts subjects is being blurred, particularly as work patterns change.

There is clearly a shift in the qualification landscape with students voting to opt for some traditional subjects at the expense of others.

The 2019 A-level - results evidenced two main influencers on students' choice of subjects. A declining trend in the number of girls choosing English A-level, but opting for STEM subjects outnumbered their male peers in Sciences, whilst young men continued to choose Mathematics, Physics and Economics, rather than English. Entries in English Literature fell by over a fifth in 2019 compared with 2018.[1] In this survey, the popularity of STEM subjects, at the expense of English and other arts subjects, was confirmed by students, parents and teachers, alike. A common view expressed was that 'English was indulgent and arty, but cannot support you financially, in comparison to a subject like Maths or Economics.'

In an age where young people are subject to social media and swamped by external influences, criticism was expressed of the GCSE English Literature exam. The absence of 'coursework', the choice of classic British authors, moving away from international literature, were not deemed popular. Respondents identified 'the mechanical, tick box' approach and the emphasis on memorising quotations, as features they did not value.

A survey on Shakespeare found that over two-fifths of 11 to 18 year-olds believed 'studying Shakespeare will not help them get a job when they leave school'.[2]

Young people reported they were challenged by the Bard's language and would understand Shakespeare's work better if the plays were set in the modern day and digital technology was used to help visualise the scenes.

The collaboration between Adobe and the Royal Shakespeare Company (RSC) resulted in a digital art series with iconic scenes from *Romeo and Juliet, Macbeth* and *A Midsummer Night's Dream*. Photography, illustration and comic book artistry made the plays more relatable to today's social media generation. '… access to arts and cultural learning improves empathy, critical and creative thinking in young people', stated Jacqui O'Hanlon, RSC. Teachers can now access creative resources and approaches to enhance their teaching of Shakespeare.[3]

These changes, with regard to the English curriculum, takes account of young people's views. A revisioning of other aspects of curriculum, with greater relevance and attractiveness for students can help broaden their choices.

## Careers Education, Information, Advice and Guidance (CEIAG) and how this impacts on destinations

Social mobility and equity in schools relies on lifting the glass ceiling for all young people; 'great careers guidance provides the first rung on the ladder of opportunity, helping everyone to achieve their full potential' (DfE, 2017, p. 3).[4]

Profound inequalities exist across different courses and jobs sectors, affecting national productivity and individual wellbeing. For instance, based on WorldSkills UK figures, 9 per cent of professional engineers are female, 99 per cent of beauty therapists are female and 95 per cent of computer game developers are male.

The Social Mobility Barometer Poll[5] shows half the people polled believe that where you end up in society is mainly determined by your background. Four in five believe that there is a large gap between the social classes in Britain with poorer people held back at every stage. Three-quarters voice that there are significant differences in opportunity, depending on where you live in the country. The poll uncovers deep social pessimism amongst students and calls for a partnership of businesses, communities, councils, schools and universities to champion a level playing field.

Post-16, further and higher education systems, in general, funnel students towards academic or vocational specialisation. Impartial CEIAG for entrepreneurship, the four levels of apprenticeships, A-levels and the new T-levels should all be given equal sway and signposted in schools against entry points into different professions. Parents are arguably the biggest influencers for young people and involving them in the CEIAG process in the same way that we involve them in their children's learning should be a priority. Many either do not understand or have a negative view of apprenticeships. They may not have been to university or even know how apprenticeships can provide a route to university. It is important that schools inform parents of developments and stress to students the cardinal characteristics of being enterprising, determined and resilient when searching for apprenticeships or choosing higher education. Young people and their parents need to see the array of choices within the context of the emerging and current landscape of employment.

## Symbiotically linked: CEIAG, curriculum intent and students' choice

Careers advice can reinforce traditional choices, because young people access limited information over the advantages of non-traditional routes. Appropriate and unbiased (CEIAG) is crucial for young people in making curriculum choices, in line with their aspirations, vocational and academic potential. Recent policy reviews have highlighted shortcomings in current provision that fail to open up academic and vocational choices for young people and do not challenge low expectations and aspirations based on stereotypes. The CBI commentary on the Augar review (May 2019)[6] reinforces the importance of a curricula review. 'The stark lack of technical and vocational options for people often frustrates employers.'[7]

Schools are statutorily required to publish detailed careers programmes, as well as a 'careers leader' responsible for the monitoring and evaluation of students' destination outcomes. The central point here is the importance of the careers leader's understanding of the complex educational choices facing students and the destinations they choose. Recruiting a careers leader in school, sharing one across a Trust or across a cluster of secondary schools within a local authority, ensures greater impartial guidance. In addition, better use of the leader's expertise and insights contributes to the planning and evaluation of the careers and enterprise programme and good practice across schools. Schools increasingly deploy 'Compass' to evaluate the school's annual careers and enterprise activity plan against the eight Gatsby Benchmarks.[8]

By the end of 2020, schools will be required to offer every student at least seven 'meaningful encounters' with employers over the course of their school career and will be inspected in 2021 on their ability in meeting all eight benchmarks. All schools and colleges now partially achieve every benchmark. Three-quarters of schools and colleges fully achieve six to eight benchmarks.

## Gatsby Benchmarks

The Gatsby Benchmark Toolkit 2017[9] endorses the involvement of local employers, in view of the importance of:

1.   a stable careers programme;

2.   learning from career and labour market information;

3.   addressing each student's needs;

4.   linking curriculum learning to careers;

5.   encounters with employers and employees;

6.   experiences of workplaces;

7.   encounters with further and higher education;

8.   personal guidance.

The Toolkit features an action plan that the careers adviser compiles with each student, sharing this with parents and tutors. Every student should have opportunities for guidance interviews with a career adviser; at least one, by the age of 16, and a further interview by the age of 18.

The key aspect here is greater understanding of the school's curriculum, linked to careers advice and guidance. Subject leaders with the adviser can map practical examples of how different subjects are used within the workplace and different careers, so that students value the skills and knowledge they are developing at school, as a means to their end point.

According to research by the Quaglia Institute,[10] there are three universal truths. Firstly, students feel more engaged in their learning when they perceive the relevance of what they are studying to their own and other people's lives. Secondly, subject teachers are highly influential – students are far more likely to be motivated to learn if teachers know their aspirations. Thirdly, students are given authentic opportunities to develop their career thinking and acquire important career management and employability skills through work experience and contact with employers. This results in a whole school approach as in the case studies below.

---

### CASE STUDY OF STABLE CAREERS PROGRAMME (GATSBY TOOLKIT, 2017)

Lilian Baylis Technology (11–19 school, London). The programme aims to transform the life chances of all students through a holistic approach to staff roles and responsibilities, including a designated link governor, senior and middle leaders and careers adviser.

The programmes activities include: enrichment activities, PSHE, employer encounters and workplace experiences. Year 10 students participate in employer-inspired extended projects and SEND students benefit from employer links to improve their transition (16–18). The Enterprise Advisers act as critical friends. Parents rated the school as outstanding for developing young people's confidence and navigating them through post-16 careers advice.

---

### CASE STUDY: CHELSEA ACADEMY (11–19) HOLD THE QUALITY IN CAREERS STANDARD ACCREDITATION

All Chelsea academy[11] students are entitled to:

Self-development, career planning and entrepreneurial skills. Impartial advice includes careers resources, a one-to-one guidance interview and action plan for all students in KS4; 'drop-in' access for students across key stages and on-going careers advice and practical support from learning coaches.

Careers support is personalised to specific needs and abilities and includes extra support for students with low levels of literacy, EAL and / or SEN.

The Academy's Careers and Transitions programme when measured using the Compass Self-Assessment Tool against the 8 Gatsby Benchmarks, scored 100 per cent in 6 out of 8 areas. The provision features Year 7 Real Game, a CEIAG lesson for Year 8 students, prior to option choices within a taster lesson program, Independent Careers Guidance for KS4 students, work experience for Year 10 and 12 students. A programme of employer contact enables all students to have at least one contact with employers from Years 7–13.

---

From Year 7 onwards, students should be taught how to find and process information so that they access local and national labour market information. This is a key factor in decision making regarding careers. In one school, some Year 8 students with high career aspirations expressed their ambitions as pilot, architect, working in robotics. Before selecting their subject choices at the end of Year 8, the careers advice they had received did not guide them on the best options to take. This was because the curriculum selection process was not formally linked to careers destinations. It is vital when students are reflecting through their subject options that they can connect National Curriculum subject specifications with careers-related content.

Information can be adapted to meet the needs of different learners. Special schools, for example, make good use of Makaton signs and symbols to support understanding of careers and employability for students with severe learning and communication difficulties.

Figure 19.2 provides an example of a school that mapped its subjects to employment sector pathways and used partnerships to good effect.

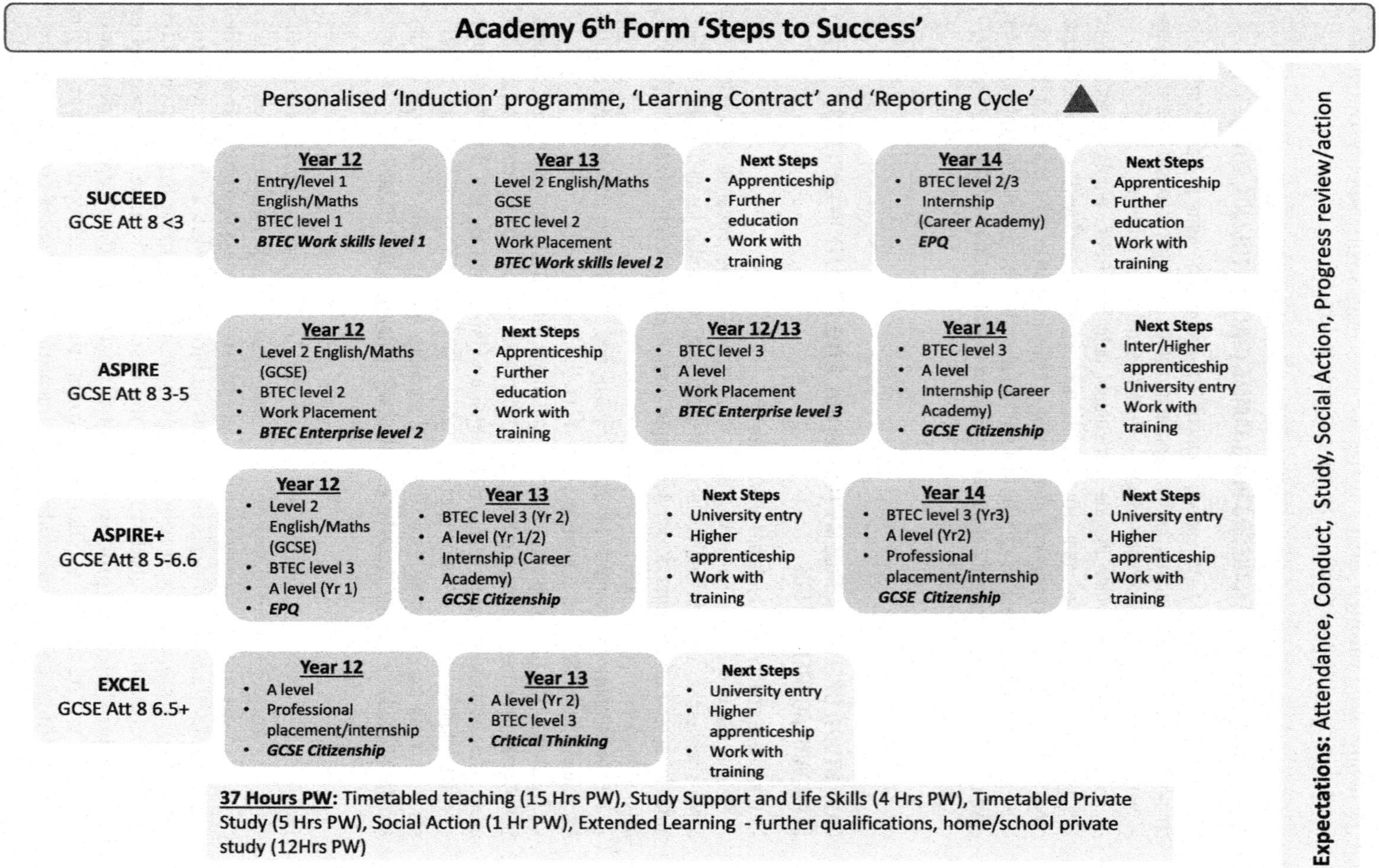

## Academy 6th Form 'Steps to Success'

Personalised 'Induction' programme, 'Learning Contract' and 'Reporting Cycle'

**Expectations:** Attendance, Conduct, Study, Social Action, Progress review/action

**SUCCEED**
GCSE Att 8 <3

**Year 12**
- Entry/level 1 English/Maths
- BTEC level 1
- *BTEC Work skills level 1*

**Year 13**
- Level 2 English/Maths GCSE
- BTEC level 2
- Work Placement
- *BTEC Work skills level 2*

**Next Steps**
- Apprenticeship
- Further education
- Work with training

**Year 14**
- BTEC level 2/3
- Internship (Career Academy)
- *EPQ*

**Next Steps**
- Apprenticeship
- Further education
- Work with training

**ASPIRE**
GCSE Att 8 3-5

**Year 12**
- Level 2 English/Maths (GCSE)
- BTEC level 2
- Work Placement
- *BTEC Enterprise level 2*

**Year 12/13**
- BTEC level 3
- A level
- Work Placement
- *BTEC Enterprise level 3*

**Year 14**
- BTEC level 3
- A level
- Internship (Career Academy)
- *GCSE Citizenship*

**Next Steps**
- Inter/Higher apprenticeship
- University entry
- Work with training

**ASPIRE+**
GCSE Att 8 5-6.6

**Year 12**
- Level 2 English/Maths (GCSE)
- BTEC level 3
- A level (Yr 1)
- *EPQ*

**Year 13**
- BTEC level 3 (Yr 2)
- A level (Yr 1/2)
- Internship (Career Academy)
- *GCSE Citizenship*

**Next Steps**
- University entry
- Higher apprenticeship
- Work with training

**Year 14**
- BTEC level 3 (Yr3)
- A level (Yr2)
- Professional placement/internship
- *GCSE Citizenship*

**Next Steps**
- University entry
- Higher apprenticeship
- Work with training

**EXCEL**
GCSE Att 8 6.5+

**Year 12**
- A level
- Professional placement/internship
- *GCSE Citizenship*

**Year 13**
- A level (Yr 2)
- BTEC level 3
- *Critical Thinking*

**Next Steps**
- University entry
- Higher apprenticeship
- Work with training

**37 Hours PW:** Timetabled teaching (15 Hrs PW), Study Support and Life Skills (4 Hrs PW), Timetabled Private Study (5 Hrs PW), Social Action (1 Hr PW), Extended Learning - further qualifications, home/school private study (12Hrs PW)

**FIGURE 19.2**  An example of a school which has linked employment sector pathways to subject areas

## Academy 14–19 'Career Pathway Progression' overview

| Sector/Careers | KS4 Portfolio | KS5 Portfolio | Additionality/Progression |
|---|---|---|---|
| **Sports and Leisure**<br>• Sports Science<br>• Coaching and instructing<br>• Sport and leisure facilities<br>• Sport enterprise | • PE GCSE<br>• Additional Science<br>• NCFE Health and Fitness (L 1-2)<br>• Core Science<br>• Business GCSE/BTEC (L2) | • Sports and Fitness BTEC (L2-3)<br>• Science A-level (Biology/Chemistry)<br>• Applied Science BTEC (L3 appropriate modules)<br>• Business/Enterprise BTEC (L2-3) | • Sports and Fitness BTEC delivered in partnership with local football team (focus on coaching qualifications)<br>• Work placement and IAG (community sport partnership)<br>➢ Apprenticeship/work with training/university |
| **Science and Health**<br>**Health Professional**<br>• Midwife/nursing, optometrist/paramedic<br>**Health and Social Care**<br>• Social Work (professional) Childcare, care of elderly, pharmacy technician, health support services, healthcare science assistant, teaching assistant<br>**Science Professional**<br>• Research, chemical engineer<br>**Science Technician**<br>• Laboratory technician, manufacturing | • Triple/additional/core Science<br>• Maths (GCSE-AS/Statistics)<br>• Humanities GCSEs<br>• Languages KS4 Portfolio<br>• GCSE<br>• NCFE Child Development CACHE (L1-2) | • Science A-level (Biology/Chemistry)<br>• Sociology A-level<br>• Science BTEC (L3 appropriate modules)<br>• Health and Social Care BTEC (L2-3)<br>• BTEC Child Development Diploma (L2-3) | • STEM programme<br>• Work placement and IAG<br>➢ Health and Science Professional still/traditional degree route (although some/higher apprenticeships in science)<br>➢ Apprenticeship and work with training route into care and technician careers |
| **Professional**<br>• Law, Accountancy, Teaching, Journalism, Engineering, Marketing, Education | • EBacc (English, Maths, Additional Science, Humanities, Language)<br>• AS-level where appropriate (e.g. Maths, Languages)<br>• Product Design GCSE<br>• Business Studies GCSE | • English Literature A-level<br>• Maths A-level<br>• Sociology A-level<br>• Business (L3)<br>• Law (L3)<br>• Languages A-level | • G&T programme<br>• 'Aim Higher'<br>• Work placement (Career Academy)<br>➢ Although traditional degree route, many accountancy and management firms recruit at end of KS5 e.g. bespoke degree or higher apprenticeship. |
| **IT**<br>• Computer Science –Programming, Software Engineer, Systems Analyst.<br>• Supporting IT/IT for business – Computer service technician, technical support, network technician/manager | • Computer Science GCSE<br>• Business GCSE/BTEC<br>• CISCO 'IT Fundamentals' (L1-2) | • Applied ICT A-level<br>• BTEC Computing Level 3<br>• CISCO 'IT Fundamentals' (L1-2)<br>• Maths A-level | • STEM programme<br>• Work placement and IAG<br>• Additional support for apprenticeship route (intermediate and higher)<br>➢ Apprenticeship/work with training/University |

**Figure 19.3** Academy 14–19 'Career Pathway Progression' overview I

## Academy 14–19 'Career Pathway Progression' overview

| Sector/Careers | KS4 Portfolio | KS5 Portfolio | Additionality/Progression |
|---|---|---|---|
| **Media Industry**<br>• Publishing, advertising, Broadcast Media, web design, creative and performing arts (TV/film/ theatre etc.)<br>• Media technician, retail | • Media Studies GCSE<br>• Film Studies GCSE<br>• Performing Arts GCSE<br>• Music GCSE<br>• Dance GCSE/BTEC<br>• Art and Design GCSE | • English Literature A-level<br>• Media Studies (L3)<br>• BTEC Creative Media (L3)<br>• Photography (L3)<br>• Performing Arts (L3) | • STEM/BIMA projects<br>• Work placement<br>• Academy enrichment (e.g. productions)<br>➢ Apprenticeship, university entry, work with training, further education |
| **Service Industry**<br>• Paralegal, secretarial, administration, HR, driving, finance | • Business GCSE/BTEC<br>• Languages (GCSE) | • Business BTEC (L3)<br>• I LEX (paralegal qualification)/Law(L3)<br>• Applied ITC A-level<br>• Maths A-level<br>• Languages | • Career Academy<br>• Work placement<br>• Extended offer<br>➢ Apprenticeship (e.g TFL), work with training, university entry |
| **Hospitality and Travel**<br>• Catering/kitchen team, event management, hotel industry, retail, ravel industry | • Catering GCSE<br>• Travel and Tourism BTEC(L2)<br>• Languages (GCSE)<br>• NCFE Food and Nutrition | • Catering GCSE/L3<br>• Travel and Tourism BTEC (L2/3)<br>• Languages (French/Spanish +Community) | • Enrichment/Social Enterprise<br>• Work placement<br>➢ Work with training, apprenticeship, further education/university entry |
| **Engineering and Construction**<br>• Construction industry (e.g. carpentry, dry-lining, surveyor, civil engineer)<br>• Transport industry (e.g. track maintenance, mechanic, electrical engineer)<br>• Manufacturing | • Core/Additional/Triple Science<br>• Maths GCSE<br>• Product Design GCSE<br>• Engineering BTEC (L1-2) | • A-level Science<br>• A-level Maths<br>• Applied Science BTEC (L3 appropriate modules)<br>• Engineering BTEC (L3) Diploma/Sub Diploma | • STEM/Transport for London/Carillion partnership<br>➢ Apprenticeship (e.g. 'Carillion', 'Intertrain'), university entry |

**FIGURE 19.4** Academy 14–19 'Career Pathway Progression' overview II

**CASE STUDY ON SIGNPOSTING QUALIFICATIONS TO CAREERS (14–19)**

A London 11–19 academy signposted its curriculum in a booklet in relation to careers helping students in selecting pathways in Year 9 and then again in Year 11, so that they could forward plan and map their chosen qualifications towards their destinations.Its partnerships with industry and the local football club helped inform apprenticeships. Figures 19.3 and 19.4 illustrate student progression based on specific subjects.

## Linking with employers is a non-negotiable

Signposting qualifications to careers is like a road map and, wherever possible, it is valuable to cultivate good relations with a local employer. He or she could be interrogated on the fitness for purpose of qualifications and skills within the curriculum and be questioned on how well they believe these choices prepare students for future employment within their sector. Employers can contribute through providing first hand testimonies for students on the linkages between work experience, skills, qualifications and careers.

The school's careers adviser or local authority can share local market information about employment trends locally, within the region, or further afield. These can be used to populate typical case studies of students' aspirations and destinations; illustrating the value of making the right subject choices. Tracking leavers' destinations over 3 to 5 years, using both a combination of quantitative and qualitative data trends, provides anecdotal narratives and quality information for curriculum planning.

To introduce the world of work to students, employers may be accessed through the local National Careers Service Inspiration Agenda. Barclays Life skills[12] offers comprehensive teaching resources on employability and digital skills that support effective employer engagement and provide a usefully linked curriculum programme, developed with teachers.There are also opportunities for students to become Life Skills Champions.

The Career Development Institute's templates include helpful employer engagement requests, checklists on managing partnerships and sample employer evaluation feedback forms, as well as webinars.[13]

## Accrediting work experience

This is integral within the curriculum, and schools need to reference work experience into the sequencing of subject knowledge and skills. In this way, students derive maximum benefit from employer encounters and work experiences. For example, at the simplest level, joined up links between curriculum and the world of work could involve a student on work experience in an administration post in a local recruitment company. As part of the personal action plan, the business studies teacher's input provides valuable subject-related information for the student to reflect on what he or she has learned, and how it relates to overall career planning.Virtually all schools and colleges identify employability skills and increased self-confidence as the key benefits of work placements.

Additionally, students can capture evidence relating to their experience through the ASDAN qualifications. These help students acquire knowledge and skills for work and life through an engaging curriculum and personalised learning. In Key Stages 3 and 4, schools, academies, alternative education providers and training organisations can use the qualifications to accredit preparation for employment training, career education, enterprise education, work-related learning and work experience.[14]

## Raising aspirations in career choice

As we saw in Chapter 16, an inequitable outcome resulting from socio-economic status and low aspiration is reflected in the proportion of young white males progressing to higher education. This amounts to less than 10 per cent of young white males in receipt of free school meals. Expanding employer and HE encounters can help broaden students' horizons. Project ASPIRES 2[15] longitudinally tracked young people over five years, to understand the changing influences of the family, school, careers education and social identities and inequalities on young people's science and career aspirations. The research relates these aspirations to students' attainment in national examinations and their post-16 and post-18 choices. One startling outcome was that although 78 per cent of Year 9 students believed that scientists did valuable work, only 15 per cent of these aspired to be scientists.

Schools partnering with colleges, employers and the Third Sector, including charities and organisations steering the youth skills agenda,[16] will clearly raise aspirations. Three examples include the *Stemettes*, a social enterprise that seeks to inspire and support young women in STEM careers, the *Engineering Development Trust*, which offers young people active learning experiences in STEAM-related careers[17] and the STEM Ambassador Programme[18] that provides inspiring role models to engage students on Science and Mathematics careers.

Volunteers from the world of work, including 'Inspiring Women' can be sourced through 'Inspiring the Future',[19] and figures across business, arts, politics and industry can be invited to schools from Speakers4Schools[20] and Founders4Schools.[21] WorldSkills UK Champions act as motivational role models for future generations of apprentices in a range of technical skills, as diverse as mechatronics and floristry.[22]

Other strategies that a school could consider include a positive culture of life-long learning, creating a learning community, inviting staff members, parents/carers, alumni to speak of jobs or vocations in assemblies. Local universities provide annual careers-related celebrations showcased in school, or students can go to national and local events. Examples include: National Careers Week, National Apprenticeship Week, British Science Week, International Women's Day, National Mentoring Day.

Information about apprenticeships for students, parents and staff can be found at: Apprenticeships 4 England. Amazing Apprenticeships provides an excellent parents' guide so parents/carers can be better informed.[23]

The following case studies are taken from the Gatsby Toolkit 2017, illustrating innovative and practical approaches to CEIAG.

## Meeting Gatsby Benchmark 7 (preparing for world of work)

### CASE STUDY: ACADEMY BROADENING PARTNERSHIPS

A network of university students, alumni and apprentices volunteer support for students alongside teachers in the classroom, and act as mentors and role models. Year 8 and 9s take part in a welcome day and evening graduation linked to choosing their GCSE and other options. Key stage 4 and post-16 students benefit from multi-subject taster days at their local university, master classes, and residential summer schools.

### CASE STUDY: WORK EXPERIENCE

Year 9 students in a 11–18 school (East Midlands), participate in a 'Take your son or daughter to work day' model. Year 10, students' one week work placement, leads to discussion in small groups and production of a mock newspaper article about their experience. Year 12 students have a one-week work experience/work shadowing placement, enquiry and problem-based; students gather information they need for an extended project qualification, subsequently outlining what they achieved within CVs, personal statements and application forms.

Interviewing skills are valuable for students. Charitable organisations offer interview experiences with one such London based example: https://reachvolunteering.org.uk/opp/mock-interview-day-school-slough (accessed 13/01/20)

### CASE STUDY: WORK EXPERIENCE

St Peter's Catholic School (Surrey), an award-winning school for best practice in engaging employers in career development, offers a progressive programme of employer encounters to students; such as the Big Bang Science Fair (Science and Engineering). At the heart of the school's programme is a *careers and employability week* for Year 10 students including:

- a Future Options Day;
- a Business Day;
- enterprise and team working activities;
- workshops on topics (personal finance and Future Pathways), Interviewing skills, volunteering.

120 external people contribute with parents actively encouraged to support students in reflecting on their own experiences, alongside a parents' guide on the school's virtual learning environment.

**CASE STUDIES OF SCHOOLS LINKING CURRICULUM LEARNING TO CAREERS (GATSBY TOOLKIT, 2017)**

**Case study 1**

Year 11 students participate in 'mock job interviews' through choosing and applying for a job from a booklet compiled by every subject leader. They prepare a CV and reflect on questions before their mock interview. The school evaluated that students perform better in their GCSE language speaking and listening skills, because they recognise the real-life purpose of the activity.

**Case study 2**

**Tomorrow's Engineers'** coordinated outreach for 11–14 year olds enables Engineering experiences with an employer.[24] Their careers resources support the National Curriculum, cover regional variations and promote routes into Engineering. Their aim is for equal numbers of girls and boys to aspire to being engineers.

A Suffolk school is working on a STEM-related project, with hands-on experience in the real world. The impact on girls is especially notable, with 45 per cent reporting they 'know a lot about Engineering', compared to 16 per cent in the UK overall.

# Post-16 pathways

## T-levels: Technical qualifications leading to vocational pathways

With regard to the binary equation of knowledge-based academia versus vocational skills, the onset of Technical levels (T-levels) has the potential to create welcome changes in our pre and post-16 vocational qualifications. These are sector based and have greater relevance than their BTEC counterparts.

From 2020 a list of 54 providers are piloting three 'T-level' qualifications in the following disciplines:

- Digital sector: Digital production, design and development T-level Design and Development – Digital Route;
- Construction sector: Design, Surveying and Planning T-level Design – Construction Route;
- Education and Childcare sector: Education T-level.

A diagram detailing the rollout is available in Appendix 19.1 (at www.routledge. com/9780367900878) with a further 7 T-levels available from 2021. The Sainsbury Report recommendations propose a framework with 15 routes to skilled employment.[25] The 'gold standard' of post-16 education is based around three possible routes for students, A-levels leading to higher education, T-levels leading to either higher education, and/or employment and apprenticeships leading to higher education and /or employment. T-levels will be worth the equivalent of three A-levels, so students either study a T-level route or an A-level route, with one T-level permitting entry to a university placement. A list of the proposed pathways is included in Appendix 19.2 (available at www.routledge.com/9780367900878).

The T-level initiative is clearly a major step forwards in preparing young people for the world of employment: 'a distinctive and prestigious offer in its own right … for skilled employment … preparing our young people for jobs of the future and for increasing automation in our economy, supporting the aims of the Government's Industrial Strategy'.[26]

The advantages are that students will spend 20 per cent of their course time with an employer and crucially, the number of qualifications will be limited. This means that they can focus on the delivery of the course rather than potentially swapping between BTEC examining bodies. Most importantly, the 'Occupational Maps' show a route from education to employment by grouping together sector-based occupations. An example is available in Appendix 19.3 (available at www.routledge.com/9780367900878).

Employers have mapped the qualifications against 'person specification requirements' by sector. These not only identify the necessary qualifications, but most importantly, the *knowledge, skills, and work behaviours for effective performance*. Employers, are less convinced by the recent mantra of 'knowledge is key' and know that occupational maps are not just tick lists of prerequisite knowledge; they essentially comprise competencies and skills, integral for access to careers.

Students will be expected to study for around 1800 hours over two years to successfully complete a T-level, including the industry placement.[27] This will mean that it should ideally be delivered in four option blocks, with 8–9 hours a fortnight, taking into account students' placements. Whilst a minimum of 45 days is allocated for placements, government guidance identifies these can last longer.[28] Students are awarded a 'pass, merit, distinction or distinction*' for completing a T-level, but A*E for their core component. Students who do not pass will be awarded a certificate as a confirmation of the units studied. This will serve as a stepping stone for students, allowing them to progress into some careers, with the experience they have gained. Although a graded component allows for a comparison with A-level results, a BTEC style final award enables a simple comparison with the BTEC qualifications that T-levels will potentially replace over time.

Students with lower graded level 2 outcomes will access, in some cases, a 'transitional year'. To this end, this path will suit students who perceive the academic school curriculum as not suitable for their future careers or inaccessible. Of note, these T-level qualifications can be more suitable for students with SEND, owing to the longer time span of three years, including greater flexibility, in completing the assessment strand in the workplace.

## Apprenticeships: Not a poor relation to academia

Apprenticeships are an excellent vocational pathway as an alternative to HE, or combined with further academic qualifications. These three examples perfectly illustrate the versality of apprenticeships. One young person completing her A-levels joined a drugs company AstraZeneca, as a level 5 laboratory scientist apprentice, worked four days in chemical development with one day towards a Foundation degree in Chemical Sciences. Having completed the level 5 successfully, she secured full time employment whilst continuing her studying. She rated the advantages as acquiring the chemistry *knowledge and skills for the job,* whilst actually learning about working in industry.[29]

Amazon's Automation Engineering Degree apprenticeship facilitated a young woman to enter a four-year scheme (a blend of classroom, training and on-the-field practice), whilst working at an Amazon Fulfilment Centre.[30]

An apprentice with Aviva who had struggled at school achieved a distinction in the Level 3 Insurance Practioner Apprenticeship – the core skills of underwriting and actuarial.[31]

Entering the world of work not only gives independence, but often motivation through greater relevance in the learning. Not every young person knows what they want to do at 14 or 16, but being given the opportunity to have a go through an apprenticeship means they can at least find out if the pathway is suitable for them.

## Post-16 tutorials

We have included in Appendix 19.4 (available at www.routledge.com/ 9780367900878) tutorial documentation that will especially help track students who are not achieving as they should against their potential. Offering students the opportunity to study the EPQ is balanced by the ASDAN Certificate of Personal Effectiveness and the ASDAN Diploma that gains eight UCAS points. Post-16, the qualification can be effectively used as part of the study programmes. It provides a good point of reference, when used in tandem with a log book that captures the students' volunteering, mentoring experiences in the school and wider community. The Individual Learning Plan is a key tutorial document, which helps students and tutors to ensure the student is on track. Through regular 1:1 sessions between student and tutor reviewing learning, the document has the potential to record and identify potential underachievement, or skills that are required during post-16 study. Conversely, it also helps record the progress made against students' starting points and is motivational.

## Summary

In conclusion, the prime importance of a school investing in quality CEIAG, is not simply because of the imperative to comply with the Gatsby Benchmarks, but most importantly, because students need to make the essential link between the curriculum they are following and their future destination, or employment. In too many cases, students choose an GCSE option in KS3 because they like the teacher, or like the subject, and give up on one that may have been more appropriate for them. Not only is the student losing out, but so is the school and the economy. STEM, creative and digital skills underpin many of the potential high-growth industries in the UK economy. Nevertheless, when choosing KS4 and post-16 courses, students can be steered by a misperception. Students gravitate towards the possibility of GCSE or A-level grades being more attractive in 'easier' subjects. This risks turning them away from subjects which might be more suitable, towards those where they believe they will perform better. This means that they may miss out on those qualifications and training routes such as apprenticeships, that might in the long term be the most valuable in the workplace and where they might excel.

T-levels offer a welcome link to employers and as a consequence, a genuine opportunity for students to develop practical working and employability skills that they need to be successful in a vocational/technical career. It is clear from the rationale that employers will be integral in the delivery of the work element, rather than schools or students themselves organising some add-on placements, separate from the overall content. It is intended that The Education and Skills Funding Agency (ESFA) and National Apprenticeship Service (part of ESFA) will work with employers and providers on industry placements. It remains to be seen how well the placements are embedded, as they are so dependent on the buy in from employers and the coordination of a national database.

## Notes

1    *Guardian*, 17 August 2019.
2    ITV News (2019) Pupils concerned studying Shakespeare will not help with jobs, poll shows. Available at: www.itv.com/news/2019-10-22/pupils-concerned-studying-shakespeare-will-not-help-with-jobs-poll-shows/ (Accessed: 2 December 2019).
3    Adobe (2019) Reimagining Shakespeare to boost classroom creativity. Available at: www.adobe.com/uk/education/rsc.html (Accessed: 2 December 2019).
4    Department for Education (2017) *Careers Guidance and Inspiration in Schools.* London: Department for Education.
5    Social Mobility Commission (2018) *Social Mobility Barometer.* London: Social Mobility Commission.
6    Department for Education (2019) *Post-18 Review of Education and Funding: Independent Panel Report.* Available at: www.gov.uk/government/publications/post-18-review-of-education-and-funding-independent-panel-report (Accessed: 5 December 2019).
7    Epon Design and Test (2019) Augar review has right approach to FE, but must protect funding for universities, say CBI & others. Available at: www.epdtonthenet.net/article/171179/Augar-review-has-right-approach-to-FE--but-must-protect-funding-for-universities--say-CBI-others.aspx (Accessed: 10 December 2019).
8    Careers & Enterprise Company (2018). Available at: www.careersandenterprise.co.uk/ (Accessed: 11 November 2019).
9    Careers and Enterprise Company (2018) *The Gatsby Benchmark Toolkit for Schools.* Available at: www.careersandenterprise.co.uk/sites/default/files/uploaded/1041_gatsby_toolkit_for_schools_final.pdf (Accessed: 18 January 2020).
10   School Voice & Aspirations (2019) School Voice & Aspirations. Available at: http://quagliainstitute.org/qisva/ (Accessed: 13 December 2019).
11   Chelsea Academy (2019) Chelsea Academy. Available at: https://chelsea-academy.org/ (Accessed: 17 December 2019).
12   LifeSkills Barclays (2019) LifeSkills Barclays. Available at: https://barclayslifeskills.com/educators/ (Accessed: 17 December 2019).
13   Career Development Institute (2019) Career Development Institute. Available at: www.thecdi.net/ (Accessed: 19 December 2019).
14   ASDAN (2019) ASDAN. Available at: www.asdan.org.uk/courses/qualifications/employability (Accessed: 14 December 2019).

15    UCL (2019) Institute of Education. Available at: www.ucl.ac.uk/ioe/departments-and-centres/departments/education-practice-and-society/aspires-2 (Accessed: 11 December 2019).

16    V. Daga (2019) Full STEAM ahead – the future of technology jobs. Available at: https://edtechnology.co.uk/Blog/full-steam-ahead-the-future-of-technology-jobs/ (Accessed: 29 November 2019).

17    EdTechnology (2019) More creative subjects needed to deliver industrial strategy. Available at:https://edtechnology.co.uk/Blog/more-creative-subjects-needed-to-deliver-industrial-strategy/ (Accessed: 14 December 2019).

18    STEM (2019) STEM Ambassadors. Available at: www.stem.org.uk/stem-ambassadors (Accessed: 5 November 2019).

19    Education and Employers (2019) *Inspiring the Future.* Available at: www.inspiringthefuture.org/ (Accessed: 5 November 2019).

20    Speakers 4 Schools (2019) Speakers 4 Schools. Available at: www.speakers4schools.org/ (Accessed: 5 November 2019).

21    Founders 4 Schools (2019) Founders 4 Schools. Available at: www.founders4schools.org.uk/ (Accessed: 6 November 2019).

22    World Skills UK Champions (2019) World Skills UK Champions. Available at: www.worldskillsuk.org/directions/our-role-models/skills-champions (Accessed: 6 November 2019).

23    Amazing Apprenticeships (2019) Amazing Apprenticeships. Available at: https://amazingapprenticeships.com/resource/parents-pack-september-2019/ (Accessed: 6 November 2019).

24    Tomorrows Engineers (2019) Tomorrows Engineers. Available at: www.tomorrowsengineers.org.uk/ (Accessed: 7 November 2019).

25    D. Sainsbury et al. (2016) *Report of the Independent Panel on Technical Education.* London: Department for Education.

26    Ibid.

27    www.gov.uk/government/publications/introduction-of-t-levels/introduction-of-t-levels

28    Ibid.

29    J. Hall (2020) *Spotlight Skills and Apprenticeships: A 21st Century Education: Astra Zeneca Case Study.* Available at: newstatesman.com/page/supplements (Accessed: 17 January 2020).

30    Amazon (2020) Amazon Future Engineer. Available at: www.amazonfutureengineer.co.uk/ (Accessed: 19 January 2020).

# Conclusion

## Summary of recommendations

- A broad and balanced curriculum ensures parity of academic, technical and creative pathways, in line with shifting global employment trends, changing societal skills needs, the impact of AI/technologies and the introduction of T-levels. The inclusion of Computing Science, Technology and Creative Arts into the EBacc suite of subjects is more vital than ever.

- Moving away from a knowledge-led curriculum to a knowledge and skills model, gives students a genuine stepping stone for future destinations, and means investment in young people's talent and potential.

- A flexible, relevant education for all students means a curriculum that is inclusive and equitable in its intent, implementation and impact. Curriculum design is flexibly steered by the needs of the national economy, together with the local context of students' needs and aspirations. Autonomy in decision making at local level is best balanced by what further/higher education and training, as well as what employers identify as requisite.

- Students must be at the heart of the curriculum; the vision and intent should take into account local context and student profile. Students with special educational needs and those at risk of exclusion should consistently have their learning needs met, so they are not at risk of disengaging from education. Deploying the skills and abilities of aspirational students, influences positive attitudes to learning for their peers.

- A resourced Engage and Achieve Unit for 'learning catch up', along with bespoke alternative Pathways for students allows targeted groups to fulfil their academic potential.

- The pernicious cycle of exclusions will continue unabated, unless schools prioritise the symbiotic links between a relevant curriculum, students' behaviours and a values-based school culture. The initial 'startup costs' of investing in the curriculum for students at risk of exclusions, create value for money and far outweigh the potential loss of students' life chances.

- The teacher is best placed to equip SEND students with the necessary skills and knowledge they need through clearly differentiated strategies. Leaders defining curriculum intent for SEND should ensure that scheduled time allows teachers and TAs to plan, deliver and evaluate the teaching. Breaking down barriers so all students access curriculum through cross subject literacy, mathematical skills and metacognitive skills training. This provides an equitable level playing field for our most vulnerable students and those most at risk of becoming NEETS.

- Moving from a three-year GCSE to two-year GCSE for all students, serves some students' interests well, but can also disadvantage those who require longer to succeed. The advantage of the three-year GCSE allows for deeper conceptual learning, development of employability skills and key skills.

- Creating a Mandatory Key Skills module should include the important 'human skills' – much needed by employers; namely, oracy, financial literacy, digital and critical literacy skills.

- As leaders of own learning: students require metacognition skills (learning to learn), self-reflection and conceptual thinking skills. Assessment is key to this, through a model of interlacing teacher feedback with 'Do Now' Actions, and a student's Learning 2 Learn Diary.

- Challenging students to develop curiosity and inquisitive minds is key to '*knowledge building on knowledge*'. The best Knowledge Organisers are adapted for students with different learning needs and encourage students to use their prior learning through elaborative interrogation and teacher feedback.

- Cross-curricular concepts and skills create memorable learning – the 'Eureka moment' – and help students retain and apply what they have learnt over time.

- Resourcing and integrating a curriculum blend of classroom teaching and digital online tutoring and learning is the best model for learning to be any place, any time and anyhow. A flip learning model provides opportunities for interactive, reflective learning and assessment.

- Evaluating the impact of curriculum through Pupil Progress Reviews (PPR) is a powerful tool within a quality assurance process. PPR outcomes identify whole school and subject based strategies; student interventions linked to a Raising Achievement Plan; as well as continuously informing professional developmental pathways for teaching staff.

- Cultural capital, creative thinking and critical literacy threaded through the curriculum subjects, form part of students' citizenship entitlement. All students need to distinguish 'fake news'; to learn of their British, Black, Asian, European heritage and importantly, of the contributions to British society from peoples of other heritages.

- Partnerships with parents, the Third Sector, businesses, universities create an Extended Learning Community. Parental engagement is best targeted in line with the students' profile, hooking in the 'hard to reach' parents; those who do not have high aspirations for their children, or do not know how to support their children academically.

- Moving away from a binary focus on disadvantaged and non-disadvantaged attainment should influence curriculum reform, as parental factors clearly have a stronger bearing in determining high attainment levels, than socio–economic status, or disadvantage alone.

- Key to the eventual success of GCSE outcomes is the sharing of quality 'Transition' information on students' prior learning (KS2-3), and critically, at points of interrupted learning, when students move to different settings, and especially, to alternative provision.

- Impartial CEIAG is prime within the curriculum's implementation, in line with the Gatsby Measures. Advisers must be forward looking; and provide curriculum mapping to changing national and global employment routes. Drawing on student outcomes, exclusions profile, destinations trends, and employers' expertise and skills are rich sources of data that better influence curriculum design.

# Index